web
PHOTOSHOP 5
to go

ISBN 0-13-011848-6

90000

9 780130 118486

web PHOTOSHOP ⑤
to go

Jason I. Miletsky

Prentice Hall PTR, Upper Saddle River, NJ 07458

Library of Congress Cataloging-in-Publishing Data

Miletsky, Jason I.
    Web Photoshop 5 to go / Jason I. Miletsky
        p.   cm.
    ISBN 0–13-011848–6
    1. Computer graphics. 2. Adobe Photoshop. 3. Web-sites—Design.
I. Title.
T385.M536   1999
006.6´869—dc21   99–2647
                                                           CIP

Editorial/Production Supervision: Joanne Anzalone
Acquisitions Editor: Tim Moore
Editorial Assistant: Bart Blanken
Manufacturing Manager: Alexis Heydt
Art Director: Gail Cocker-Bogusz
Interior Series Design: Rosemarie Votta
Cover Design: Anthony Gemmellaro
Cover Design Direction: Jerry Votta
Page composition/color insert design: Meg Van Arsdale

The publisher offers discounts on this book when ordered in bulk quantities.
For more information, contact

    Corporate Sales Department,
    Prentice Hall PTR
    One Lake Street
    Upper Saddle River, NJ 07458
    Phone: 800-382-3419; FAX: 201-236-714
    E-mail (Internet): corpsales@prenhall.com

Printed in the United States of America

10 9 8 7 6 5 4 3 2 1

ISBN 0-13-011848-6

Prentice-Hall International (UK) Limited, London
Prentice-Hall of Australia Pty. Limited, Sydney
Prentice-Hall Canada Inc., Toronto
Prentice-Hall Hispanoamericana, S.A., Mexico
Prentice-Hall of India Private Limited, New Delhi
Prentice-Hall of Japan, Inc., Tokyo
Prentice-Hall (Singapore) Asia Pte. Ltd., Singapore
Editora Prentice-Hall do Brasil, Ltda., Rio de Janeiro

*To my Mom and Dad,
who are not only great parents,
but are also my best friends.*

CONTENTS

CHAPTER 2

CHAPTER 3

CHAPTER 4

CHAPTER 5

CHAPTER 7

CHAPTER 10

ACKNOWLEDGMENTS

A lthough mine is the name on the cover, there are a lot of people who played a part in making this book a reality. I'd like to take a moment to thank some of those people. There are a lot, so if your name doesn't appear please don't think you've been forgotten! Everyone who played a role was important to me.

I owe a lot of gratitude to Jim Markham, my Development Editor, who helped rne get organized and provided me the structure I needed to finally meet a deadline. This is also true for my Acquisitions Editor, Tim Moore, who helped me to finally get it all together, as well as offered me the opportunity to continue writing for Prentice Hall. I'd also like to thank Bill Camarda, even though I didn't like his revisions at first, he really helped make this book more marketable. The same holds true for "EHB"—I may not know your name, but you're more than just initials to me. Thanks, too, to Joanne Anzalone, my brilliant Production Editor.Thanks for the help.

Thanks, too, to Stephen Solomon, my original Acquisitions Editor, who gave me the initial chance to get into writing, and to Leabe Berman, who introduced me to the wonderful world of computer books in the first place. (I still owe you a drink for that.)

Special thanks to the people at PFS New Media: Dennis, Valerie, Jerges, Marianna, Mike, and Jill who worked extra hard to make up for the time I was writing instead of working. You guys are the best—thanks for hanging in there.

Even though I didn't use his advice like I should have, I cannot forget my uncle for looking over and revising all my original contracts for me. Thanks, Rob.

I also cannot leave out friends who hung in there with me and kept me company while I was writing, or just offered me continuing support: Lidia Becz, Michali Lerner, Deb Schaff, Stacy Silverman, and Renee Sileno.

Thanks to Led Zeppelin and Jimmy Buffet for recording enough songs to keep me awake through long nights at crunch time, and to Eros Café in Rutherford, NJ, who let me sit there writing for hours every night.

Lastly, I want to thank my personal guardian angel. When I finally see this book on a shelf, Lisa, I'll know that you're watching, and that you're proud of me. I miss you.

INTRODUCTION

THINGS YOU SHOULD KNOW

If you're reading this book, you probably don't need me to tell you what an exciting program Adobe Photoshop is. Throughout the graphics industry, Photoshop is the recognized tool of choice for creating digital images. With the populization of the Web, Photoshop's usefulness has expanded to become one of this generation's most powerful shapers of information presentation.

Okay, now that I've gotten the obligatory Adobe brown nosing (essential to any book on the topic) out of the way, let's move on with the important stuff. You're probably anxious to get started building some really cool graphics, impress your boss or your girlfriend, prove that 14-year-olds don't really know more about computers than you do, or satisfy some other motivation you have for spending long, sleepless hours absorbing cancer waves from a computer monitor. Before you jump right in, though, you way want to at least skim this Introduction to help you better understand this book.

WHO SHOULD READ THIS BOOK

Because talent is a tough quality to measure, it's nearly impossible to write a book like this for everybody. Have you won awards for your amazing Photoshop abilities, or regularly give seminars on the secret design tips of Photoshop experts? If so, this book may not be for you, Is your copy of Photoshop still in its box and your dedication to learning how to use it dwindling faster than your weekly trips to the gym? If so, this book may move a bit too fast for you.

Basically. this book was written for the following people:

◆ Your Photoshop ability falls somewhere between "basic working knowledge of" and "strong control over" the program, and/or

◆ You've been using Photoshop for print or other media, and now either need or want to get involved with Web design, and/or

◆ You've been working with Photoshop 4.0 or an even older version, and want a practical resource through which to understand the improvements in version 5.0, and/or

◆ You're a relative of the author and are willing to buy at least a dozen copies to keep sales up.

If you fall into one or more of these categories, this book is for you. It's not important to have any real knowledge of HTML to understand this book, and the few pages that do reference HTML tags will explain how they are used.

HOW THIS BOOK HAS BEEN WRITTEN

Like the title says, this book is good "to go." That means that any information that is deemed unnecessary, boring, or wasteful has been deleted. For example, the section about file types gives you what you need to choose a proper file type for your images, but stops short of explaining how a JPEG image is built, or how color palettes are indexed. I know you want to get right into the creation process as quickly as possible, so besides my witty interjections now and then, most of the fluff, or "fat" if you will, has been removed.

It is not necessary for you to read this book in a linear fashion—in fact, I'd recommend jumping around from section to section. If possible, try to read this book while at your computer. There are a lot of follow-along examples for each topic, and practicing while you read is the best way to learn.

Throughout each chapter, you'll be confronted with an array of various symbols to help you better understand what you're reading. The symbols are:

Note *

Note icon gives a more detailed explanation of the topic.

Warning

The Warning graphic tells you when there is a potential for a problem. You'll see very few of these—in my opinion, as long as you end up in your bed at the end of the day, there are a few problems worth stressing about.

The tip icon provides additional information of the topic.

Another thing that you may notice as you read is that most all references, including screen shots, are taken off the Macintosh version of Photoshop. When I give an example and include a keyboard command, the command configuration will be for Macintosh, and the equivalent Windows command will follow in parentheses.

WHAT YOU WILL NEED

In order to get full use out of this book, there are a few things you should have available to you, not the least of which is a computer. Photoshop 5.0 is a RAM hog, and I would recommend having at the very least 32 megs of RAM installed in your system (more is better, but who am I to spend your money.)

Photoshop version 5.0 would also be a bonus to have around, but it's not terribly necessary. You can get a lot out of this book even if you are still working with version 4.0 or 3.0. Completing examples may take a few extra steps with an older version, and there are a scant few pages that will not be applicable at all to older versions. But for the most part, as long as you have a version that supports layers, you'll get a lot out of this book.

Some of the chapters will give you supporting HTML code. For that, you'll need a text editor. For Mac users, SimpleText will work just fine, and for Windows users, Notepad will do the trick. Both of these text editing programs am probably already installed on your system.

The last important item you'll need (I'm not going to go into all the non-essentials, such as an bottomless pot of coffee and the phone number of an all night pizza place), is a Web browser to check your work. Personally, I prefer Netscape, but Microsoft Internet Explorer will be fine as well (actually, my preference is unimportant—when you build Web sites you'll need to check your pages on both of these browsers anyhow).

QUESTIONS, COMMENTS, AND OTHER GIBBERISH

Although my writing style sometimes takes a playfully caustic tone, I'm a pretty friendly guy. And as long as you have only great things to say about this book, I'm pretty open-minded. So if you ever want to contact me, ask me a question, or show me some of your own work that you've created using this book's techniques, you can e-mail me at `jasonm@fulllscope.com`.

That address can also be used to hire me for your next wedding or bar-mitzvah (nothing thrills a crowd more than a rousing analysis of JPEG compression techniques), or to ask me out on a date (I'm single, and like long walks on the beach). If you are Katie Couric from the Today Show (who I have an enormous crush on), you can contact me privately through my publisher, Prentice Hall.

If you'd rather use US Mail, you can drop me a line at the following address:

Prentice Hall
Attn: Jason Miletsky
One Lake Street
Upper Saddle River, NJ

Unfortunately, neither Prentice Hall nor myself can act as a technical resource for hardware or software concerns. While I will make every effort to answer all inquiries as best and as quickly as I can, please consult the reference guide that accompanies your software or hardware to help with difficulties.

Thank you for your interest in this book, and I hope you get a lot out of the help it is meant to provide. If you don't, and you feel like you've completely wasted your time by reading it, please just ignore the e-mail address given above.

chapter 1

PHOTOSHOP
REVIEW

As design quickly made the transformation from traditional rubyliths and hand-drawn sketches to computer-based art, Adobe Photoshop rose to the forefront and has become a staple in the graphic design industry. It's almost impossible to look at a billboard, flip through a magazine, or browse through a CD-ROM without seeing at least a few images that have passed through Photoshop for one reason or another. With the popularization of the Web, Photoshop has become even further entrenched as a must-know tool for designers.

But you undoubtedly know all of this already—after all, you've probably been working with Photoshop for a while now. But there's a difference between knowing Photoshop and *knowing* Photoshop, and that's where *Web Photoshop 5 to Go* comes in. You're probably anxious to learn the exciting techniques that set Photoshop experts apart from everyone else. Even more importantly, you're anxious to get in on the ground floor (yes, it's still the ground floor) of the whole Internet explosion. You're ready to learn ins and outs of how to make Photoshop useful for more than just a printed flyer, brochure or letterhead, how to make it your tool of choice for creating Web sites that dazzle your audience.

So use this chapter as a resource for understanding version 5.0 upgrades, how the new tools work, or even as a quick refresher for any Photoshop aspect that you don't know too well or have forgotten. This chapter and the rest of this book, are set up to share with you the tips, tricks, and techniques I've learned over the years, designing printed pieces and Web sites for some of industry's largest companies, as well through teaching hundreds of graphic designers in New York's leading Adobe Training Facility.

So rev up the mouse, launch the application, place your seat back and tray table in their upright and locked positions, and get ready to take full advantage of Photoshop 5.0 on the Web.

NEW FEATURES IN PHOTOSHOP 5.0

Even if you've been using Photoshop for years, there's tons new in the upgrade to version 5. Although many designers seemed to think that the upgrade from 3.0 to 4.0 was less than satisfying, the large majority will agree that the jump from 4.0 to 5.0 was something to cheer about! Although Adobe continued their slightly annoying habit of changing keyboard commands for no apparent reason, that fact is forgiven with some of the exciting new additions and improvements. Here's a brief review of some of what's new in this version, and what it means to you, the professional.

The Text Editor

Arguably the most exciting of all the Photoshop improvements, the new Text Editor not only allows you to use varying font sizes and styles in one placement, but it also gives you control over kerning and tracking. More importantly, all text is saved on its own layer and re-editable at any time. This particular feature helps turn Photoshop into a complete layout program, and makes it very useful for mapping out an entire Web page before converting to HTML (see Chapter 10 for more on laying out a Web page in Photoshop). Chapter 5 reviews the new Text Editor in more detail.

The History Palette

Finally! The always frustrating and often detrimental single undo of previous Photoshop versions has been replaced by the History Palette. Although it takes up significant memory, the History Palette lists a preset number of changes that you make to your image and allows you multiple undo's. The History Palette is reviewed further later in this chapter.

Layer Effects

The cure for the people in a constant rush has arrived! Nowadays, nearly every site and graphic uses a drop shadow or bevel to some extent. But what used to be a time-consuming process has been made easier with the new Layer Effects. Layer Effects provides quick and easy methods for creating drop shadows, bevels, embosses, and glows, leaving you more time to concentrate on more advanced aspects of Photoshop. Layer Effects are explored in more detail throughout this book, especially in Chapters 5 and 6.

Magnetic Lasso

While sometimes difficult to discipline, this new tool makes selections by finding the differences in color tones and contrasts in your image. A valuable addition to Photoshop's already powerful arsenal of selection tools.

Freeform Pen

A new twist in creating paths, the Freeform Pen allows you to draw the shape you want as it places adjustable anchor points.

Magnetic Pen

Similar to the Magnetic Lasso discussed above, the Magnetic Pen will create a re-editable path around your desired selection.

PDF Import

As PDF continues to grow in popularity, Web designers will be expected to have more tools to work with it. PDFs now can be opened and rasterized in Photoshop, as well as saved directly as a PDF. Watch for PDF to play a larger role in Web sites in the near future, with companies using its full potential to provide catalogs, annual reports, financial histories and other information to increase the level of service it provides. Find out more about PDF in Chapter 10, including how to create high-quality PDFs with small file sizes.

Measure Tool

A funky new addition, the Measure tool let's you accurately measure the length, width, angle and location of portions in your image. Working in conjunction with the Info Palette, the Measure tool will help you come as close as possible to laying out your site for viewing cross-platform and on various monitor sizes. This will prove extremely useful to you as you make the transition from your Photoshop page lay-out to actual Web layout. You'll see how this comes into play in more detail in Chapter 10.

Expanded Scratch Disk Support

Although this upgrade is more important for designers of print and hi-res images than it is for Web designers and other users of low-res files, it is still a great upgrade. Now you can designate up to four sources of scratch space, for a grand total of 200 GB, so you should never have to worry about being stopped by those annoying messages that Photoshop cannot complete a command due to lack of memory. Check out Chapter 10 for more on Scratch Disks and other ways to work with memory.

Improvements in Color Management

Photoshop 5.0 uses new ICC profiles to assist in keeping colors consistent.

HOLD IT!!

Many users of Photoshop 5.0 have been having problems with color shifts and a deterioration of color quality. Responding to these problems and complaints, Adobe released Photoshop 5.0.2, a minor upgrade which addresses and solves the color problems associated with the 5.0 version.

You can get the upgrade for free by downloading it at `http://www.adobe.com/photoshop/updat502.html` If you'd rather have it on a CD-ROM, you can order one for $7.45 plus shipping (as of the time of this writing) by calling Adobe Customer Services at 1-800-492-3623.

The upgrade includes a Color Management Wizard to make configuring your color management setting easy as well as a few other color adjustments. Other, noncolor issues that this upgrade resolves are better support for certain Illustrator 8.0 features and correct kerning values for auto-kerning text when using the Type tool.

THE TOOLBAR

Figure 1-1 shows the Photoshop 5.0 Toolbar. The tools are sectioned off into various groups, conveniently dividing them into their respective functions. Each of the tools, and most of the other commands, has its own keyboard shortcut. To get the most use out of Photoshop, I recommend using the keyboard shortcuts instead of the mouse whenever possible. Keyboard shortcuts are provided in Figure 1-1, or can be obtained by leaving your mouse on a tool for a couple of seconds. Other shortcuts are provided in Chapter 10, or on the Website accompanying this book, found at `http://www.phptr.com/togo`.

Some tools have small arrows next to them. Holding the mouse button down on these tools for a couple of seconds reveals alternative tool choices.

The contents of the toolbar are as follows:

Selection Tools

Elliptical and Rectangular Marquee

These allow you to make selections in circles (or ovals), or squares (or rectangles), respectively.

Row and Column Marquee

These allow you to select an entire row or column of pixels. Although I personally have never found a use for them, there are rumors that they are somehow helpful in certain instances.

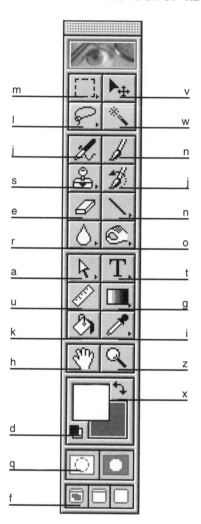

m
l
i
s
e
r
a
u
k
h
d
q
f

v
w
n
j
n
o
t
g
i
z
x

Figure 1–1: *The Toolbar. The letters pointing to each tool are the keyboard shortcuts for activation.*

 Crop

Selecting part of an image and pushing "return" ("enter" for Windows) will cut away and eliminate everything outside of your selection, as will double clicking inside your image. Handles on all corners and sides allow you to manipulate the selection, and pushing "esc" will escape from the crop feature. This will be a vital tool in removing edges that will otherwise just increase file size and make your images download more slowly.

Magic Wand

One of the coolest tools (besides the Rubber Stamp), you can use the Magic Wand to select a specific color in your image. All adjacent colors will also be selected, within a certain hue range (established in the magic wand's option palette).

Lasso

The Free-Form Lasso allows you to make free-form selections, while the Polygon Lasso makes selections using straight lines and corners.

Magnetic Lasso   NEW TOOL!

A new selection tool, the Magnetic Lasso creates a selection by finding the edges between two colors or color tones.

Move

The Move tool lets you move the part of the image you've selected to another area of your canvas. Actual selections do not need to be made for the Move tool to be functional—even without selections, it will move everything on the active layer.

Airbrush

Allows you to airbrush over your image. See Figure 1-2 for a sample.

Paintbrush

Allows you to paint over your image. See Figure 1-3 for a sample.

Figure 1–2: The Airbrush at work

Figure 1–3: The Paintbrush at work

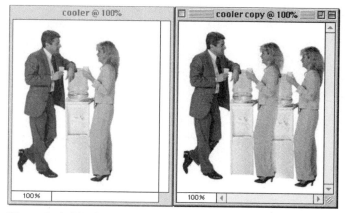

Figure 1–4: The Stamp Tool clones the girl at the water cooler.

Rubber Stamp: Clone and Pattern

One of the truly awesome tools, the Rubber Stamp tool lets you clone one part of your image onto another. Figure 1-4 shows a sample of the Clone Stamp. The Pattern Stamp allows you to select a portion of your image and use that selection as a pattern.

History Brush   NEW TOOL!

This tool works in conjunction with the History Palette. It allows you to erase back to an earlier version of your image. With this new addition, you can feel free to experiment more, and not be afraid to lose your work if you make a mistake. Read more on how to use this tool later in this chapter.

Eraser

Allows you to erase part or all of your image or layer.

Line

Allows you to draw lines on your canvas.

Pencil

Allows you to draw as you would with a pencil.

Smudge

Use this to "finger-paint" over your image. Figure 1-5 shows a sample.

Blur

Blur portions of your image. See Chapter 7 for other ways you can blur an image.

Sharpen

Sharpen portions of your image (honestly, I don't think this is a really great tool). Better techniques for sharpening a blurry image can be found in Chapter 7.

Figure 1–5: The Smudge Tool at work.

Burn

Use this tool to burn, or darken portions of your image, as you might in a darkroom.

Dodge

Use this tool to lighten portions of your image, also as you would in a darkroom.

Sponge

Kind of a neat tool, the Sponge lets you saturate or desaturate colors in your image.

Pen

A somewhat intimidating tool, the Pen tool occurs in a number of other programs as well. Utilizing Bézier Curves, the Pen tool is the most powerful yet for making selections, outlines, or paths for export.

The Pen establishes points to determine where and when your path will change direction.

The Magnetic Pen tool creates a path between tonal differences in color, placing editable points.

The Freeform Pen NEW TOOL! creates a path and places anchor points as you draw freehand around your image.

The Plus and Minus Pens add or subtract points from your path.

The Arrow tool allows you to select, move, and adjust a path or path segment.

The Convert-Anchor-Point tool allows you to, well, convert an anchor point between a smooth point and a corner point, or vice-versa.

Text   NEW TOOL! (some)

The text feature is one of the best improvements in version 5.0. This tool is detailed further in Chapter 5.

Ruler   NEW TOOL!

For use with the Info Palette, helps measure lengths and angles.

Gradient   NEW TOOL! (some)

Let's you set a multiple color gradation across part or all of your image in various configurations. More detail about the Gradient tool is given in Chapter 4.

Paintbucket

Let's you fill an area or selection with a chosen color.

Eyedropper and Color Sampler

Think of the Eyedropper as "absorbing" a color from a particular point. The Color Sampler tool NEW TOOL! is pretty useful, allowing you to anchor a number of points around your image for color comparison in the Info Palette.

Hand

When your image is too large to fit in a given window, you can use the hand tool to move it around. Access the Hand tool instantly by pressing the space bar, no matter what tool is active.

Magnifying Glass

Not super important, the Magnifying Glass allows you to zoom in and zoom out of your picture. Keyboard commands are a better alternative to this.

Colors

Photoshop allows you instant access to two colors at once, provided as your foreground and background colors.

Clicking on either color will access Photoshop's Color Picker (explored in detail later in this chapter).

The curved arrow in the top right corner switches your background and foreground color, while clicking the black and white boxes in the bottom left turns your colors to black and white.

Edit Modes

Standard mode, accessible with the left-hand button, is the default and usual mode of working on your image. Quick Mask mode creates a temporary mask, which can be used to edit active selections, or make new selections.

View Modes

Each selection will affect how you view your image, as well as which menu items you have access to.

Standard Screen Mode, the default option, displays your canvas in a widow with a titlebar and scroll bars on the side and bottom. It allows you complete access to the menu bar, as well as the ability to view multiple open images at once, as well as the images on your desktop. Figure 1-6 shows an example.

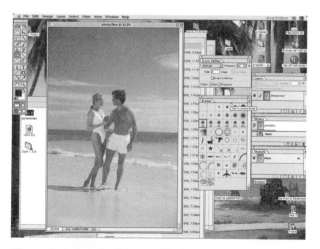

Figure 1–6: Standard Screen Mode. The underlying desktop shows behind Photoshop, while the image appears in an adjustable window. The menu options are available.

Figure 1–7: Full Screen Mode (Gray). A neutral gray acts as the background. Menu options are still available.

Figure 1–8: Full Screen Mode (Black). The background is completely black. The menu and its underlying options are hidden and inaccessible.

Full Screen Mode (Gray) hides other open images and your desktop. The titlebar and scroll bars disappear, and your image is placed on a full- screen gray background, as shown in Figure 1-7. You still have access to all menu options.

Full Screen Mode (Black) is similar to the grey version, except that the background your image is placed on is black instead of grey, and you will not have access to the menu bar (shown in Figure 1-8).

PALETTES

"Floating" palettes are a primary resource for functionality in Photoshop. They are the control center for organizing many Photoshop capabilities, giving you easy access to tools and their options, as well as a place to enter essential information. Much of what happens on your canvas will be a direct result of what type of information appears in your palettes. Some palettes, such as the Layers and Channels palettes, will rely on your input. Other palettes, such as the Info and History palettes, are geared more toward providing you with information based on what's going on in your image. Still others act more like toolboxes, holding items and information until you need it, such as the Brushes, Action, and Swatches palettes.

Palettes can be opened or closed directly through the Windows menu in the menu bar. You can also customize them by literally dragging one palette into another palette window. Personally, I keep my Layers, Channels, and Paths palettes in one window and open all the time, and my Options, Info, and Brushes palettes in another window and open all the time. Over the years I have found that this configuration works best with my particular style. All the other palettes I keep closed until I need them.

The following sections describe the various palettes Photoshop provides.

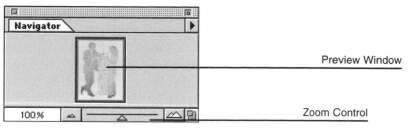

Figure 1–9: The Navigator Palette

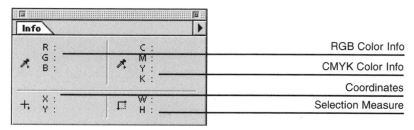

Figure 1–10: The Info Palette

The Navigator Palette

Particularly useful for large images, this palette offers the most specific options for navigating through portions of your image (Figure 1-9). Use the slider to make your image larger or smaller within its current window, or type in a zoom in/out percentage for more precise control. If your image falls outside the boundaries of the window or your monitor, move the red square in the Navigation palette preview window to find the exact spot in your image that you wish to use.

Info Palette

This palette (Figure 1-10) provides information on relative color values for CMYK and RGB images, the location of your mouse pointer, the width and height of any selection, and the angle and distance of measurements being made. More can be learned about the Info Palette in Chapter 4.

Options Palette

Double clicking on a tool in the tool bar brings up its corresponding Options Palette. Each Options Palette offers different variables for customizing the settings of your tools. (Figure 1-11).

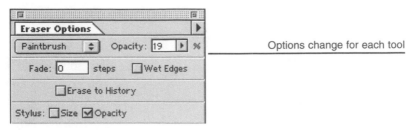

Options change for each tool

Figure 1–11: The Options Palette

Color Palette

One of several ways that Photoshop gives you to choose a specific foreground or background color. Use the sliders or enter a numeric value (Figure 1-12). Many Photoshop users find it to be a convenient means of accessing and mixing colors, although I'm personally not a huge fan—after sitting in front of a monitor day in and day out, the last thing I want to do is try to discern color shades in that tiny preview box. I find the Color Picker much better for choosing the color and shade that I want.

Swatches Palette

Kind of a neat tool, this palette (Figure 1-13) acts as a storage center for colors, allowing you to save specific shades that you like for later use. This palette will also help you reduce the file size of your image, as well as assist in solving problems associated with transparent portions of your images. Find out more about this in Chapter 2, "Preparing Images for the Web" and Chapter 3, "Transparency".

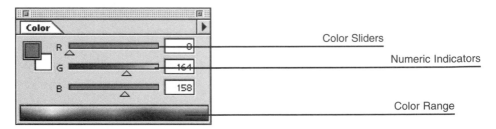

Color Sliders

Numeric Indicators

Color Range

Figure 1–12: The Color Palette

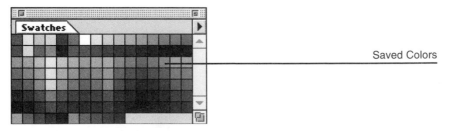

Saved Colors

Figure 1–13: The Swatches Palette

Brushes Palette

Provides a number of preset brushes (Figure 1-14), plus a storage area for your own custom brushes. Change the size, angle, and softness of any brush in the palette or create new ones for unique painting needs. Photoshop also provides a set of brushes you can load that is made up of various shapes, including five point stars, running deer, ducks, flying birds, and semi-circles. To add the Adobe-provided brushes to your palette, choose Load Brushes from the palette pull-down menu (the arrow on the top right). Find your Adobe 5.0 folder in your local drive, and open it. Open the subfolder marked Goodies, and then another subfolder marked Brushes. Inside you'll find a few choices for different brush types you can load and use.

Layers Palette

One of the main features that really separates Photoshop from the crowd, the Layers Palette (Figure 1-15) is your window into how your image is being built. Acting like a stack of acetates, you can add to your image on one layer without affecting portions of your image on other layers. A full description of the Layers Palette can be found later in this chapter.

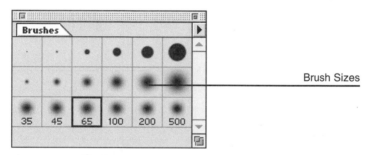

Brush Sizes

Figure 1–14: The Brushes Palette

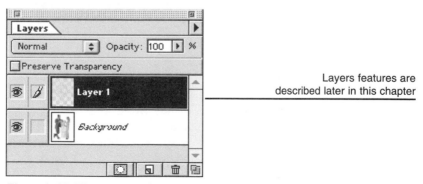

Layers features are
described later in this chapter

Figure 1–15: The Layers Palette

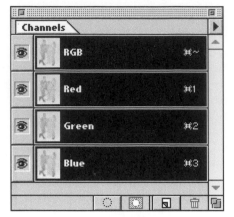

Figure 1–16: The Channels Palette

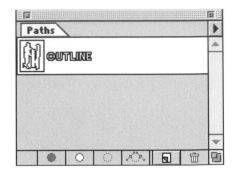

Figure 1–17: The Paths Palette

Channels Palette

This palette (Figure 1-16) acts as a storage area for image color and saved selections, as well as allowing you to create cool effects with masks. It is a treasure chest of color-mixing capabilities, and version 5.0 includes a new feature for creating spot colors to really excite print designers. Channels are explored in many chapters throughout this book.

Paths Palette

For use with the Pen tool, the Paths Palette (Figure 1-17) retains path information and allows for path adjustments. Use this palette to turn paths into selections, fill them with color, or stroke your path with varying widths of color outlines.. For print designers, save paths to isolate images for use in page layout programs (Web designers can make use of this feature as well, by laying out a page in Quark or PageMaker to be turned into a PDF, as explained in Chapter 10.

History Palette

This palette (Figure 1-18) saves a preset number of moves and changes to your image. Use it in conjunction with the History Brush tool for recapturing portions of your image at earlier stages. Because it allows for multiple undos, you can experiment on your image with little fear of mistakes becoming permanent. This feature is explored in greater detail later in this chapter.

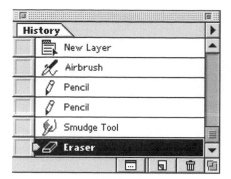

Figure 1-18: The History Palette

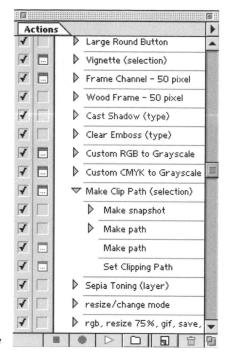

Figure 1-19: The Actions Palette

Actions Palette

A useful tool, this palette (Figure 1-19) creates and remembers sequences of actions as macros so you can expedite otherwise mundane Photoshop functions. A total time saver, it is especially helpful for Web designers, who often have to repeatedly perform a tedious chain of events. It is explained in more detail later in this chapter.

WORKING WITH LAYERS

Unlike earlier versions of Photoshop, versions 4 and 5 literally force you to use layers. Any time you place text, paste a new item into your image, or drag an image from one canvas to another, a new layer will be created. In addition, certain functions will be unavailable to you until you create a new layer, including color blend modes and the new Layer Effects.

In a nutshell, you can use layers to alter, add, subtract, or otherwise experiment on your image without having to disturb other aspects of your work. Each layer acts as a transparency, so that its contents remain independent from the rest of the image and allow all other layers to be viewed at the same time if needed.

CREATING AND DELETING LAYERS

Figure 1-20 shows and describes the Layers Palette, while adjoining Figure 1-21 graphically illustrates how layers are created.

When you open a new file, you automatically begin work on the background layer. This is the only layer that remains unchangeably opaque (although you can remove the layer if necessary—see "Renaming Layers" further ahead. As you draw on or change the canvas in your layer, you will notice that the icon in the Layers Palette changes also (Figure 1-20).

To add a new layer to your image, you have a number of choices, including:

◆   Place text on your canvas, or paste something from the clipboard into your image. (Don't worry that the image you paste will no longer retain its selection.) To select the items in a particular layer at any time, command (Ctrl. in Windows) + click on the desired layer.

◆   Push the "new layer" icon at the bottom of the palette.

◆   In the Layers Palette menu (accessed by pushing the arrow on the upper right) choose "New Layer."

◆   From the menu bar, choose Layers -> New -> Layer (kind of an out-of-the-way method, but it's there, and I'm just the messenger...).

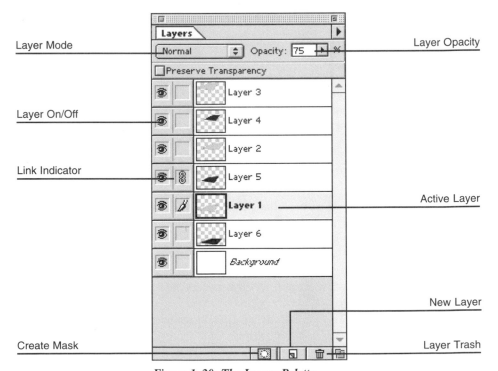

Figure 1–20: The Layers Palette

Figure 1–21: Graphical depiction of layers

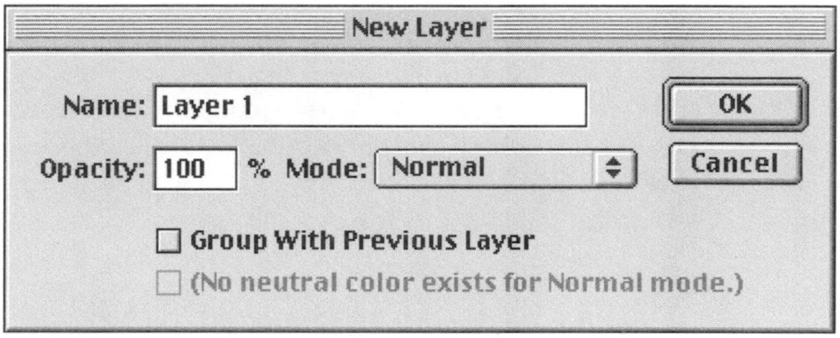

Figure 1–22: New Layer dialog box

If you choose either of the latter two methods, you will be presented with the dialog box shown in Figure 1-22. Among other things, you can use this dialog box to give your layer a unique name. This could help later, when your image has 30, 50, or more layers and you need to find something in particular. If you choose not to name your palette, it will be given the name "Layer 1" (or "Layer 2" or whatever is the next number). (You can always rename any layer whenever you like—see ahead, "Renaming Layers").

Layers stack upward, so that each new layer that you create is directly above the active layer (the layer that is currently being worked on—highlighted in the Layers Palette).

To delete a layer, you do one of the following three things:

◆ Simply drag the layer to the garbage can in the lower right corner of the Layers Palette, or

◆ From the Layers Palette menu, choose "Delete Layer," or

◆ From the menu bar, choose Layer -> Delete Layer.

Renaming Layers

After you put part of an image in a layer, you may want to name it so that object can be easily found again. For example, if your image has multiple shadows, each with its own layer, you may want to give names like "shadow under car," so that you can quickly identify it.

To rename an existing layer, double click on the layer desired in the Layers palette. A dialog box will appear, providing the option to create a name.

If you double click on the background layer and rename it, it will take on the same properties as other layers—you can change it's opacity, move it, and so on.

MANAGING MULTIPLE LAYERS

As you've probably experienced, it's easy for a simple image to turn into a monster, and have 50, 60, even 100 layers of text, images, shadows, and the like. So how do you manage all of these without spending all of your time trying to figure out where things are? Well, naming each layer as described above is a start, but another good way is to use the keyboard. If you can see the layers that you want to work on, hold down the Command (Ctrl. in Windows) key and click on the image in your canvas. The layer that that image is located on will become active.

MOVING, LINKING, AND MERGING LAYERS

At any given time, it may become necessary to bring layers forward or send them further into the background. To move a layer, simply drag it from its original position in the Layers Palette to whereever you want it.

A feature new to Photoshop 5.0 is the ability to send your layer one level backward or forward, or directly to the front or back, by choosing from the menu bar Layer -> Arrange -> (your preference).

If you want the contents of two or more layers to move in conjunction with one another, simply "link" them together. Figure 1-20, shown previously, illustrates the chain-link icon that links your active layer to other layers. When you use the Move tool to move the contents of one layer, the contents of all linked layers move as well.

Another new feature to Photoshop 5.0 is the option of aligning your linked layers either flush left, right, top, bottom, vertical center, or horizontal center. You can do this by choosing Layer -> Align -> (your preference). If you have three or more layers linked, you will also have the option of choosing Layer ->Align -> Distribute Linked.

To merge the contents of two or more layers together into a single layer, the following options are offered to you:

◆   If your layers are linked, choose "Merge Linked" from either the Layers Palette menu or the menu bar Layer menu.

◆ To merge with the layer below the active layer, choose "Merge Down" from either the Layers Palette menu or the menu bar Layer menu.

◆ If any of your layers are turned off (see below), choose "Merge Visible" from either the Layers Palette menu or the menu bar Layer menu.

VIEWING LAYERS: TURNING THEM ON OR OFF

As shown in Figure 1-20 you can turn a layer on or off by clicking the eye icon on the left-side column. Turning it off means that it will be invisible in your canvas, although you will still be able to see the contents in the Layers Palette. You will not be able to manipulate or add elements that reside on invisible layers.

FLATTENING LAYERS

When you save an image that has multiple layers, "Photoshop" will be the only format option available to you. To save your image in any other format, so that you can use it when putting together your Web site, you have to first "flatten" your image, which means that all visible layers will be merged into the Background layer. To do this, choose "Flatten Image" from either the Layers Palette menu or the menu bar Layer menu.

The Layers Palette's features don't end there, however. There are many more exciting features that the Layers function has to offer, which unfortunately fall out of the scope of this book. Look for the *Fat Free Guide to Photoshop 5.0* for a more detailed discussion of how Layers work.

SAVING TIME WITH ACTIONS

The hi-tech version of creating macros, the Actions Palette helps to streamline your work and save you loads of valuable time. By recording actions, you can perform a complex set of functions that can replay repeatedly through any number of images. The Actions Palette is shown and described in Figure 1-23.

As for any differences between the Actions Palette in Photoshop 4.0 and 5.0, they are significant and welcome. Rather than collect all Actions directly in one palette, Photoshop 5.0 allows you to separate Actions, saving and loading them as individual Sets. Also, the extent to which the palette will save functions has increased, allowing you to include color modes and other commands that version 4 would not recognize.

As an example of a simple Action, let's say that you are going to be building a series of buttons for your Web site. All of the buttons are going to look the same, although each is going to say something different, such as "Home," "Products," "Contact", and

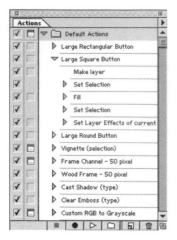

Figure 1–23: The Actions Palette

Figure 1–24: Predesigned buttons for my site

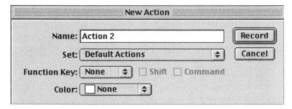

Figure 1– 25: New Action dialog box

so on. As Figure 1-24 shows, the buttons have already been built, and they are made up of three layers each, in RGB color, and are obviously too big to be useful on a Web site. You want them to be 50% smaller, flattened, and changed to index color mode (so you can save them as GIF images—see Chapter 2, "Preparing Images for the Web").

To make this sequence of commands into an Action, follow these steps:

1. In the Action menu options (accessed through the arrow in the upper right of the palette) choose "New Action." The dialog box in Figure 1-25 appears. I recommend giving new actions a name. For this example, I've named my Action "Flat, 50%sm, Index" to later remember what this action does. I have also allocated a keyboard command for the action by selecting the function key "F1" + Shift, which I knew was available. Hit OK.

2. Notice on the Actions Palette that the "record" icon (the classic red circle) is highlighted to show that it is recording.

3. Choose "Flatten Image" from the Layers Palette.

4. Choose Image -> Image Size and reduce the Print Size width to 50%. As long as the "constrain proportions" box is checked, the height will also reduce by 50%. Hit OK.

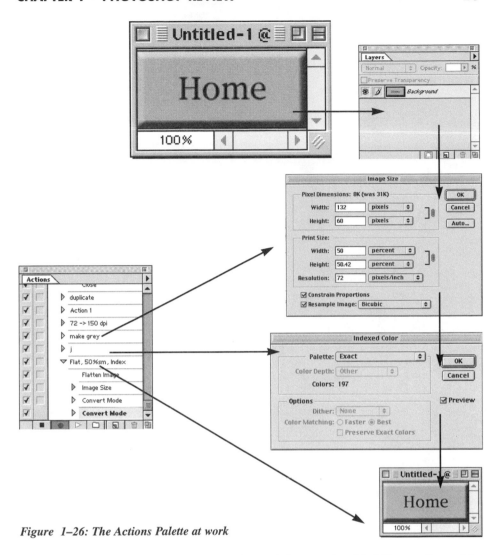

Figure 1–26: The Actions Palette at work

5. Choose Image -> Mode -> Index Color, and, for now, just hit OK regardless of the selections in the dialog box.

6. Push the "Stop" icon (the universal square) at the bottom of the Actions Palette to stop recording. You have just finished making your first Action.

7. Make a different button your active canvas. Play your Action by either pushing the "Play" icon (the universal triangle) at the bottom of the Actions Palette, or by using the keyboard command, (which I had set as F1 + Shift).

The Action "plays" without you having to go through each tedious step. Figure 1-26 shows the process.

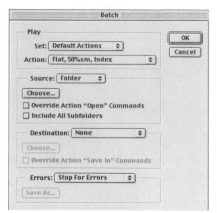

Figure 1–27: The Batch Palette

BATCHING ACTIONS

What's even easier then having an Action do all the work for you on open images? Having an Action do all the work for you on closed images, of course! (Who knows, by Photoshop 7 or 8 maybe our images will just design themselves.) Use the batch option to perform your Action on a folder full of images.

1. Simply select your desired Action and choose File -> Automate -> Batch to access the dialog box shown in Figure 1-27.
2. Select the folder where all the images that you want to run this Action on are located.
3. Sit back and relax.

If your images are not located in the same folder, either batch process multiple times—once for each folder—or move all the images into one directory before you begin this process.

VIEWING AN ACTION BEFORE COMPLETION

If you create a particularly long and involved Action (or even a short one, for that matter), you can program it to stop in midstream to judge for yourself the progress of the Action and decide if you wish the Action to continue. To do this, choose Insert Stop from the Actions Palette menu. Enter any message you wish in the text field and check the box for Allow Continue. When an Action is played and the stop is reached, your message will be displayed and you're given the choice of stopping or continuing. You won't be able to make any changes, but you'll at least be able to judge whether you want the action to complete.

FORCING MENU ITEMS TO WORK

There may be instances when you try to record a command and you cannot because it's grayed out. You can force the Actions Palette to recognize it by choosing Insert Menu Option from the Actions Palette pull-down menu. Type in the name of the command and click the Find button. You'll be able to insert functions into your Actions that would otherwise be unavailable to you.

CHANGING THE LOOK OF THE PALETTE

Due to the specific nature of the commands placed in each Action, the palette can get somewhat jumbled. One way that you can alleviate this problem is the obvious—close any of the triangles on the left side that are open, hiding the Action contents.

The more efficient way to clean up the palette is the convenient ability to turn each Action into a button. To do this, make sure you are not currently recording an Action and choose Button Mode from the pull-down menu. The benefit of this is in its simplicity: if you've named your Actions well, or applied a specific color to them (in the New Action dialog box), each will be easy to find. You also won't need to click on the Play button anymore—just push the button that applies to the Action you want to run.

The downside is that you cannot edit or move an Action while in Button Mode. You also cannot create new Actions. If you need to do any of these things, simply choose Button Mode again from the palette pull-down menu.

CREATING AND SAVING SETS

Although this is a relatively simple process, you'll find it useful as you work on images for your Web pages, especially for aspects like buttons that often assume the same properties and dimensions. To begin a Set, choose New Set from the Actions Palette pull-down menu. You can create new Actions within this Set, or you can move already existing Actions into it by dragging them into the Set folder.

To save a Set, click on the Set name and choose Save Actions from the palette pull-down menu. Place the Set in your desired directory.

The next time you want to use that particular Set, simply choose Load Actions from the palette pull-down menu.

SOME USEFUL ACTIONS—MY PERSONAL LIST

There are any number of combinations of commands you can put together to create an Action. The following constitutes a short list of the Actions that I have found useful in creating content for the Web. I have also tried to assign keyboard commands to as many as possible, also in the name of timesaving and convenience (Isn't it amazing that I have to resort to an actual *key* to run an action, instead of using the mouse to push the Play button? A hundred years ago, people still churned their own butter...).

- Duplicate
- Duplicate 2x
- Duplicate 4x
- Add Emboss
- Cut & Paste
- Create New Layer
- Duplicate Layer
- Save: Close
- Save Selection

- Add Drop Shadow 50%
- Add Drop Shadow 75%
- Copy & Paste
- Change Hue + 10
- Change Hue + 30
- RGB: GIF
- GIF: RGB: Resize 75%: GIF: Save
- GIF: RGB: Resize 50%: GIF: Save
- RGB: GIF Web Palette: RGB: GIF Exact Color

PHOTOSHOP COLOR

Understanding color can be a vital part of utilizing Photoshop well. It can also be a major factor in causing you to send your computer hurtling through an open window 20 floors above street level. For those of you who, like myself, have a print background, you know how frustrating it can be trying to match the color off a press to the color you see on your monitor. Color for the Web can be just as exasperating, as trying to match colors from one operating system to another becomes a major chore. These problems can be minimized by understanding how to access and work with colors in Photoshop.

COLOR MODES

By selecting Image -> Mode from the menu bar, you'll see a list of various "color modes" that you can choose to work in. Although each has its own separate set of properties, the modes you'll be concentrating on for Web design are RGB, Grayscale, and Index.

- RGB is the mode you will usually create and manipulate your images in. In this mode, images are comprised of Red, Green and Blue pixels that mix to create other colors. RGB is used when creating electronic material, as monitors can accurately display the color ranges. This is different from CMYK, (Cyan, Magenta, Yellow, and Black), the mode used for printed material, which is generally comprised of fewer colors.

- Grayscale is, as you may guess, the mode that allows you to work only in shades of gray. It is not used often on the Web, except for aesthetic purposes or to reduce file sizes.

- Index color is a mode that will reduce the amount of colors in your image to 256 or fewer—to reduce file size and create GIF images (see Chapter 2 for more information on Index color and GIFs).

Selecting Index Color will flatten your layers. Save your document as a Photoshop file to preserve your layers for later editing.

In most cases, you will be working in RGB color and then switch to Index color for preparation of GIFs.

THE COLOR PICKER

Clicking on either the foreground or background color in the Toolbar gives you access to the Color Picker shown and described in Figure 1-28. Although there are many different ways to view the color options, my personal favorite, and probably the most popular, is the one that allows you to work in the default "hue" (select one of the other radio buttons to see how the color wheels change).

You can choose which color or color family you want by using the slider to the right of the main color field. Once you have chosen your color, the field will offer you all the available shades for the color you have chosen.

1. Move your cursor throughout the field until you're happy with the color and shade you have selected. The before and after color boxes to the right of the slider show you the new color (top box) and your original color (bottom box).

2. When you have chosen your desired color, click OK and that color will be in either your foreground or background color in the toolbar, depending on which you used to access the Color Picker.

If you or your client needs to match a PMS color for the Web site, you can select it by hitting the "Custom" button on the Color Picker. The Custom Color dialog box, shown in Figure 1-29 lets you choose from a number of different color matching systems often used in printing for logos or corporate identification. If you know the exact number of the color you want to use, simply start typing it to find it quickly.

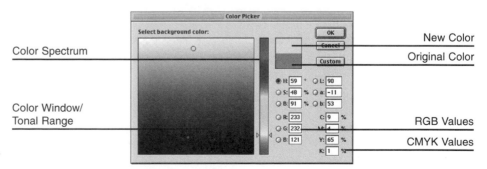

Figure 1–28: The Color Picker

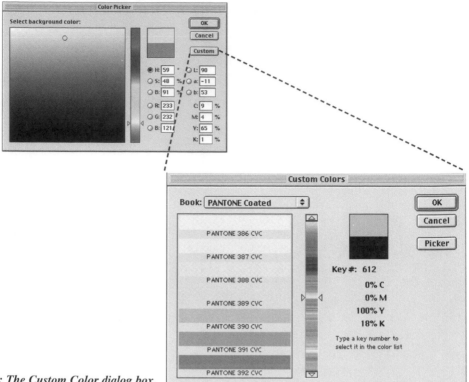

Figure 1–29: The Custom Color dialog box.

If a client gives you a PMS color to use in their Web site, don't be suprised when they ask why it looks different on screen than it does on their printed pieces. RGB Web graphics will display slightly differently from CMYK print colors.

FREEDOM OF EXPRESSION:
THE HISTORY PALETTE

Okay, stop the presses! The History Palette has arrived! This is the best new tool since Photoshop introduced us to Layers. Up until now, designers have had to deal with working under the pressure of only one undo—make two drastic mistakes in a row and get ready to find the Revert command.

The main function of the History Palette is to provide for multiple undo's—make 18, 19, even 20 mistakes in a row, and you can still go back to fix what you've done.

Maybe even more importantly, the History Palette allows you to experiment in ways you never could before. In earlier versions of Photoshop, you would apply a color correction, filter, or other effect, and then have to undo that before trying something else or accept your original experiment as permanent. With Photoshop 5.0's History function, you can apply an effect, then apply an effect to that effect, and continue for up to 20 new manipulations with the option of undoing any one of them.

THE HISTORY PALETTE

Figure 1-30 shows and describes the History Palette. Above the solid black line is a picture of the original image, as it was before any manipulations. By double clicking on it, the picture will revert back to its original state.

 You can make a snapshot of your image at any point and revert back to that in similar fashion. From the Palette menu box, choose New Snapshot, and name it if you like. The snapshot will save below the picture of your original image, above the solid black line. As you continue to manipulate your image, just double click on your snapshot to revert back to it.

In the palette, each state of manipulation is given its own title, such as "Paint Bucket" or "Blur Tool," and are stacked downward in the order that they are completed. By clicking on any title in the palette, your image will go back to that state. The History Palette will hold 20 states as its default (changing the default is discussed soon) —any states after that will be added at the expense of the oldest states.

Once you revert to an older state, all of the states that came afterward will disappear. This is the default, but we will soon learn how to change this.

SETTINGS

Choosing History Options from the Palette menu brings up a dialog box. The following options will be available to you:

◆ Maximum History States: You can set the number of states that the History Palette will remember. The maximum number allowed is 100. There are obviously advantages to having more, but the more you have the more memory you'll be wasting.

◆ Automatically Create First Snapshot: Checked by default, this is what causes the History Palette to save the original image as a constant for instant reversion (see above for more details). Remove the checkmark and the Palette won't automatically save your starting point as a snapshot.

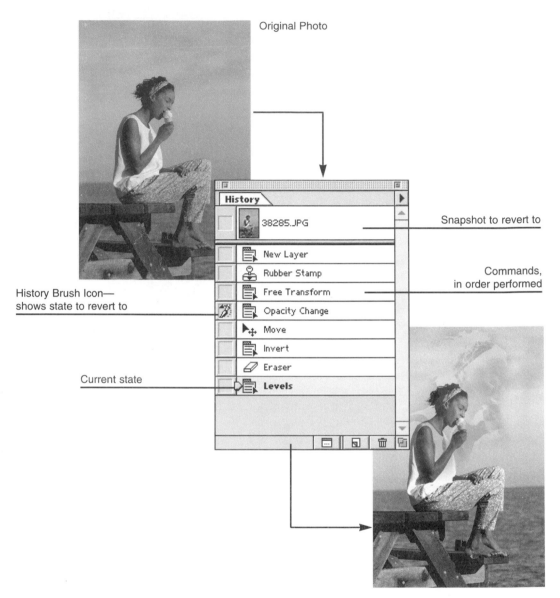

Original Photo

Snapshot to revert to

Commands,
in order performed

History Brush Icon—
shows state to revert to

Current state

Manipulated Photo—the steps taken are
remembered in the History Palette

Figure 1–30: The History Palette

◆ Allow Non-Linear History: As I explained earlier, once you revert to a state, all of the states that had come afterward will gray out. By checking this button, you will be able to revert to one state, but keep all subsequent states intact. This is a great feature, but also consumes memory.

BAD THINGS HAPPEN...

There are some negatives that are associated with the History palette, the two most prominent of which are:

◆ **Megatonnage:** The History Palette takes up *a lot* of memory. You're likely to run into a lot more "out of memory" type errors than you did in previous versions of Photoshop. To reduce the possibility of running out of memory, or to regain lost memory, take one of the following steps:

  • Open the History Options dialog box (as described above) and reduce the number of states that the Palette will save, or

  • Choose Edit -> Purge -> Histories (You cannot undo this option, so make sure that you really want to do it before making this choice).

◆ **Too Much of a Good Thing:** Don't get too confortable with the idea of the History Palette saving you from mistakes. I've fallen into the trap of continuing to make corrections to my image without saving, thinking that I can always go back to a previous state if I want to. But when I unhappily crash (yes, I use a Macintosh), my History Palette is completely cleared when I reopen my image. The information in this palette does not remain between uses of Photoshop.

THE HISTORY BRUSH

The History Brush works in conjunction with the History Palette. While clicking on one of the titles in the History Palette will bring your image back to that entire state, the History Brush will do the same but only for the portions of your image that you paint over.

Each manipulation title in your image has a small empty box next to it on the left. Clicking in one of these boxes will cause an icon of the History Brush to appear. That icon marks the state on the History Palette that you will revert to. As you use the History Brush to paint over your image, it will revert back to the marked state in the areas the you brush over. Figure 1-31 illustrates this, as does Color Figure 1.

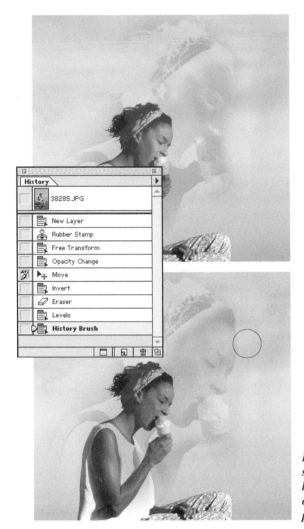

Figure 1–31: The History Brush,
shown as the large circle in the
lower picture, reverts just a portion
of the picture to the point in the
palette marked by the icon.

THINGS I MISSED

Of course there's more to Photoshop 5.0 than just what was covered in this chapter, and
there are other features, such as the Channels Palette, that deserve their space in this
book as well. But trust me, everything that you will need to become a bang-up Web
designer and Photoshop expert will be covered in one place or another, depending on
where they are most relevant. The four main features covered here—Layers, Actions,
Color, and the History Palette—are more universal items that, when creating content
for the Web, will apply in some way to nearly everything you do. Some features, such

as the Layers, are unavoidable—you can do little in Photoshop without them. Other features, like Actions, are universal in their convenience and will make your life easier and help to streamline your workload.

SUMMARY

Photoshop takes practice—there's no doubt about that. However, by knowing the basics, and following the examples in the remainder of the chapters, you'll have enough tools at your disposal to create some great Web graphics. But don't stop here, though—Photoshop 5.0 has such great depth as a graphic design tool that you'll be limiting yourself by not practicing continually and learning the aspects covered in this chapter in more detail, as well as the aspects of the program not covered in this book. It won't take you long before you'll get the hang of the many functions Photoshop has to offer, with the basics serving as your springboard. Combine this knowledge with some of the unique aspects of the Internet that we'll see in upcoming pages and you'll be on your way to a profitable and productive experience in Web design.

chapter 2

PREPARING
IMAGES FOR THE
WEB

Creating anything is always a blast. Whether you're working in a kitchen cooking up a great meal, sitting at an editing system splicing together a movie, or sweating it out in a woodshop building furniture, there's nothing more satisfying than watching your own work come to life.

Well, that is, almost nothing as satisfying—cashing the check for watching your work come to life enjoys a slight edge.

Unfortunately, no matter what your medium—food, video, wood, or any other, the creation process cannot begin without a certain amount of tedious preparation. At some point, the chef needs to shop for food and preheat ovens, the video editor has to digitize footage, and the wood worker has to ... well, I don't really know what the wood worker has to do to prepare, but I'm sure it's not fun.

Anyway, Web graphics are no different. The Photoshop part is a limitless challenge of creativity and talent. And for the most part, this book reviews techniques and aspects of design and Web creation that are fun. But unfortunately, before you get to that, there is some really boring, tedious information you must know first. Color palettes, file types, image sizes—all of these are important aspects of the "infrastructure" of Web design, and will be vital to you as you forge ahead in creating Web sites.

So just keep telling yourself that the best part is still ahead and you'll be able to ease through this chapter. Although I am only providing the bare bones of what you need to know, you'll find this information an important resource to your work.

GETTING IT ALL TOGETHER

The existence of multiple popular browsers and computer operating systems has turned Web designing into more than just an art form; it's transformed it into a scientific and educational subject to be studied and understood. Netscape and Internet Explorer can read spacing between objects differently, while Mac and PC computers display colors with varying intensities. Monitors that only display a few colors may radically change your intended image, and one file format may cause images to download slower than other formats. This chapter will help you to better understand the differences in many of the Web variables, so that when you finally begin your Photoshop work, the designing of your site can be both efficient and fun.

LIMITATIONS OF IMAGE AND SPEED: (NEARLY) UNIVERSAL RULES OF THE WEB

Until speeds get faster, and T1, ISDN, or cable lines become more commonplace, your toughest job will be to balance speed with design quality. A few ways to do this are:

◆ Try to keep pages below 100K whenever possible to reduce download time.

◆ If your page scrolls, try to put your text before the graphics, so that your users will have something to read while they wait for your images to download.

◆ Use transparency to reduce file size (see Chapter 3, "Tranparency").

◆ Interlace your images (more information on this is provided later in this chapter)

◆ Break up your images. If you need to put a large amount of graphics on a Web site, break them up into smaller pieces and rearrange them in a table if you have to, to allow each segment to load individually. (See chapter 9 for more information on recreating Photoshop images in an HTML table).

Following these guidelines will help ensure that people who come to your site will stay there, find it useful, and come back again. As the next section will explain, it is important to set a least common denominator, to give as many people as possible access to your information.

ESTABLISHING A LEAST COMMON DENOMINATOR

Before you go wild creating amazing, award-winning graphics that, due to speed limitations or browser availability, only a handful of people will have access to, set up a least common denominator that you can create for.

Because there are so many different variables when it comes to computers and the Internet, you'll find it nearly impossible for everyone to see and enjoy your Web site and Photoshop graphics exactly as you intended them. The best you can do is to understand the current environment and try to create for the largest possible audience.

When I first began building Web sites, I would build them for the following least common denominator technical specifications:

◆ 14.4 modem, 640 x 480 monitor resolution, AOL 2.5 browser

The general idea is that if people who fit that description could happily view my Web sites, then the majority of users would not have a problem. Times change rapidly, however, and as of the writing of this book, the new least common denominator is:

◆ 28.8 modem, 640 x 480 monitor resolution, Internet Explorer 3.0 browser

It is arguable that 14.4 modems are no longer the norm and have given up their reign to 28.8 modem speeds. This will give you a little (not much) more flexibility in creating your graphics. In the future, we can look forward to a day when file size may be irrelevant, and we can be as imaginative as we'd like. But for now, though, the reality is that the Web is still somewhat simplistic, and we have to build within certain limitations.

So what does my lowest common denominator mean? Well, it means that I'm going to use Photoshop to create my graphics in such a way as to keep each page below 100K in file size, in order to accommodate 28.8 modems. I'm also going to allow myself to create graphics for more complex page layouts, because AOL now supports Internet Explorer. I'm also not going to jeopardize my page by building for larger monitor resolutions than 640 x 480—most people will be using monitors that don't support much else, and of the remaining folks who have better monitors, many don't even know they can change the resolution from the factory preset.

With the impending merge of AOL and Netscape and the expansion of cable modems, I don't think an upcoming reevaluation of my least common denominator can be far off.

MACINTOSH VERSUS WINDOWS/NETSCAPE VERSUS INTERNET EXPLORER

Because of some boring, techy reason involving color palettes, graphics will look different on a Macintosh computer than they do on a Windows platform. Simply stated, try to keep in mind that most of the time, your image on a Windows computer will be darker that the same image on a Macintosh.

Keep this in mind when you are creating your graphics. Remember that even though you are most likely creating your Web sites on a Mac (the dominent Web design platform), most of the people visiting your site will be using Windows (if this weren't the case, Bill Gates wouldn't be as rich as he is). Pay special attention to maroons (which will look brown on Windows), dark blues (which could look black), and lime greens.

At the same time, remember that your page set up for Netscape may be a bit different than the same exact page viewed in Internet Explorer. This is especially true for spacing issues, which can throw off a layout, and keep your page from looking the same from one browser to the next.

 Although this is not really classified as a Photoshop situation, it's important enough that I thought it should be mentioned

FILE TYPES FOR THE WEB

Web designers will rarely miss an opportunity to talk at mind-numbing length about the importance of file types and proper compression techniques. Most would love nothing more than to spend their lives in the Cyber Café, spewing numbers faster than a ticker at a stock exchange.

Besides dazzling you with war stories of working with 8-bit color palettes, and horror stories of dithering complex photographs, most will endlessly recite to you the widely accepted mantra, "Use JPEG for photographs, and GIF for flat colors or line art."

Now, throw in the marketing aspect.

This philosophy and stressed importance on knowing all ins and outs of color palettes and compression comes largely from those who know a great deal about computers and the Web, but relatively little about marketing. The truth is, yes, there can be some difference in picture quality by using one file type over another, but who cares? Unless your audience is part of the small percent of the population that works in graphic design, nobody will notice. And the savings in download time will often make up for a lack of definition in an image.

I am not a fan of JPEGs. However in the interest of fairness, I will not grandstand the issue simply because my name is on the front of the book. So to appease those who fall on the side of the fence that demands a more unbiased approach to the file type and color discussion (particularly PTR editors who expressed a difference in opinion on this particular issue), here it is.

There are a few key differences between GIF and JPEG that you should understand in deciding which format to use for any given image:

GIF Format	JPEG Format
GIF uses a color index, and supports 8-bit color, (up to 256 colors)	JPEG supports 24-bit color, (16 million colors)
GIF images can be transparent and made into basic animations.	JPEG images cannot.
The GIF format is lossless compression, meaning that it does not lose information when you save it.	JPEG uses a lossy compression,which eliminates what it considers to be useless information. Each time you open and resave a JPEG image, the quality will deteriorate.
GIF will work better with images that have a high amount of specific detail that is important to the success of the piece.	JPEG is a better bet with photographs, or other images that use a lot of colors.

You'll want to treat each of your images individually. That is, rather than decide on one format to be used throughout your entire site, you could use a combination of formats for different purposes, depending on the nature of your image.

◆ Do you want to place an image without the rectangular edges and corners? Then you'll want to use GIF for its transparency support.

◆ Is your image photographic, or continuous-tone with gradual gradations and changes of color? Then you'll most likely want to use JPEG.

◆ Do you want to make sure that the colors stay the same cross-platform? Then use the Web-safe color palette in the GIF format (Web-safe color is discussed later in this chapter).

◆ Are you trying to create something on your Web site that has some movement? Then use GIF to create a small animation.

◆ Do you have an image with text, or other elements with hard, detailed edges? JPEG won't work as well as GIF.

Of course, you may come across situations in which these rules don't apply. Plus there is plenty to consider in terms of the quality/file size ratio. Color Figure 2 shows a number of different picture types with varying attributes to show a quality comparison and their resulting file sizes.

The million dollar question, then, is how much quality are you willing to sacrifice for a smaller file size? Keeping in mind that most people are still using 28.8 modems, reducing your file sizes as small as possible is an important part of creating graphics for the Web. In my own opinion and experience, people are more forgiving of images that they see on the Web than they would be of images they see in a printed magazine. And most people would gladly trade in a reduction in image quality for a faster-loading Web page.

UNDERSTANDING AND USING GIF

The story of how a GIF is created and where it came from is about as interesting as watching a coat of paint dry. Suffice it to say that GIFs are currently the most popular format for images found on the Web. They are considered to be a "lossless" format, because although they are compressed, the image will look the same when decompressed (this is as opposed to JPEG, which can be a "lossy" file format).

When working with GIFs, you will be limited to a maximum 256 colors in your color palette. Because of this, your file size will generally be greatly reduced as fewer colors require less space. On the flip side, you may be limited in the amount of detail your image will have with only 256 colors. In very extreme cases, your image may even look blotchy or posterized. As I stated in the opening, however, the smaller file size is well worth it; most people are either conditioned to seeing less-than-magazine-quality images on the Web and would prefer to have them download faster, or they really could'nt see a difference anyway.

WORKING WITH COLOR ON THE WEB

Are you still awake? Well, just when you thought it could'nt get any more boring, let me introduce you to the wonderful world of Web color management. I'm still doing my best to plow right though this chapter and move on to the aspects of the Web that are more interesting and fun, but the truth is you really should at least skim the following pages, boring topic or not.

If you have a print background, as many new Web designers do, you may be uncontrollably excited at the prospect of finally working in a medium that frees you from the constraints of CMYK color. No more having to explain to clients why their project looked different on the monitor than it does on paper. No more print checks, or dealing with IRIS proofs or match prints.

Wow, do I miss those days…

The Web is a wonderful medium in terms of convenience and display, and when it comes to having an outlet for creativity, it's fantastic. Like everything else, though, it is not without its frustrations. The harsh truth is that color management on the Web can often be as complex, if not more so, as printing. Different platforms, various monitor resolutions, and other obstacles work to provide hazards that make it difficult to ensure that everyone can view your site as you meant it to be viewed.

As we'll continue to see, there are many ways that you can use Photoshop to help combat these problems and make your images as accessible as possible for all viewers.

BROWSER-FRIENDLY COLORS

As I've mentioned earlier (and will surely mention again), small file sizes are a key to building a successful Web site. Besides reducing the actual physical size of an image, to help achieve a lower file size you can limit the number of colors used. Understanding the very basics of how computer color works will go a long way toward helping you maximize your file size reduction efforts.

Color Management Systems are used by computers to allow us to see colors on our monitors. While most of these CMSs work in a similar fashion, each one has its own way of rendering any given color. This presents one of the basic problems that many Web designers face: they create a great-looking Web site on their Macintosh (where most of the creative community still is) only to receive angry calls from their clients who see the Web site as being very dark. This is because the Macintosh CMS will typically present color as lighter and brighter than a PC will. Dark blues on a Mac will look like black on a PC, and Macintosh orange will look like a muddy brown to its Windows counterpart.

As a designer, you're likely to work with a professional, high-end monitor, capable of displaying all 16.7 million possible colors, and a relatively powerful computer. The rest of the world is not quite up to these standards, however, and if you don't keep this in mind, you may find that you've included colors in your site that other computers are incapable of displaying. When that happens, the computer's CMS will try to compensate for this by substituting what it believes to be the closest available alternative. You can image the results—would you ever call a printer and tell him to run the job with whatever color he likes best? Of course not. When you allow the computer to choose a color for you, the end result can be disastrous.

An 8-bit system has the capability of displaying 256 colors. Of these, CMSs will usually claim 40 colors as reserved for the computer's system software, leaving 216 colors for Web designers to work with in designing sites. Mercifully, both Microsoft and Netscape use the same palette of 216 colors for their Web browsers. I see this as Bill Gates' way of apologizing for having created IE in the first place, but scientists say it has something to do with math. Either way, it's a happy bonus.

Photoshop 5.0, in a successful effort to become more of a Web-friendly program, has made it easy to use the standard 216-color palette:

1. Open your Swatches Palette by choosing Windows -> Swatches, as shown in Figure 2-1 and Color Figure 3.

2. Click on the right arrow of the palette to access the pull-down menu and choose Replace Swatches.

3. Find the Adobe Photoshop 5.0 folder in your computer, and locate and open the Goodies folder.

4. Choose and open the Color Palette folder, and select Web Safe Colors. Click Open. The result will change your Swatches Palette to contain the 216 Web-safe colors.

5. You can use any of these colors by placing you cursor over your desired color. Notice that the Eyedropper tool appears, as shown in Figure 2-3 (Color Figure 4 shows the Web-safe color palette.) Clicking on it loads it as your foreground color.

You'll see that 216 colors don't give you much to work with—there is a significant lack of lighter colors, and an overdose of blues and greens. In the end, it will be up to you, and the audience you are trying to reach, to decide what to do. Disregarding the palette altogether will allow for much nicer designs, but may not appear to users as intended. Using the 216-color palette will somewhat limit you in design, but gives you a safe haven from the growing number of inconsistencies between browsers.

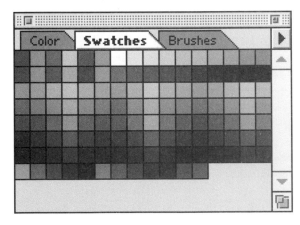

Figure 2–1: The Swatches Palette

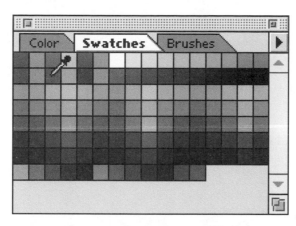

Figure 2–2: Your cursor turns to the Eyedropper tool, and clicking loads the chosen color as your foreground color.

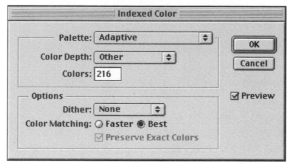

Figure 2–3: The Index Color dialog box

CREATING A GIF

When creating a GIF image, Photoshop 5.0 reduces the color palette by "indexing" the colors. To do this, choose Image -> Mode -> Indexed Color.

Photoshop will provide the dialog box shown in Figure 2-3. You have a number of palette options when it comes to creating a GIF:

◆ *Exact*

If you're using 256 colors or less, this option will be available. It will create a palette consisting of the exact colors used in your image, but cannot allow dithering (see below for more information on dithering).

◆ *System (Windows or Macintosh)*

Will use either the Windows or Macintosh default 8-bit color palette, respectively. Based on a uniform sampling of RGB

colors, it could be a good choice if you're creating an intranet that will only be seen on one platform.

◆ *Web*

Saves your image with the browser-safe web colors. Described in greater detail earlier in this chapter, the browser-safe color palette consists of 216 colors, and will most often be seen as you intended by both Netscape and Internet Explorer web browsers.

◆ *Uniform*

The uniform method will create a palette based on a uniform extraction from the spectrum. It starts getting too mathematical to explain well, and really—why bother? In my experience, it's largely useless.

◆ *Adaptive*

A popular method, and my personal favorite, the adaptive method does an excellent job of analyzing your image and assembling a palette consisting of the best possible colors. This choice will give you the best possible results with the least amount of work on your part. Although this one will cost you the most in terms of file size, you'll want to use it when working with photographic or other continuous-tone image work that

originally contained more than 256 colors.

◆ *Custom*

The custom method lets you use your own palette for your image. The menu in the Swatches Palette allows you to save swatches for later use, and the custom method in the Index Color dialog box allows you to choose any saved color palette.

◆ *Previous*

This feature lets you use the same palette on multiple images. It cannot be accessed unless you have already converted an image using either the adaptive or custom method.

So which do you choose? Well, there are a number of variables to determine before answering. The easy answer is to say "just use the Adaptive method and let Photoshop do the work for you," but that's also a tad irresponsible. The truth is that there are times when you may want to use any one of these methods. Adaptive is used most often, and I would recommend using it as your primary weapon. But if cross-browser consistency is important to you, then choosing the Web method may be your best option.

Additionally, keep in mind that just because you use only 256 colors in your images, your Web page may still look bad from a color perspective. If your viewer is using a monitor that only supports 256 colors, you could be in trouble. One image on your Web page may be fine, but suppose you use three different images, each with its own 256-color palette. That's more colors than an 8-bit monitor can handle, and so it may compensate in undesirable ways, as illustrated in Figure 2-4 and Color Figure 5. If this is a major concern, you may want to consider designing a palette that you like and using the Custom or Previous method.

Also, while GIFs do handle most photographic images more acceptably than many people will give them credit for, they don't always handle large blocks of colors well. Figure 2-6 on page 47 shows red text over a yellow background and how the dithering has created an odd pattern within the letters. Avoid this by choosing the Web method when indexing. (Read further into this chapter for information on CLUTs and reducing the number of colors kept in a Web palette.)

When you choose Index Color for an image with layers, you will first see a dialog box asking if you want to flatten your layers. Click OK to continue conversion to Index Color mode. If you click Cancel, the conversion is aborted.

Figure 2-4: Eight-bit monitors may present your graphics as very posterized if you don't use web-safe colors, or use multiple but different web-safe color palettes.

Color Depth	Number of Colors
3	2x2x2=8
4	2x2x2x2=16
5	2x2x2x2x2=32
6	2x2x2x2x2x2=64
7	2x2x2x2x2x2x2=128
8	2x2x2x2x2x2x2x2=256

Figure 2–5: The arithmetic behind color depth

COLOR DEPTH

When you choose either the Adaptive or Custom color palette, you will have the option of selecting the bit depth as well. Bit depth is calculated as 2^{nth}. For example, an 8-bit graphic is 256 colors, and an 8-bit monitor is capable of displaying 256 colors. This is determined as 2 to the 8th power, or 2 x 2 x 2 x 2 x 2 x 2 x 2 x 2 = 256. Although it's simple arithmetic, Figure 2-5 shows a chart of how many colors are in various bit depths.

If you index color to create a GIF and you select the Adaptive (or Uniform) palette, you can select the color depth of your image. It won't take much time to experiment—try to use this option to your advantage in reducing file size. Before you accept 8-bit color, reduce the depth to 7 bit. If it looks good, reduce the depth to 6 bit, then 5 bit, and so on until your image is starting to be affected by the lack of color. Doing this can produce huge results in terms of faster download times.

DITHERING

If you look at a printed piece through a loupe (a small magnifying glass), you can see that the cyan, magenta, yellow, and black are printed in certain patterns, too small for the human eye to see without help. The patterns and close proximity of the colors create an illusion of other colors that are not printed. Photoshop uses the limitations of the human eye to do this with index color palettes as well. When 256 colors are not enough to accurately represent your image, Photoshop will use its dither feature to create the illusion of a color in graphics consisting of various hues.

The index color dialog box gives you the option of turning the dither feature on or off. You'll have to judge for yourself when dithering is appropriate. If your image is made up of just a few colors, it may not be necessary and cause your file to grow unnecessarily larger in file size. Additionally, if you are using large blocks of colors, as shown in Figure 2-6, dithering may have a negative effect on the overall appearance. Conversely, dithering is a definite must if you are indexing an image with a wide tonal range, multiple color hues, or subtle shading. Figure 2-7 shows the difference between dithering and not dithering images that require it.

To apply dithering to an image:

1. Choose Image -> Mode -> Index Color from the menu bar.

2. Select Adaptive or Web for the desired palette.

3. For Dither, select Diffusion.

4. Choose either Faster or Best for Color Matching, and check the box marked Preserve Exact Colors for the best results.

CLUTS

As I will discuss in more detail later in this chapter, when you are creating a GIF image for the Web, you will do so in Photoshop by choosing Image -> Mode -> Index Color. Doing this will reduce your color palette to 256 colors (or less). These colors are stored in a palette called the Color Lookup Table (CLUT), which is invisibly attached to your GIF image.

You can help reduce the file size of your image by reducing the number of colors in a CLUT. To see how many colors are in your CLUT, index your image and open your color palette. If you index your image using the browser-safe color palette (Web palette), your Swatches will show all 216 colors. It will show 216 colors even if your image is made up of less. There is a simple way to reduce the CLUTs—although it can be tedious. You may want to make the following into an Action, to expedite the process.

1. Open an RGB image and index it by choosing Image -> Mode -> Index Color. Select Web from the pull-down menu.

2. Change the image back to RGB by choosing Image -> Mode -> RGB.

3. Index the file again, but this time choose Exact from the palette pull down. Notice the reduction in the number of colors.

4. Save the image as a GIF.

Figure 2–6: Dithering doesn't work well with large blocks of colors. The left image is the original, red text on a yellow background, in RGB. The right image is after indexing the colors, using the Web palette and a diffusion dither.

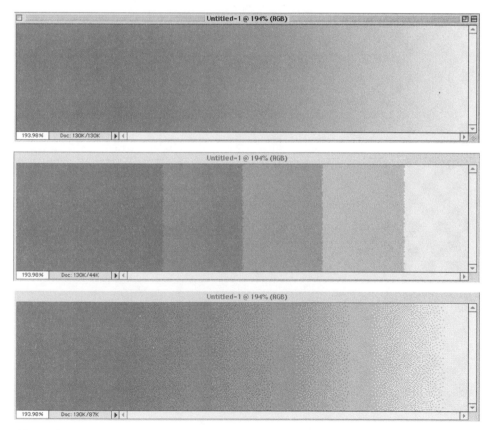

Figure 2–7: Top image: shows an extreme gradient in its original TIF format.
Center Image: Index Color: Web palette, no dithering
Bottom Image: Index Color: Web palette, diffusion dithering

INTERLACING IMAGES TO RELIEVE WEB FRUSTRATION

Graphics on a Web site can download in two ways: annoying and nonannoying. The annoying way has them downloading from the top downward, making the user wait until it's completely finished before deciding whether or not the image is important. The nonannoying way is called interlacing. Interlacing, in a nonscientific description, allows the image to appear as a whole immediately but very blurry. As it downloads, it becomes more clear, so that the user can tell more quickly whether or not they want to wait for the full picture.

When you go to save your index image as a GIF, you'll get the simple dialog box shown in Figure 2-8 asking whether or not to interlace. Click the radio button that turns interlacing on. Figure 2-9 shows an example of how a dithered image loads in a browser.

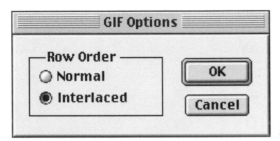

Figure 2–8: The Interlace dialog box

Figure 2–9: Interlaced GIFs load in gradually.

ANIMATION AND TRANSPARENCY

Because both of these features are such an important aspect of GIFs, and each carries its own unique complexities, they each have their own chapter in this book. See Chapter 8 for more information on Animation, and Chapter 3 for more information on Transparency.

CREATING A JPEG

As I stated earlier, JPEGs are the format of choice if tight photographic detail and allegiance to color is a priority.

Creating a JPEG is decidedly easier than creating a GIF, however, as there is no need to index the colors or concern yourself with any particular color palette. There is no such thing as Web-safe colors when working with JPEGs—they are capable of displaying more than 16.7 million colors. However, don't forget that your image will still be limited to the type of browser that your user will be using. Figure 2-4 and Color Figure 5, presented earlier, show how a beautiful photographic image saved as a JPEG will appear on an 8-bit color monitor. Obviously, situations like this are undesirable and will take away from the overall effect.

THE COMPRESSION SLIDER

The most important tool when creating a JPEG is the Compression Slider, shown in Figure 2-10. Updated from Photoshop 4.0, this new slider is more Web-designer friendly, offering more compression options ranging from 0 to 10 (0 being maximum compression/lowest quality, 10 being lowest compression/maximum quality). You can open the slider when you choose File -> Save As -> JPEG.

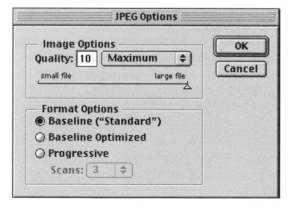

Figure 2–10: The JPEG Compression Slider.

Obviously, by choosing a quality setting of 8, 9, or 10, you can ensure a great-looking image that may take forever to download, while a quality setting of 0, 1 or 2 probably won't be worth downloading in the first place, no matter how fast.

Don't be fooled, though. Choose a quality setting of 0 and hit OK. Your image will look like it hasn't changed at all! Great—maximum compression with no loss of quality. Actually, the truth is you won't see the effect on your image until you close it and open it again. However, once you do, don't do any further edits—JPEG is a "lossy" compression method, literally destroying certain data from your image. You will notice a progressive deterioration in your image as you continue to reedit and resave it.

 As you'll read in other places in this book, it is a good idea to save your original, layered graphics as .psd files (Photoshop format). In the future, if you need to make any changes to your images, you'll want to work off the original.

Figure 2-11 shows the differences in image quality for various quality settings. As a designer, when working with JPEGs, you will have to decide for yourself how much quality you are willing to give up for a smaller file size.

As you can see from the figure provided, there is a big difference in file sizes between the lowest quality setting and the highest quality setting. With enough comparison of file compression, you'll probably find a number of lower quality image settings that have smaller sizes than comparable GIFs. Although some of the file sizes seem very small and thus very attractive, it is important to note that the figures could be a bit misleading: in a download race between two images, one GIF and one JPEG, both 50K in size, the GIF will win, as the compressed JPEG file must first spend time to decompress before it loads.

FORMATTING OPTIONS

Besides the slider, you will have to choose between three different format options:

◆ *Baseline (Standard).* The universally supported format, Baseline (Standard) will load your images from top to bottom, with one pass. This can be rather annoying, as your user will have to wait a while before deciding whether or not the image is important enough to the site's content to wait for downloading.

◆ *Baseline (Optimized).* This option will optimize the color information of the image, resulting in smaller file sizes, without losing the quality people seek when using JPEGs. But it's not a recognized format by all browsers, so not everybody will be able to view images saved this way.

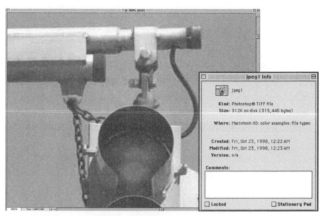

Figure 2–11: Various quality and file sizes for different JPEG compression settings.

Quality setting: 1 (low)
File Size: 36K

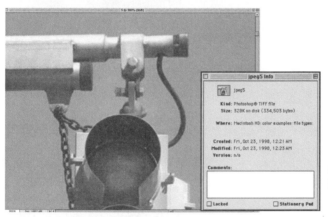

Quality setting: 5 (medium)
File Size: 64K

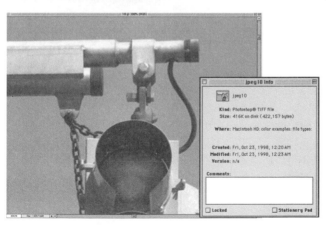

Quality setting: 10 (high)
File Size: 329K

◆   *Progressive.* The Progressive format will act much like the interlaced GIFs we spoke about earlier. The image will appear on screen seemingly as a blur, and get more clear with each pass or "scan." You set the number of passes that the image will make until completion. The prices you pay are a more hefty requirement of RAM by the user for viewing, and the danger of this format not being recognized by all browsers.

Although current support for the latter of these format options is not widespread, time moves quickly when it comes to the Internet. It won't be long before all three formatting options will be universally accepted, and you'll need to be familiar with their use differences. And as speed becomes less of a factor on the Web (whether through faster modems or an increasing move toward cable lines), and new HTML tags emerge, the popularity of GIF for anything other than animation may wane and shift toward the higher quality JPEG format. However, along with all of these changes come additions to formats as well, and it may not be long before both GIF and JPEG are replaced as the hometown hero by the up-and-coming PNG contender (see page 55).

BLURRING THE LINES TO REDUCE FILE SIZE

JPEG works best when there are smooth transitions between colors. So a trick that is popular among Web designers who favor the JPEG format is to selectively blur certain parts of your image.

Much of the photography that you will use in you Web pages will contain a main subject, surrounded by supporting data. Figure 2-12 shows my original picture of a man and a woman sitting in what appears to be a hay field or a hay truck. They are obviously the main subjects of the image and everything surrounding them is necessary for the idea behind the picture but will not be the object of focus.

Figure 2-12 is the picture in its original state, saved as a JPEG with a quality compression setting of 8, saved as Baseline (Standard) for a resulting file size of 140K. However, when I make a selection around everything but the two people, feather it with a feather radius of 2, and apply a Gaussian Blur (choose Filter -> Blur -> Gaussian Blur) with a blur radius of 2, the resulting file size is only 120K, a significant difference. Comparing this picture with the original, shows a negligible difference in photo quality—Figure 2–13 shows the slight blur on everything but the people. Apply an additional blur of 1 to the entire image and the file is reduced even more, down to 100K (Figure 2-14) with still very little visible difference to the image quality.

Figure 2–12: The original picture saved as a JPEG with a quality of 8 has a file size of 140K.

Figure 2–13: By blurring the background slightly, the file size is reduced to 120K, with no major quality loss detectible.

Figure 2–14: File size is reduced further to 100K when the blur is expanded to include the main subjects.

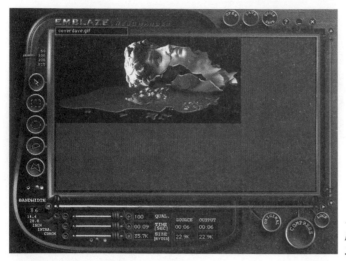

*Figure 2–15: Emblaze Web Charger
program can help reduce file sizes for
your web graphics.*

REDUCING FILE SIZES FURTHER: THIRD-PARTY PROGRAMS

There are a number of various third-party programs that can help you reduce file sizes and offer better compression than Photoshop. My personal favorite is Emblaze Web Charger, by GEO Publishing, Inc. This software, whose interface is shown in Figure 2-15, works with JPEG and GIF (as well as PICT and BMP).

An extremely easy tool to learn and use, you can import your GIF, JPEG, BMP, or PICT original file into Web Charger, and after adjusting a few settings, you can see a resulting JPEG-compatible file with as much as a 400% reduction in file size. Figure 2-16 shows the differences in file sizes between images both before and after using the Web Charger software.

The idea behind Web Charger is that after your image is imported, you can select which portions of your image you wish to have the most clarity. The program will then set about reducing the remainder of the image for maximum compression. However, even if you want the entire image to have the highest quality detail, Web Charger will be able to make the size of your file smaller than a similar GIF image. If you are setting a maximum file size that you are trying to keep your Web pages under, Web Charger will allow you to view your file at various compressions before completion, so that you can balance quality versus file size before your final save.

You can reach GEO Publishing for more information on the Emblaze Web Charger at: www.emblaze.com

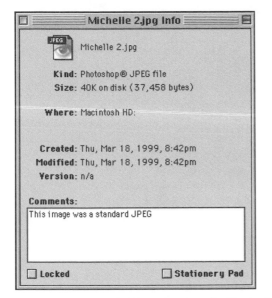 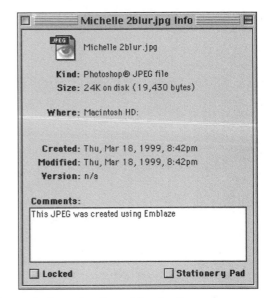

Figure 2–16: Differences in file size before and after using the emblazed software for compression.

PNG: THE NEW KID ON THE BLOCK

The PNG format is a fairly new Web format, developed as a third alternative to GIF and JPEG. PNG has caused a lot of excitement in the Web graphics community, and while it's used less than GIF and JPEG, I would implore anybody who is serious about Web design to learn PNG as a preparation for the future.

PNG has a number of interesting features, including:

◆ Like a GIF, it has a lossless compression technique.

◆ It supports 24 bit color, for the clarity of a JPEG.

◆ It includes an 8-bit mask for GIF style transparency.

◆ It can adjust colors for consistency across platforms.

◆ It has higher quality interlacing.

Of particular note is PNG's ability to take the guesswork out of how your graphics look on different systems. The frustration of getting colors to look similar cross-platform can be enough to make even the most die-hard Macintosh user go out and buy an NT system.

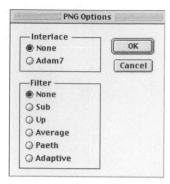

Figure 2–17: The PNG dialog box

Unfortunately, at this point, the 3.0 versions of both Netscape and IE don't support PNG, and it may be a while until Communicator and IE 4.0 filter their way into the masses and you can actively design for them without excluding older browsers.

CREATING PNG FILES

Figure 2-17 shows the dialog box that comes up when you choose File -> Save As -> PNG when saving a flattened RGB, grayscale, or indexed color image. The top section of the dialog box offers you the opportunity to have your image open progressively on your Web site, as it might by choosing "interlacing" when creating a GIF image. As the name Adam7 infers, the graphic will load up in 7 passes, as opposed to just a couple for GIF, or 3, 4, or 5 for a Progressive JPEG.

The bottom portion of the dialog box decides the way the PNG will compress your image to create smaller file sizes. Choosing None results in no compression and ultimately larger file sizes. The other choices each have a few subtly different features, all of which will reduce file sizes in varying amounts depending on the type of images you have. An in-depth discussion of each choice is beyond the scope of this book, as PNG is not yet widely used. Experiment with each though, to see which works the best with your particular files, although the differences in file size between each setting will be somewhat negligible. Figure 2-18 shows some file size differences.

CROSS-PLATFORM COMPATIBILITY

There's nothing worse than being a Macintosh Web designer working on a client's project, spending long hours hours to get the colors of your client's site just the way they want them, only to receive a phone call that the site is way too dark on his Windows computer. The PNG format will reduce the probability of this happening—it saves the gamma values used in any particular image, which neither JPEG or GIF does. When a PNG image is opened on a system other than the one it was created on, it will self correct itself by comparing the gamma settings of both the system on which it was created and the one on which it was opened. To ensure that this works properly, how-

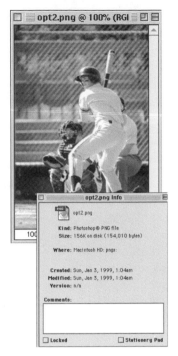

Figure 2–18: File size differences using the PNG format. The first one was saved using the "None" setting (176K), the second with the "Average" setting (156K), and the third with the "Adaptive" setting (152K).

ever, you'll want to make sure that you properly calibrate your system. (See the Photoshop Users Manual that came with your program for step-by-step instructions on how to calibrate your system.)

PNG TRANSPARENCY

PNG transparency is actually a more powerful transparency technique than the GIF89a format (see Chapter 3, "Transparency"). The GIF transparency allows you to choose certain colors to make transparent, but does not allow for a gradual transition of colors, so you cannot make any color only partially transparent. PNG allows for more realism than GIF because it uses masks (alpha channels) for a smoother transition of colors.

You create transparent PNGs not with a separate dialog box, but right in your image by creating a mask and saving it as a separate alpha channel. One of the ways you can create a mask is by making a selection and choosing Select -> Save Selection. You can manipulate the selection in the Channels Palette, including the variable transparency percentage.

Although support for PNG in general is gaining, even the newer browsers have been slow to implement support for masks. As of the writing of this book, Netscape Communicator supports PNG, but not alpha channels, while Internet Explorer 4 only partially supports each of them.

Saving a channel will add approximately 20% or more to your file size, unlike GIF transparency, which actually *reduces* your file size.

SUMMARY

Knowing the advantages and disadvantages of each format is important in creating a Web site that is functional, attractive and quick to download. While each designer may have his or her own special reason for why they prefer one format over another, each format provides useful tools for putting your image and info out on the Web. Experimenting with each is the best way for you to conclude which is the right file format for you, and keeping your eyes opened to all of the new advances and changes in format standards will help you prepare for how your work will be viewed in the future.

TRANSPARENCY

NOW YOU SEE IT, NOW YOU DON'T

How useful would it be if you had the ability to make unimportant things suddenly disappear? By one touch, any undesirable thing in your life would no longer hold any significance or be in your way? Credit card bills, toxic waste, mimes, and children who cry on airplanes would suddenly vanish as the world breathed a sigh of relief, wondering whether we could get rid of Barbra Streisand records just as easily.

I'm sorry—I got lost in a personal daydream. Obviously, these things can't happen. To better illustrate my point on transparency, I'll provide a better example:

See that white space directly above? Well, it's not really white space—it's a transparent paragraph. I wrote it, but decided that because it was boring and unnecessary to the rest of this chapter, I'd make it transparent. It's still there, but you can see the white of the page below in its place. I've saved myself the cost of the ink that would have been used to print it, and it is no longer able to detract from my primary message.

Transparency on the Web works in much the same way—you make a portion of your image vanish, so it is no longer visible. It will still act as a placeholder, but, like my transparent paragraph saved me the cost of the ink I would have used to print it, transparent portions of my Web graphics save me the cost of large file sizes, and help my images download faster.

Photoshop provides you with the resources you'll need to create transparent images, while the rest of this chapter will give you information on how to effectively use the power of transparency to streamline your graphics for better Web use.

TRANSPARENT FILES

If you read or even skimmed the chapter on file types for the Web, you know that as of the time of this writing, there are two main file types for Web graphics: JPEG and GIF. While each has its pros and cons, one of the main benefits of using GIF is its ability to make images or parts of images transparent, unlike JPEG files, which do not have that option.

Transparency in Photoshop can only be achieved with images that have been indexed. However, unlike the standard GIF format, which you access via the File -> Save As menu, transparent files must be exported as GIF89a through the File -> Export -> GIF89a option.

To make a portion of an image transparent:

1. Open or create a new image and change the mode to index color. I am using the image shown in Figure 3–1—a navigation bar that I created, that is simple and deliberately constructed to provide both curves and straight edges for this chapter's demonstration.

Figure 3–1: This sample navigation bar has angled edges, curves and flat lines.

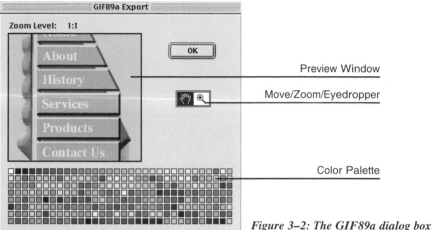

Figure 3–2: The GIF89a dialog box

2. Choose File -> Export -> GIF89a.

3. This export selection gives you access to the dialog box shown and described in Figure 3–2. A preview screen of your image is displayed in the top left of the dialog box. Directly below is the palette containing all of the colors in your image (maximum of 256 because the image has been indexed—boxes in the palette that are not used will appear with an x through them). On the right are three tools for you to use in making your transparency:

   ◆ Use the Hand tool to pan through your image if it is too big for the Preview window.

   ◆ Use the Magnifying Glass to zoom in and out of your image for more detailed work.

   ◆ Use the Eyedropper tool to select the colors you wish to make transparent, either from the image itself or from the color palette. Clicking on a color designates it as transparent—Option + clicking on a selected color takes away its transparency.

4. Change the preview color for your transparency by clicking the gray colored box marked Transparency Preview Color. Use the Color Picker to choose a color not represented in your image.

In my image, I only wanted the white pixels to be transparent, so I clicked on the white pixel in the color palette.

As Figure 3–3 shows, there is a dark outline around the white pixel box. Even more startling is the preview window, which shows that all of the white in my image has now turned to gray. Gray is the default color that Photoshop uses to show which areas of your image are transparent.

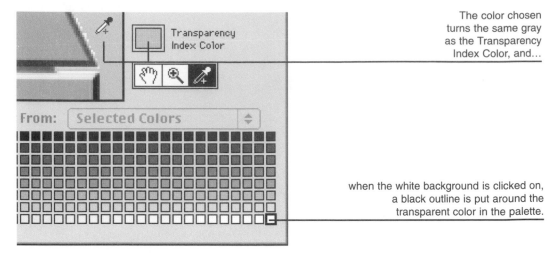

The color chosen turns the same gray as the Transparency Index Color, and...

when the white background is clicked on, a black outline is put around the transparent color in the palette.

Figure 3–3: Turning a color transparent makes the color change to the default gray and puts a black outline around the color in the palette.

This is fine, unless you use gray in your image. Then it will be difficult to know what turned transparent and what didn't.

If you later open your exported transparent image in Photoshop, the color you chose as your preview color will appear as part of your image in the areas that were meant to be transparent. Although your browser will not see the color, Photoshop will, and this makes for rough times in later edits. Avoid problems by saving your export with a unique name, rather that saving over your original file.

GIF89A PROBLEMS AND HOW TO OVERCOME THEM

Although transparency is one of the most attractive features of working with GIFs, there are a few problems:

◆   There is no partial anything when working with transparent GIFs. You cannot make a pixel only 50% transparent to allow for smooth gradations—each pixel must be either on or off.

◆   Choosing a color is not like working with the Magic Wand tool: pixels do not have to be touching each other to be selected. In other words, if I choose to eliminate the white surrounding my picture, but there is an equal tone of white within my picture, all whites will be made transparent.

Figure 3–4: The letters are white just like the background, so by making the background transparent, I also make the button letters transparent.

Figure 3–4 illustrates this last problem—as you can see, my original image contained white letters as well as a white background. Unfortunately, even though I only want to make the background transparent, I have made the letters transparent too (there is a gray color over them to indicate this in my preview window).

The first and easiest solution is to simply replace the background color in your original Photoshop document. As Color Figure 6 shows, since there is no red in my image, I changed the background from white to red, and then made the red transparent.

However, that same figure also shows that I have a new problem—there is a red "ring" around much of my image (notably the curved areas) also referred to as a "halo." Considering my image will appear on a slightly textured background, this is unacceptable. (Figure 3–5 also shows the halo problem, although you can see it more easily in the Color Figure).

We can solve these problems in Photoshop before we ever open the GIF89a dialog box. As we'll see in the following example, we can use a few different techniques, your choice of which may change depending upon the type of file you are working with.

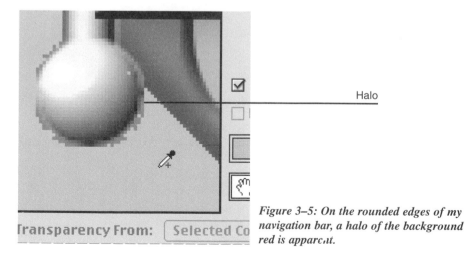

Halo

Figure 3–5: On the rounded edges of my navigation bar, a halo of the background red is apparent.

Solution 1: Choosing Your Background Wisely

If your Web site is a solid color, then there's not too much to worry about—simply use that same color for the background of your graphic, and there's no problem. The problem comes when your background is a texture. Solutions for this assume that you have preplanned your Web site to some extent and know in advance what your background will be.

Figure 3–6 and Color Figure 7 show the background texture that I will be using on my Web site.

It is fairly complex, using a number of red/orange shades. I could try to avoid transparency altogether, and just use the background graphic as the background for my image, but it would be practically impossible to make it line up properly on my Web page. Even if I could, there is no way to ensure how it will line up on other systems, browsers, etc.

What I'll do instead is use a solid color for the background of my image, but I'll choose it by taking an approximate average of the colors in my background. In this situation, you would take the following steps:

1. Index the colors in the background image, originally RGB, by choosing Image -> Mode -> Index Color.

2. For the Palette, choose Web, to ensure that all the colors in the palette would be browser safe, with a diffusion dither.

3. Choose Image -> Mode -> RGB and turn your image back to RGB color.

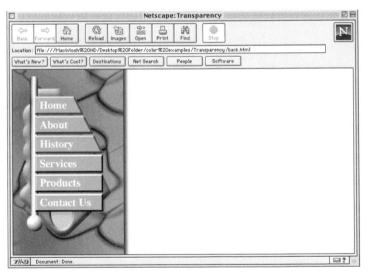

Figure 3–6: The background, shown also in Color Figure 7,
has a sidebar with multiple shades of red and orange, as well as
a black line design through it.

4. Back to indexing again, choose Image -> Mode -> Index Color, and select Custom for your palette. That will bring up the Custom Table shown in Figure 3–7 and Color Figure 8. This table lets you see the basic colors that make up your image, and since you had turned them into browser-safe colors (Step 2), you can be confident of not getting any surprises with them.

5. With your eye, choose one of the colors in the table that looks like it would be an average of all the colors. Clicking on it brings up the color palette, as shown in Figure 3–8. Write down the RGB values on a piece of paper.

6. Revert your image back to it's original state by choosing File -> Revert and fill your background color with the average color that you selected from the color table.

7. When you go to make your image transparent this time, it will still have a halo, but, as you can see in Figure 3–9 and Color Figure 9, it is practically imperceptible.

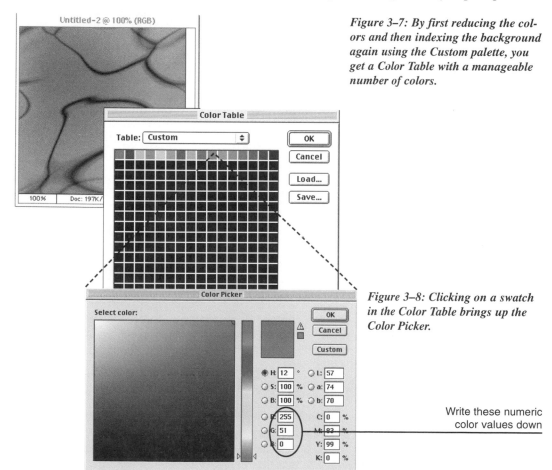

Figure 3–7: By first reducing the colors and then indexing the background again using the Custom palette, you get a Color Table with a manageable number of colors.

Figure 3–8: Clicking on a swatch in the Color Table brings up the Color Picker.

Write these numeric color values down

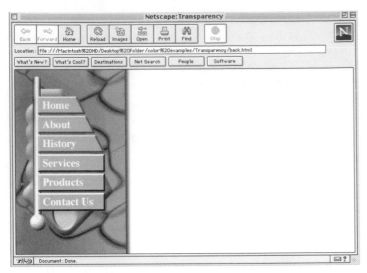

Figure 3–9: The halo is imperceptible because of the color I chose.

Solution 2: Using Channels

Alpha Channels are some of the most powerful tools in Photoshop, and can be helpful even when creating transparent GIFs. For this next example, we'll be using the same navigation bar that we used in the previous example, starting back at a point before the image was indexed, and was still unflattened. This time, instead of relying on an average color to minimize any halos, take advantage of Alpha Channels to provide a sometimes more effective transparency:

1. Command + click (Ctrl + click in Windows) on Layer 1, the layer which contains your image. Doing so will select everything on that layer.

2. Choose Select -> Save Selection, which creates an Alpha Channel named Alpha 1 in your Channels Palette.

3. Although the color channels will merge when you index the colors, Alpha 1 will remain intact. Index your image by choosing Image -> Mode -> Index Colors and select Adaptive for your palette.

4. In the GIF89a Export Palette, check the pull-down menu in the Transparency From selection. Select Alpha 1 and the preview window displays the default grAy transparency indicator color in the areas outside your mask.

Solution 3: Making Transparencies from Layers

Oftentimes Web designers lay out their entire Web page in Photoshop. Although Photoshop was never intended to act as a layout program such as Quark or PageMaker, it works pretty well for laying out your Web site. The Layers feature allows you to put different elements on your page and have an idea of how it should lay out in your browser.

Figure 3–10 and Color Figure 10 shows how my navigation bar will interact with the other elements on my sample page. The Layers Palette shows how each of the elements is in a separate layer. Because indexed color images cannot support layers, you would have to make the transparency of each object from the individual layers themselves (the alternative would be the arduous task of moving each object from its layer into its own separate canvas). Because everyone's general Photoshop layout of their Web page is going to differ, I'll be able to explain this section better by writing the steps that I took, with Figure 3–10 serving as the reference point:

1. Starting with my navigation bar in Layer 1, I make all other Layers invisible. I do this by turning off the "eye" icon on the left of all layers except Layer 3. The checkerboard behind my image indicates that the area surrounding it will be transparent. This is the way your canvas looks by default when you make the background layer invisible.

2. I crop the image so that there won't be a lot of empty space around my navigation bar to get in the way of other images in my browser.

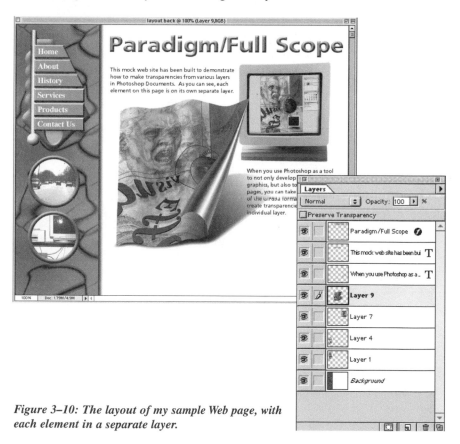

Figure 3–10: The layout of my sample Web page, with each element in a separate layer.

3. I choose File -> Export -> GIF89a. Because the image I am exporting is a layer in an RGB image rather than a flattened Index Color image, I don't get the usual dialog box for GIF89a. Instead, I get the dialog box shown in Figure 3–11. Within this dialog box, I choose how I want my image to be indexed, much as if I had chosen Index Color from the Image -> Mode menu. I choose Adaptive as my preferred color palette.

4. To see which areas of my image will be transparent, I push the Preview button. This button gives me access to what looks like the traditional GIF89a dialog box, with the color palette and the preview window, as shown in Figure 3–12. This time, however, I cannot change the areas of transparency—those have been designated by my layer. I still have the pan and zoom tools available to me, so I can check to make sure that everything is as it should be. I click OK and name the image.

As you'll come to see in your work, there are plenty of situations that could pose challenges to you as you try to make your images transparent for the Web. Keep experimenting to discover which solution will most effectively help you achieve your goal.

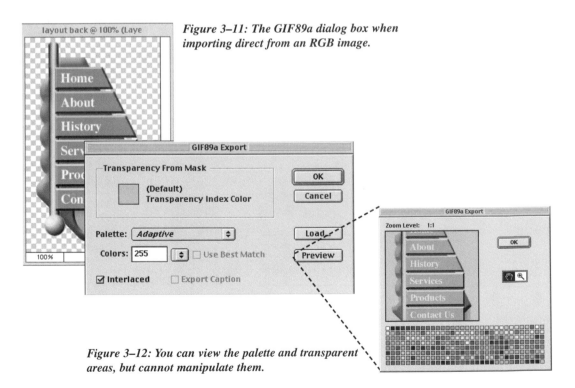

Figure 3–11: The GIF89a dialog box when importing direct from an RGB image.

Figure 3–12: You can view the palette and transparent areas, but cannot manipulate them.

THE TRUTH BEHIND SHADOWS AND GLOWS

There are some who claim to have developed fairly elaborate methods of preserving shadows and glows when they are part of transparent GIF. The truth is, however, that there is really just one basic rule that must be followed: put your shadowed or glowing image over your background color or the average color of your background texture and hope for the best.

If you worked through the first solution to the transparency problems presented earlier, you'll have noticed that the halo you were left with was no more than a pixel or two deep. Because your images had fairly hard edges (I'm including anti-aliased edges as "hard"), you were able to keep the halo to insignificant levels, even if the background color you chose was only the average of all the colors in your site background.

Shadows and glows pose a different problem. Figure 3–13 shows an example of each. As you can see, both effects have extremely soft edges, and to make them look realistic, there has to be a gradual transition from its core to its edge. In that span of transition, the background behind the image can be seen in greater detail. As Figure 3–14 shows, using an average color for the background of my image when my browser window has a complex design doesn't help much—the 1 or 2 pixel halo is around my shadow, instead of around the title. Since the color is showing through the lighter portions of the shadow, the average color is more obvious.

Figure 3–13: Shadows and glows are partially transparent pixels, so the background shows through them.

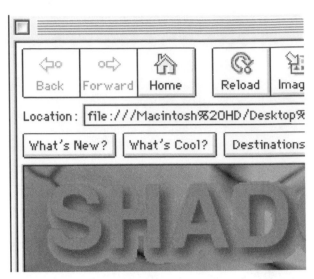

Figure 3–14: The average color technique is obvious behind images with shadows or glows.

This problem stems from the fact that, as mentioned earlier, pixels in a transparent GIF are either on or off—there is no partial transparency. This will be less of a problem when the PNG format plays more of a part in Web graphics (see Chapter 2), since PNG allows for a more natural gradation of colors.

But the reality is that as of the writing of this book, PNG is not a widely used format, so GIF transparency is the best you're going to get. For the best effects, try to use shadowed images over areas of your Web site that will contain solid colors. If you must use a texture, try to use one that is seamless by virtue of the design, such as woven cloth, or sandstone. Backgrounds like the ones I used in the last few examples will make it more difficult if not impossible to properly make a shadowed image transparent.

SUMMARY

Square shapes, hard edges, and sharp corners are not always welcome on the Web. Neither are unnecessarily large file sizes. Understanding how transparency works provides a partial solution to both of these matters. The GIF89a file format for indexed graphics allows you to turn any desired color in your image into a transparency. And by carefully taking the time to understand the colors that surround your image in the background, you can take steps toward ensuring that even partially opaque elements like shadows and glows will be largely unaffected by a transparency effort. And the future of the Web, with the PNG format rapidly becoming more of a staple, promises to embrace transparent images even further and allow you considerably more flexibility in creating content for the Web.

chapter 4

CREATING BACKGROUND GRAPHICS AND EFFECTS

Arguably the background image or color is the most important element for setting the overall theme and layout structure of your Web page. A well-done background can subtly promote organization and class, as well as provide the shell for the other site items and information. A poorly done background can obstruct copy, draw too much attention to itself, even drive your audience away. Backgrounds composed of tiles, borders, watermarks, frames, and even entire photographs litter the Web as we see it today, and are often the impetus for judgement of an entire site. Understanding not only how background images are made, but receiving insight as to what works and what doesn't will play a major role in deciding how much a part your background will play in the success or failure of your Web site.

Photoshop 5.0 provides the tools that you need to create both great and horrible backgrounds. This chapter will show you the difference between the two of them, and provide ideas, recipes, and suggestions to ensure that your background image is an effective part of your site. In addition, by combining creative graphic skills with the color, file types, and transparency information reviewed in previous chapters, you'll learn to design backgrounds that are not only interesting and detailed, but assume a minimal amount of file size.

MAKING DECISIONS

Okay, so you have a basic knowledge of HTML and Photoshop, and you're ready to start building your Web site. One of the first decisions you'll have to make is what your background will look like. This may not be as easy as it sounds, and its importance really shouldn't be overlooked. Your background, whether it is a solid color or an image, will set the graphic tone of your site. Consciously or subconsciously, your viewer is going to be affected in some way by your background, so try to keep the following points in mind while making your choice:

◆ **Know your audience.** Who is going to be looking at your Web site? If it's a personal home page, then go as crazy as you'd like—reflect your own personality. If you're building a site to sell a product or service, you may want a more professional look, such as a solid color with a subtle border. You will want to be more or less conservative depending on the industry.

◆ **Text can be tough to read.** If your background is too outrageous, or has a lot of colors or designs, it may be very difficult to read any text that you write. Make sure that the information you provide is clear and legible. More detailed information about intrusive backgrounds is coming up later in this chapter.

◆ **Watch your file size.** It's easy to get carried away with backgrounds. Can you put a full-blown picture of a corporate headquarters in the background for everyone to see? Sure you can—but it may take a year and a half to download. (see Chapter 1, "Photoshop Reviews"). Don't drive your audience away by making them wait too long for your background image.

HOW BACKGROUND IMAGES APPEAR IN YOUR BROWSER

You establish the way your background will look within the <BODY> tag of your HTML document. Basically, there are two separate commands associated with it:

 Throughout this book are HTML references when necessary to help illustrate a point. You'll notice that tags are written in all caps—that is not an HTML requirement, just a personal method I use to quickly separate commands from other text.

<BODY BGCOLOR=#000000> This uses a hexidecimal setting to create a solid color (more on this later in the chapter).

<BODY BACKGROUND="imagename.gif"> This places your background image in your browser, starting at the top left, and tiling it infinitely down and to the right.

You can also change the Link color as well as the color of the Links you have visited with LINK=#hex and VLINK=#hex respectively.

The background image is different from other images that you'll use in three distinct ways:

◆ It is the only image that can touch the sides of the browser window. All other images, depending on the browser, will come no closer that 15–50 pixels away.

◆ It cannot be animated.

◆ It is placed in the top corner of your browser window, and will tile (repeat itself) infinitely down and to the right to cover the entire browser body.

This last point can be a bit tricky. As said earlier, you want to watch your file size—if you create an image for your background that is 1250 pixels square, it will take a long time to download. However, a very small background can take a long time, too. If your background image is only 125 pixels square, the browser will need considerable time to repeat the image over and over again. You'll want to experiment to come up with a good compromise for your background image.

BALANCING DESIGN WITH FUNCTIONALITY

While creating graphics, images, and colors are largely the fun part about building a Web site, keep in mind that your main purpose is to get your information out to your audience. Wild designs and unwise color choices can make your site difficult if not impossible to understand, and potentially drive your viewers away from your site.

Figure 4–1 shows how a dark, wild design can interfere with the text on a Web site. The text color in this case is the browser default of black. In this example the image used to create the background has become the focus, and prohibits the user from gaining any real use from visiting the site.

In Figure 4–2, the background has stayed the same, but this time I have taken into consideration that the image used is dark and so I've chosen to set my text in white instead of black. This helps a little, but there is still far too much attention given to the background.

A different background design was used in Figure 4–3, which is a vast improvement over the previous examples. This time, I used an image that was far more subdued—not only does it help the text to be more pronounced, but due to its simplicity, its color palette was reduced and therefore became a smaller file size.

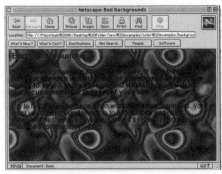

Figure 4–1: This background is so busy and dark that the text is nearly impossible to read.

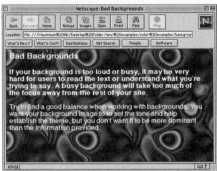

Figure 4–2: Changing the font color to white over the same background makes it easier to read.

Figure 4–3: Using a less complex background helps the text be more legible, although it is still too dark in general.

Figure 4–4: By making the same background lighter, our page still holds graphic interest, and also allows the text to be read with ease.

One last improvement, in Figure 4–4 of making my background lighter, and I finally have a Web page that has some character in the back but allows my information to be read without distraction.

CREATING A SEAMLESS TILED BACKGROUND

Your background image should, whenever possible, be seamless so it doesn't call unnecessary attention to itself. By "seamless," we mean that you cannot easily tell where the image ends and the tiles begin.

1. In Photoshop, open a new file, 200 pixels wide and 200 pixels deep.

For all of the images you will be creating for the Web, you'll want to open new documents as RGB images at 72 ppi (pixels per inch) with a white background (unless you will be using black as your background color).

2. With black and white as your respective foreground and background colors, fill your canvas with clouds by choosing Filter -> Render -> Clouds. You now have a canvas filled with clouds, which, if you were to use it as your background, would look something like what you see in Figure 4–5. As you can see, it is very obvious where the seams are.

3. Choose Filter -> Other -> Offset and change the settings so that your clouds are offset 100 pixels to the right and 100 pixels down (half the distance of your canvas

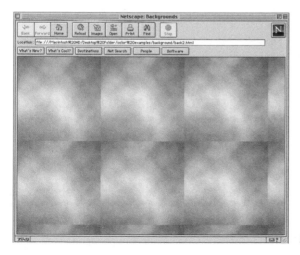

Figure 4–5: The seams are obvious

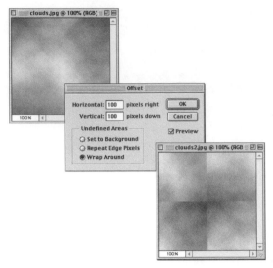

Figure 4–6: The Offset filter at work. Lines in the center are apparent, although the edges will now wrap properly.

in both directions). Make sure you choose "Wrap Around." Figure 4–6 shows how this filter changes the clouds picture. The edges in our pictures are now aligned to create a seamless tile, but as you can see in Figure 4–6, the middle of our picture has very apparent lines.

4. Use the Rubber Stamp tool or the Blur tool (or a combination of both) to carefully erase the lines in the middle. Be careful not to touch the edges of the picture. (For more info on these tools and how they work, see Chapter 1).

5. Change the color mode to Index Color by selecting Mode -> Colors -> Index Color (see Chapter 2 for more information on creating GIFs.).

6. Give your file a name, and save it as a GIF (don't forget to give it the .gif file extension). Make sure that you save the file in the same folder or directory as your other Web files. Read through Chapter 10, "Tips, Tricks, and Suggestions" for more information on how to set up your folders and files for Web documents.

7. In your HTML document, reference your new file in the `<BODY>` tag:
`<BODY BACKGROUND="imagename.gif">`

If you're not familar with HTML, the code that I used to begin my HTML text to the point of placing my background is:

```
<HTML>
<HEAD>
<TITLE>My Web Site</TITLE>
</HEAD>
<BODY BACKGROUND="imagename.gif">
```

Your browser window should now look similar to the one in Figure 4–7.

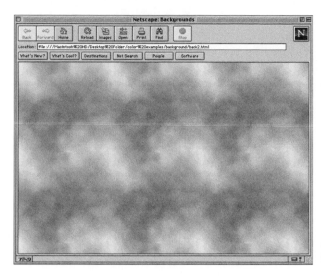

Figure 4–7: Seamless texture in the browser

SPECIFIC SEAMLESS BACKGROUND SAMPLES

Here are just a few of the infinite variations of tiled backgrounds you can create.

CREATING A WOOD TEXTURE BACKGROUND

1. Open a new file, 300 pixels by 300 pixels, with a white background.
2. Choose Filter -> Noise -> Add Noise.
3. Set the Noise level to 210, with either distribution choice. Click OK and your canvas looks like a television with no reception, as shown in Figure 4–8.
4. Choose Filter -> Blur -> Motion Blur and set the angle to 0, the distance to 39 pixels, and hit OK (Figure 4–9).
5. Save your file in Photoshop format somewhere you can easily find it with a simple name like "noise." Do not close the canvas.
6. From either the Swatches Palette or the Color Picker, choose a light brown color for your foreground color.
7. Fill your canvas with your color by clicking Option + delete (Alt + backspace in Windows).
8. Choose Filter -> Texture -> Texturizer to access the dialog box shown in Figure 4–10. Choose "Load Texture" from the Texture pull-down menu.
9. Locate the file "noise" that you saved earlier, and hit "Open."

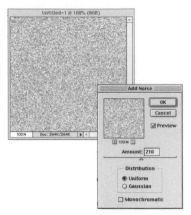

Figure 4–8: The Noise filter sets the base of the texture.

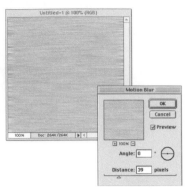

Figure 4–9: The Motion Blur filter will be the grain in the wood

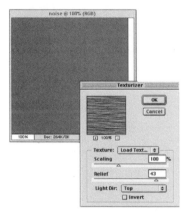

Figure 4–10: The Texture filter after filling the canvas with light brown.

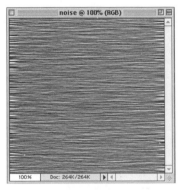

Figure 4–11: Applying the blurred noise to the light brown creates a wood effect.

10. Keep "scaling" at 100% but experiment with the "relief" slider: a higher relief for deeper grooves in the wood, lower for less of an effect. (In this example, I used a Relief of 43). Figure 4–11 shows the canvas.

11. Click OK and your canvas will have a pretty realistic wood effect. Ordinarily, the Texturizer filter will create a seamless image for you. However, due to the way the "blur" filter works, you may see some discoloration on the sides of your image. If so, use the crop tool to cut the sides away and follow the previous example to create a seamless background. Figure 4–12 shows the result in a browser.

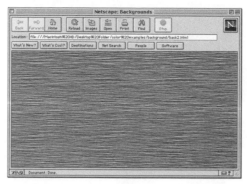

Figure 4–12: The wood texture in the browser.

Figure 4–13: The Brick texture in the Web browser

CREATING A BRICK WALL BACKGROUND

1. Fill your canvas with a maroon color of your choice.
2. Choose Filter -> Texture -> Texturizer.
3. Select "Brick" and set the Scaling to about 150% so that it will be obvious that your wall is made out of bricks. Click OK.
4. Select Filter -> Texture -> Grain and establish the settings as you'd like them. Click OK.
5. If your initial canvas is square, the brick texture will be seamless from left to right—you may have to crop a bit to make it seamless top to bottom. The result is shown in Figure 4–13.

CREATING A CRACKED STONE BACKGROUND

1. Fill your canvas with a light beige color.
2. Choose Filter -> Texture -> Craquelure.
3. Change the settings in the dialog box until you like the result. Don't make your crack depth too deep—it will impede some of the text that will later appear on your page. Click OK when through.
4. Choose Filter -> Texture -> Texturizer.
5. Select Sandstone from the pull-down menu. Click OK.
6. The result should automatically be seamless and is shown in Figure 4–14.

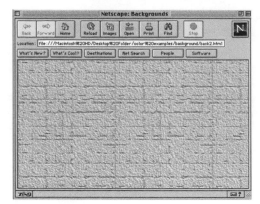

Figure 4–14: The Cracked Stone texture in the Web browser

CREATING A WATERMARKED BACKGROUND

In case you have that annoying desire to see your name or company logo repeated endlessly on your background:

1. Open a new file that is a perfect square.

2. Choose a color for your text (for the purposes of this example, we'll assume that you just want to write your or your company's name—you can follow the same procedure with any logo image as well).

3. Use the Text Editor to write your name or other text.

4. Use the ruler to make sure that your text is perfectly centered on your canvas.

5. Choose Edit -> Transform -> Numeric. Within the dialog box, set the Rotate option to 45°. Click OK when through.

6. Use the opacity slider on the Layer to make your text more transparent. A sample is provided in Figure 4–15.

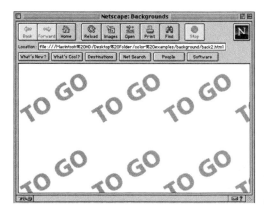

Figure 4–15: The Wallpapered name

USING HEXIDECIMALS TO CREATE A SOLID COLOR BACKGROUND

Using a solid color in the background of your Web site has two advantages: there is no file size associated with it, so there is no download time, and, as we'll see later, it can help when we create other background images.

The default color on most browsers is either a dull gray or white, depending on which browser and version is being used. To change it, you work in the <BODY> tag, as described before:

```
<BODY BGCOLOR=#000000>
```

The six numbers in the hexidecimal code are three sets of two—the first set representing the red value, the second the green value, and the third for the blue value.

By using Photoshop's Color Picker, as shown in Figure 4–16, or the Info Palette as shown in Figure 4–17, you can choose the exact color you want, and, on a sheet of paper somewhere (see? paper is not dead yet!) write down the RGB values as they appear. There are a lot of places on the Web that can help you turn RGB values into hexidecimal, however your current computer may already be able to calculate hexidecimals, and you may not even know it! Macintosh users who are working with System 8.0 or higher can determine hexidecimal values by doing the following:

1. In the Finder, Choose Edit -> Preferences.
2. Double click on any of the Label colors.

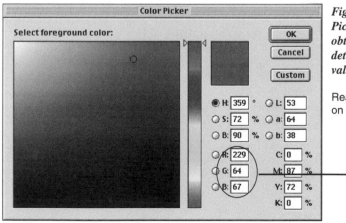

Figure 4–16: The Color Picker can be helpful in obtaining information for determining hexidecimal values.

Read Chapter 1 for details on the Color Picker.

RGB Values

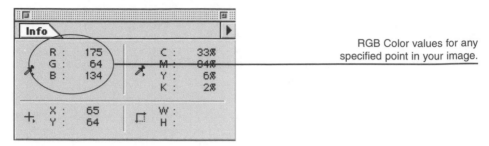

RGB Color values for any specified point in your image.

Figure 4–17: The Info Palette provides important information, including color values.

3. Scroll down the left menu to HTML Picker.

Windows users can take advantage of the scientific calculator that comes with the operating system:

1. From the Start menu, choose Programs -> Accessories -> Calculator.

2. If the calculator is in Standard Mode, open the View menu and choose Scientific.

3. Make sure the Dec option button is selected and enter the decimal number you want to convert.

4. Click the Hex option button to convert the numbers to hexidecimal.

COLORS BY NAME

There are 140 colors that you can program into your HTML code by name without having to type in a hexidecimal code. Some of the names are very obvious, such as "blue" and "red," while other names are more like crayons on acid, with names like "salmon" and "lemonchiffon." Regardless of the name, though, it would be a good idea to put a bookmark in this page—remembering and typing a proper color name is often easier than calculating a hexidecimal.

The following list contains the 140 color names that you can use in creating your site. Although they are all viable names, only ten of them are from the Web-safe color palette. These ten are listed in **bold** face. Color Figure 11 shows what these colors will look like. Note that all ten have values of either 255 (FF) or 0 in each RGB column.

Use the colors shown in Color Figure 11 as a vague reference, and not as an exact color representation. Remember these pages were printed in CMYK, a color model whose gamut is less extensive than your monitor's RGB gamut.

Name	Hexidecimal	RGB Color
white	**FFFFFF**	**255 255 255**
snow	FFFAFA	255 250 250
seashell	FFF5EE	255 245 238
floralwhite	FFFAF0	255 250 240
oldlace	FDF5EC	253 245 230
linen	FAF0E6	250 240 230
ghostwhite	F8F8FF	248 248 255
whitesmoke	F5F5F5	245 245 245
gainsboro	DCDCDC	220 220 220
lightgray	D3D3D3	211 211 211
silver	C0C0C0	192 192 192
darkgray	A9A9A9	169 169 169
lightcyan	E0FFFF	224 255 255
azure	F0FFFF	240 255 255
aliceblue	F0F8FF	240 248 255
lavender	E6R6FA	230 230 250
lavenderblush	FFF0F5	255 240 245
mistyrose	FFE4E1	255 228 225
mintcream	F5FFFA	245 255 250
honeydew	F0FFF0	240 255 240
beige	F5F5DC	245 245 220
cornsilk	FFF8DC	255 248 220
antiquewhite	FAEBD7	250 235 215
papayawhip	FFEFDS	255 239 213
ivory	FFFFF0	255 255 240
lightyellow	FFFFE0	255 255 224
lightgoldenrod	FAFAD2	250 250 210
lemonchiffon	FFFACD	255 250 205
palegoldenrod	EEE8AA	238 232 170
khaki	F0E68C	240 230 140
blanchedalmond	FFEBCD	255 235 205
bisque	FFE4C4	255 228 196
moccasin	FFE4B5	255 228 181
bisque	F5DEB3	245 222 179
navajowhite	FFDEAD	255 222 173
peachpuff	FFDAB9	255 218 185
lightsteelblue	B0C4DE	176 196 222
lightblue	ADD8E6	173 216 230
skyblue	87CEEB	135 206 235
lightskyblue	87CEFA	135 206 250

Name	Hexidecimal	RGB Color
deepskyblue	00BFFF	0 191 255
dodgerblue	1E90FF	30 144 255
cornflowerblue	6495ED	100 149 237
steelblue	4682B4	70 130 180
royalblue	4169E1	65 105 225
blue	**0000FF**	**0 0 255**
mediumblue	0000CD	0 0 205
darkblue	00008B	0 0 139
mediumslateblue	7B68EE	123 104 238
slateblue	6A5ACD	106 90 205
darkslateblue	483D8B	72 61 139
indigo	4B0082	75 0 130
navy	000080	0 0 128
midnightblue	191970	25 25 112
mediumpurple	9370DB	147 112 219
blueviolet	8A2BE2	138 43 226
darkviolet	9400D3	148 0 211
darkorchid	9932CC	153 50 204
darkmagenta	8B008B	139 0 139
purple	800080	128 0 128
thistle	D8BFD8	216 191 216
plum	DDA0DD	221 160 221
magenta	**FF00FF**	**255 0 255**
fuchsia	**FF00FF**	**255 0 255**
violet	EE82EE	238 130 238
orchid	DA70D6	218 112 214
mediumorchid	BA55D3	186 85 211
pink	FFC0CB	255 192 203
lightpink	FFB6C1	255 182 193
hotpink	FF69B4	255 105 180
deeppink	FF1493	255 20 147
palevioletred	DB7093	219 112 147
mediumvioletred	C71585	199 21 133
burlywood	DEB887	222 184 135
lightsalmon	FFA07A	255 160 122
salmon	FA8072	250 128 114
darksalmon	E9967A	233 150 122
rosybrown	BC8F8F	188 143 143
lightcoral	F08080	240 128 128
coral	FF7F50	255 127 80
tomato	FF6347	255 99 71
orangered	FF4500	255 69 0

Name	Hexidecimal	RGB Color		
red	**FF0000**	**255**	**0**	**0**
indianred	CD5C5C	205	92	92
crimson	DC143C	220	20	60
firebrick	B22222	178	34	34
brown	A52A2A	165	42	42
sienna	A0522D	160	82	45
saddlebrown	8B4513	139	69	19
darkred	8B0000	139	0	0
maroon	800000	128	0	0
tan	D2B48C	210	180	140
sandybrown	F4A460	244	164	96
orange	FFA500	255	165	0
darkorange	FF8C00	255	140	0
chocolate	D2691E	210	105	30
peru	CD853F	205	133	63
darkseagreen	8FBC8F	143	188	143
darkkhaki	BDB76B	189	183	107
yellow	**FFFF00**	**255**	**255**	**0**
gold	FFD700	255	215	0
goldenrod	DAA520	218	165	32
darkgoldenrod	B8860B	184	134	11
olivedrab	6B8E23	107	142	35
forestgreen	228B22	34	139	34
green	008000	0	128	0
olive	808000	128	128	0
darkolivegreen	556B2F	85	107	47
darkgreen	006400	0	100	0
seagreen	2E8B57	46	139	87
mediumseagreen	3CB371	60	179	113
limegreen	32CD32	50	205	50
yellowgreen	9ACD32	154	205	50
chartreuse	7FFF00	127	255	0
greenyellow	ADFF2F	173	255	47
lawngreen	7CFC00	124	252	0
lime	**00FF00**	**0**	**255**	**0**
mediumspringgreen	00FA9A	0	250	154
springgreen	00FF7F	0	255	127
lightgreen	90EE90	144	238	144
palegreen	98FB98	152	251	152
cyan	**00FFFF**	**0**	**255**	**255**
aqua	**00FFFF**	**0**	**255**	**255**
paleturquoise	AFEEEE	175	238	238

Name	Hexidecimal	RGB Color
powderblue	B0E0E6	176 224 238
turquoise	40E0D0	64 224 208
mediumturquoise	48D1CC	72 209 204
darkturquoise	00CED1	0 206 209
aquamarine	7FFFD4	127 255 212
mediumaquamarine	66CDAA	102 205 170
lightseagreen	20B2AA	32 178 170
cadetblue	5F9EA0	95 158 160
darkcyan	008B8B	0 139 139
teal	008080	0 128 128
lightslategray	778899	119 136 153
slategray	708090	112 128 144
gray	808080	128 128 128
dimgray	696969	105 105 105
darkslategray	2F4F4F	47 79 79
black	**000000**	**0 0 0**

Not all names will work in all browsers, especially in early browser versions, such as Netscape and IE 1.0. To be safe, use the RGB hexidecimal values.

CREATING A TOP BACKGROUND BORDER

By understanding how backgrounds work and combining graphic elements, hexidecimal values, and GIF Transparency (see Chapter 3), you can create not only attractive but creative backgrounds.

1. Open a file in Photoshop that is 72 pixels wide and 1440 pixels deep. Make sure you have the rulers turned on.
2. With the square marquee tool, start from the top and make a box 72 pixels wide and 72 pixels deep.
3. Choose a color from the Color Picker or the Swatches palette, and fill your box with that color.
4. Change the color palette to Index Color, name your file, and save as a GIF.

As we showed earlier, background images will start in the browser window at the top left and tile infinitely down and to the right. If you place this image in your body tag, you can see that the infinite tiling will give you what looks like a border at the top of your browser, similar to the page shown in Figure 4–18.

As the image tiles to the right, the border is created by the color at the top lining up next to itself over and over again. And by creating our original file 1440 pixels deep, we won't see the color at the top repeating unless we create a Web page that scrolls for longer than that.

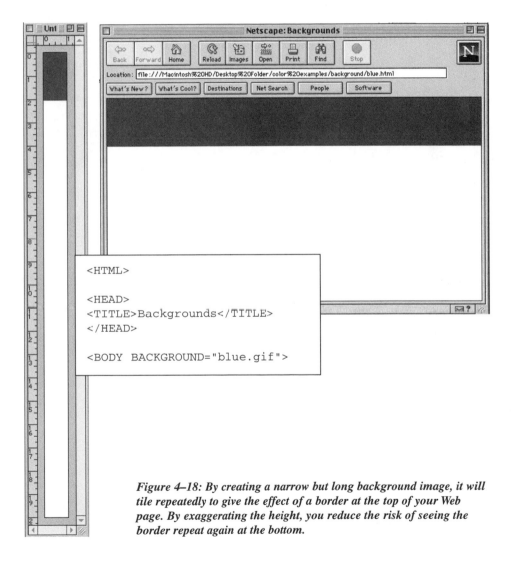

Figure 4–18: By creating a narrow but long background image, it will tile repeatedly to give the effect of a border at the top of your Web page. By exaggerating the height, you reduce the risk of seeing the border repeat again at the bottom.

If your Web page is very long and will make your user scroll signifi-cantly, you may encounter problems with your background repeating (tiling) itself vertically. It will look unattractive, unprofessional, and possibly cover some information. If this happens, go back to Photoshop and increase the height of your background image.

COMBINING BACKGROUNDS AND HEXIDECIMALS: TRANSPARENCY FACTORS

If you just worked through the last segment, you may notice that there is a slight problem: throughout this book, I have been preaching against the evils of large file sizes. However, the background image, being 1440 pixels high, is 102K even as a GIF! That's far too large for a simple background.

The way we reconcile this problem is to work with transparencies and combine the background image with the hexidecimal color selection.

MAKING AND USING TRANSPARENCY

1. If the GIF image you created in the last section is closed, open it up again and make it the active canvas. Choose File -> Export -> GIF89a Export. Figure 4–19 shows the GIF89a dialog box.

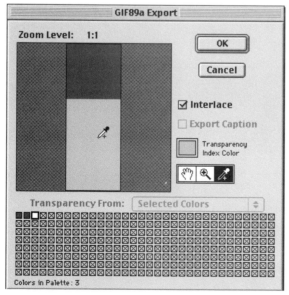

Figure 4–19: The GIF89a palette for creating transparencies. Read more about this in Chapter 3.

2. With the Eyedropper tool, select the white part of the image. You can do this either by:

   a. clicking on the white part of your image inside the preview window, or
   b. clicking the white color swatch shown in the color palette.

You'll notice that when you choose the white, it automatically turns gray. The gray represents that part of your image that is now transparent. You can change the gray to any other color by clicking on the box marked "transparency index color."

3. Choose "interlace."

4. Save your image under a different name (personally, I find it easier just to add a numeral "2" after my original name. For example, if I named the original GIF image "back.gif," I would name this "back2.gif.") Although it's not necessary, you'll find it's a good idea to keep a copy of both the original GIF and the transparent image.

5. In your HTML document, utilize both attributes of the <BODY> tag:

```
<BODY BGCOLOR=#FFFFFF BACKGROUND="imagename.gif">
```

Figure 4–20 compares your new background to the one created earlier. You'll notice that your browser looks exactly like it did back in Figure 4–20, but this time, instead of using an image that is 144 pixels black and 1296 pixels white, your image is 144 pixels black and 1296 pixels *transparent*. The transparency, which holds no file weight, is allowing the white background (BGCOLOR=#FFFFFF) to show through. If you check the folder where your images are kept, you will see a significant difference in file size between your original GIF and the transparent GIF.

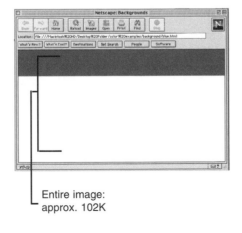
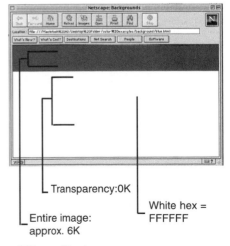

Entire image: approx. 102K

Transparency:0K

Entire image: approx. 6K

White hex = FFFFFF

Figure 4–20 Two different pages, same result, very different file sizes.

To fully understand how the transparency is working, change the hexidecimal in your <BODY> tag. Try changing it to black or any other color.

Chapter 3 deals with GIF Transparency in greater detail.

We just made a background with the border on the top of the browser. Try to make the same thing with the border going down the left-hand side of the browser window.

CREATING MORE EXCITING BACKGROUND BORDERS

There are a lot more interesting borders you can make besides the simple one-color band used for illustrating the previous example. By using some of the following techniques, you will be able to create some backgrounds that really stand out and help to frame your pages.

CREATING A BORDER WITH SHADOWS AND RIDGES

1. Open a new file 72 pixels by 1440 pixels.

2. Add two new layers to your image. Do this by first opening the Layers Palette by choosing Windows -> Show Layers, or pushing the F7 button. Figure 4–21 shows that you can quickly create a layer by clicking the "Add Layer" button at the bottom of the palette. The new layers will automatically be named "Layer 1" and "Layer 2" respectively, with the newest layer also being the topmost layer.

3. Click on Layer 2 to make it the active layer.

4. Use the Square Marquee tool to make a box about 108 pixels wide, and 72 pixels deep (the entire height of your image).

5. With the Color Picker or the Swatches Palette, choose a color you like for your foreground color. Fill the square marquee with this color by pushing Option + Delete (Alt + Backspace in Windows).

6. Make Layer 1 your active layer by clicking on it.

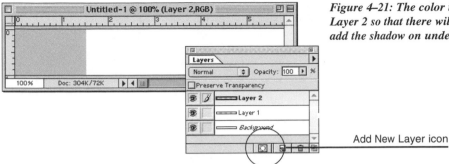

Figure 4–21: The color is added to Layer 2 so that there will be room to add the shadow on underlying layers.

Add New Layer icon

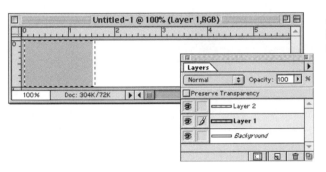

Figure 4–22: On Layer 1, the selection is moved. Anything done on this layer will not affect the green box on Layer 2.

7. With your square still selected, push the right arrow key three or four times to move your selection on Layer 1 to the right of the selection on Layer 2 as shown in Figure 4–22.

8. Feather your selection by choosing Select -> Feather, or by hitting Command + Option + D (Ctrl + Alt + D in Windows). Feathering makes your edges soft instead of hard.

9. Choose to feather your selection by 3 pixels and hit OK.

10. Make black your foreground color and fill your selection with it. Play with the opacity slider to select an opacity that gives it a realistic shadow look. Your image should look similar to the image in Figure 4–23.

11. Now that we have our color field with a shadow under it to give it some depth, we'll put ridges on the edges to make it pop even more. Make Layer 2 your active layer again by clicking on it.

12. Add 2 new layers the same way you did earlier. These new layers will be at the top of the Layers Palette, and be named "Layer 3" and "Layer 4" respectively. Make Layer 4 the active layer by clicking on it.

13. With the Square Marquee tool again, start at the top and make a selection 1 inch high and approximately 18 pixels high.

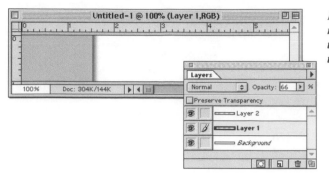

Figure 4–23: The shadow, made realistic by feathering the selection, adds depth to the border.

14. Make black your background color. For your foreground color, use the same color that you used to fill your initial selection. (If you need to recapture that color, use the Eyedropper tool and click anywhere on the field of color in your canvas.)

15. Double click on the Gradient tool. Double-clicking on any tool automatically brings up its Options Palette. The Gradient tool options dialog box is depicted in Figure 4–24.

16. The options for the Gradient tool will, by default be set to "Foreground to Background." Push the "Edit" button to get the Gradient Editor shown and described in Figure 4–25.

17. The gradient bar should show a smooth transition from your foreground color to your background color, with an arrow under the bar at each extreme. The arrow with the "F" represents the foreground color and the arrow with the "B" represents the background color.

18. Click the left arrow with the "F" in it. Notice the very tip of it turns black to show that it's been selected. Below are three arrows in boxes, showing your choices—the first allows you to add other colors besides the foreground or background colors, and the other two you are already familiar with. Push the arrow with the "B" in it. This will change your gradient to all black.

19. Add colors simply by clicking anywhere below the gradient bar. Add one color as close to the middle of the bar as you can. It will have a "B" in it and your gradient bar will not have changed much. Go back to the three selection arrows and click on the one for your foreground color. You gradient bar now looks like Figure 4–27, with black on either edge and your selected color in the center.

20. Click OK to go back to your image.

21. With the Gradient tool, start on the left of your marquee selection. Hold the Shift button, to ensure a straight gradient, and pull over to the right of your marquee selection. You will have what looks like a ridge at the top of your image.

22. Put the same ridge at the right of your color field by hitting "v" to select the Move tool. Position your cursor over the ridge, and, holding the Option key to access the copy feature and the Shift button to restrict movement, drag downward until you come to the end of your color field. The result will look like Figure 4–26.

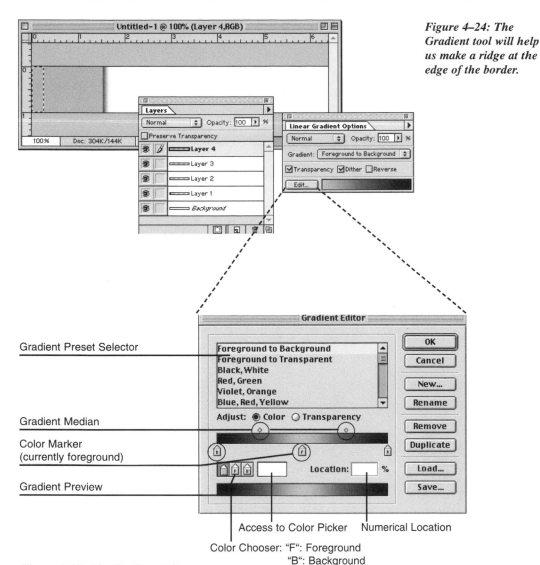

Figure 4–24: The Gradient tool will help us make a ridge at the edge of the border.

Figure 4–25: The Gradient Editor

23. If you like, use Layer 3 to put a shadow under your ridges by using the techniques taught earlier. This is illustrated in Figure 4–27.

24. Flatten your image and turn change modes to index color. Make the white body of it transparent, and save as a GIF. When you put it in your <HTML> document, the resulting background will look like the browser shown in Figure 4–28.

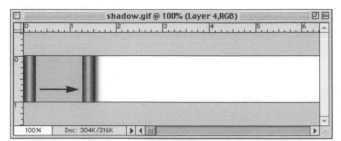

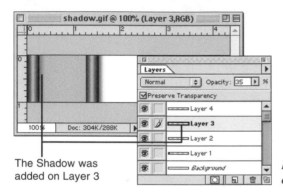

Figure 4–26: After applying the gradient, copy the ridge by selecting the Move tool and dragging while holding the Option + Shift keys.

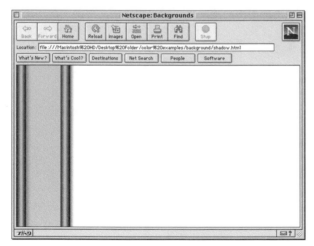

The Shadow was
added on Layer 3

Figure 4–27: Add a shadow on an empty layer.

Figure 4–28: The final product in a browser.

Twenty-four steps is a lot of work—you're not going to want to do this more than once! Before you flatten your image and save it as a GIF, save it as a Photoshop document to retain the layers—that way if you need to come back and edit the image in any way you'll save significant time and energy.

CREATING BACKGROUNDS WITH PUZZLE BORDERS

1. Open a canvas 1440 pixels by 144 pixels. Immediately create a new layer, "Layer 1."

2. Using the Pen tool would be the best way to make the curves, but mastering the Pen tool also may take significant practice. If you are unsure of how to use it, well:

3. Create a circle 72 pixels in diameter. Fill it with a light color.

4. Cut the circle in half. Put the bottom half at the top of the canvas and the top half at the bottom of the canvas as shown in Figure 4–29.

5. Create another 72-pixel circle between the two halves, so that all three curved pieces are touching.

6. Inverse select, as illustrated in Figure 4–30.

7. Use the Square Marquee tool and, holding down the Option key (Alt key in Windows) to deselect, drag a square over the right portion of the selection.

8. Fill in the remaining selection with the same color that you used to fill the circle (Figure 4–31).

9. Deselect and place a shadow beneath your puzzle, as described previously in "Shadows and Ridges." Figure 4–32 shows the image as the background in a Web browser.

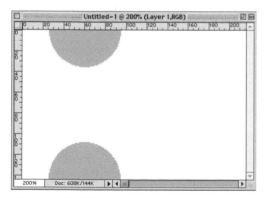

Figure 4–29: Fill a circle with color and divide it in half. Put the top half at the bottom of the browser and the bottom half at the top of the browser.

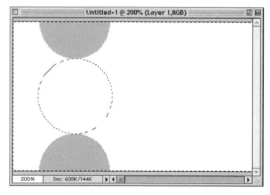

Figure 4–30: The "marching ants" or dotted line shows the selection is the inverse of a new circle, right in between the two original halves.

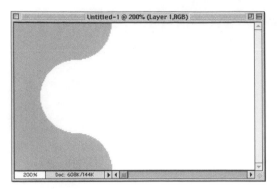

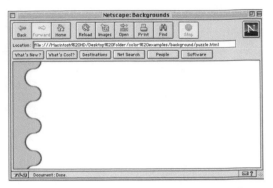

Figure 4–31: Fill the remaining selection on the left with the same color as the original circle halves to create the puzzle.

Figure 4–32: In the browser window, the puzzle image repeats infinitely and matches seamlessly to create a cool border.

CREATING BACKGROUNDS WITH BOOKSHELF (OR SIMILAR) BORDERS

This is a pretty simple but effective border. I am going to illustrate it using a bookshelf, but you'll be able to do the same for any number of items, depending upon what is called for in your Web site design.

1. Open a new file, 1440 pixels wide by 559 pixels deep.

2. Get or make a short row of books. For this example I quickly and unceremoniously created a bunch of books by filling in random colors into various rectangular selections. Don't allow your row of books to exceed much more than 144 pixels in width.

3. Make at least two or three shelves of books, so that the repetition of colors and book sizes isn't as obvious.

4. Make sure that the shelf you'll use between the books is cut exactly in half on both the top and bottom of your image, so that there won't be any problems with the background not being seamless. The final image looks similar to Figure 4–33.

RIPPED, CRINKLED PAPER BORDER

1. Open a new file 216 pixels by 216 pixels.

2. With black and white as your foreground and background colors, respectively, choose Filter -> Clouds. Keep hitting Command + F to redo the filter until you get clouds that have a good amount of contrasting areas, such as those shown in Figure 4–34.

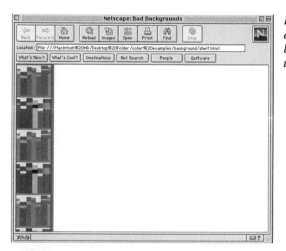

Figure 4–33: A crude illustration of a few book shelves becomes an entire library when tiled as a background in the browser window.

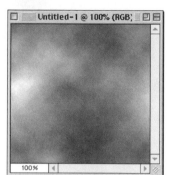

Figure 4–34: Clouds will form the basis of the paper texture.

Figure 4–35: Texturizer Filter

3. Save your file in Photoshop format, named "clouds."

4. Open a new file, 1440 pixels by 144 pixels. Create a new layer.

5. Make a square selection at the far left of your new canvas, 144 pixels by 144 pixels. Fill your selection with a light brown/beige color.

6. Choose Filter -> Texture -> Texturizer to access the dialog box shown in Figure 4–35. Choose "Load Texture" and select your file named "clouds." Set the scaling to 100% and experiment with the "relief" control (depending upon how your clouds looked, and the exact shade of brown that you chose, the exact amount of relief you'll need will vary). The preview window should show your brown plane as having "crinkles" in it. Hit OK.

7. Use the Free-Form Lasso tool to jaggedly select the right edge of the paper. Hit Delete.

8. Select the paper edge by first using the Magic Wand tool to select all the white on the right side of your canvas. Press Command + Shift + I (Ctrl + Shift + I in Windows) to select the inverse.

9. Give the edges of your paper a "burnt" look. Choose the Paint Brush tool with a 50% Opacity (manipulate this with the Opacity slider in the Options palette. Click the Wet Edges box in the Options palette. Brush along the edge of the crumpled paper border to give it a "burnt" look. Figure 4–36 illustrates this.

10. What you have at this point will not be a seamless tile when you place it in your browser. And because of the odd canvas size, you won't have much luck using the "offset" filter described earlier. Create a rectangular selection around the bottom half of your image.

11. Copy your selection, and paste it back into your image. It will paste back into the area that held your selection but on a new layer.

12. Select Edit -> Transform -> Flip Vertical. Move the pasted image to the very top, so that the outer edge kisses the top and left border of your image, as shown in Figure 4–37.

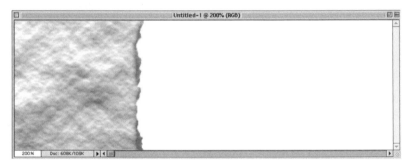

Figure 4–36: Cut the edges for the ripped effect, and use the brush with Wet Edges to create a "burn" edge.

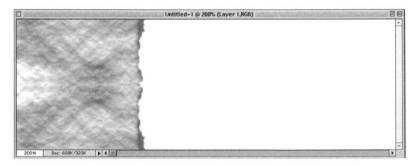

Figure 4–37: Notice the mirror effect of copying, pasting, and inverting the bottom half of the wrinkled paper. Erase a portion to ensure a seamless quality.

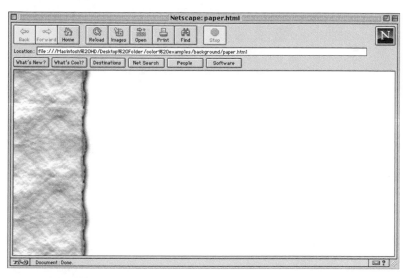

Figure 4–38: The wrinkled paper as a border in a browser window.

13. Lightly erase the bottom of the pasted image so that it blends in with the rest of the paper border.
14. Add a drop shadow as described earlier in this chapter. The final image in your browser will look similar to that in Figure 4–38.

PICTURE AND WATERMARK BACKGROUNDS

By now you're probably starting to realize that with the combination of transparent GIFs and background colors, there are a lot of fun and interesting background designs you can create.

Figures 4–39 and 4–40 are a few of the different full-screen backgrounds I have created for various clients. Most were made with a canvas that was 1440 pixels x 1440 pixels (to prevent the user from seeing the image tile), but, because the majority of the image was transparent, it carried an average weight of about 15K.

You can measure things out with some precision to make your images work in conjunction with your background. For example, in Figure 4-40, the office and its components are part of the background image, while the computer, which has an animating monitor, is a separate image, placed on the desk separately. In Photoshop, I used the measure tool to calculate the exact number of pixels down from the top and left that I wanted the computer to be placed, which is on top of the desk. In my HTML text, I set this by using the HSPACE=(number of pixels) and VSPACE=(number of pixels) so that the computer ends up on the desk in the relative proximity of where I would like it.

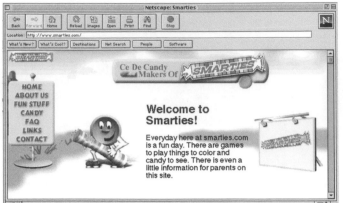

Figure 4–39:
www.smarties.com

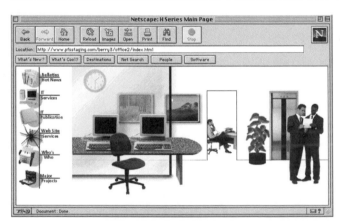

Figure 4–40: This home page for an intranet site is currently under construction.

Netscape and Internet Explorer have this annoying habit of measuring space differently. That could badly throw off your layout for certain users. Make sure that you test your site on both Netscape and IE before publishing. In this last example, I took the extra precaution of making the desk a little larger than I wanted to, to help make sure the computer always landed on top of it.

USING FRAMES TO DEVELOP BACKGROUNDS

Figure 4-41 and Color Figure 12 shows the site that my agency created for BMC Communications Group (www.bmccommunications.com). A public relations firm for biopharmaceutical companies, they needed a look that was corporate but progressive and different. Establishing the background was our first challenge.

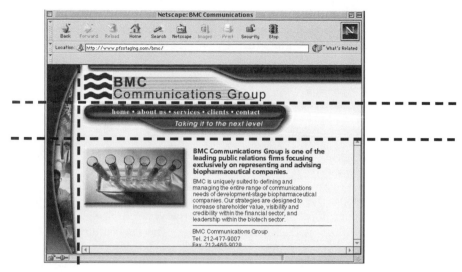

Figure 4-41: The site we created for BMC Communications. To make all the elements fit in properly, and to reduce download time, the site was broken up into 4 frames.

The background that you see in the example posed a few problems:

◆ The background involves graphics with a significant amount of blue and continuous tone photographs that make it a large file for download.

◆ Many of the pages are very long, and have to scroll to reveal the text. I needed to make sure that visitors could scroll but not lose the navigation bar at the top.

◆ Since the BMC name and logo are meant to be fixed in their position through the entire site, I didn't want them to "flash" on and off as visitors moved from page to page.

Both problems were fixed by using frames to create my page. In Figure 4-41, the dotted lines show the edges of where the three frames. The HTML code for this page is:

```
<FRAMESET COLS="78,*" FRAMEBORDER=0 FRAMESPACING=0 BORDER=0>

<FRAME SRC="side.htm" NAME="ts2lefttb" NORESIZE SCROLLING="no"
MARGINWIDTH=0 MARGINHEIGHT=0 BORDER=0>


<FRAMESET ROWS="80,75,*" FRAMEBORDER=0 FRAMESPACING=0 BORDER=0>

<FRAME SRC="top.htm" SCROLLING="no" NORESIZE MARGINWIDTH=0 MAR-
GINHEIGHT=0 BORDER=0>
```

```
<FRAME  SRC="hmbut.htm"  SCROLLING="no"  NORESIZE  MARGINWIDTH=0
MARGINHEIGHT=0 BORDER=0>


<FRAME SRC="main.htm" NAME="main" SCROLLING="yes" NORESIZE MAR-
GINWIDTH=0 MARGINHEIGHT=0>


</FRAMESET>
</FRAMESET>
```

In the top and left frames, I set the backgrounds that would be static and unchanged on every page of the site. As users move from one page to another, these backgrounds remain in place, without having to reload. The navigation bar is also in a separate frame, so that it can change colors for each page, but not be lost when the main frame, where the information is presented, has to scroll. The main frame, which is beige, holds no weight, and is set with a hexidecimal color.

SUMMARY

The background of your Web site will be one of the first things that your visitors see, and will be a deciding factor in whether or not they ever return! By using some of the techniques in this chapter, you can create borders, edges, transparencies and frames for your backgrounds that will not only upload quickly, but will also help to organize your information.

CREATIVE

TEXT

EFFECTS

Photoshop has never been known in the design industry as a premier text editor. Setting type for anything other then special effects was almost pointless since changing sizes, colors, fonts and styles was clunky, and even worse, uneditable. But the gears have been grinding over at Adobe, and they've finally started to address the text layout issue.

Photoshop's text editor has been vastly improved with version 5.0. Now, you can set type, easily change colors, set your own kerning and leading, even use different font faces and sizes at the same time. More importantly, the text is editable. Photoshop 5.0 will now saves all text attributes, so you can go back and reedit your work later on without having to type it all over.

These improvements are only a beginning, however. There are still improvements to be made. But no matter how great the text editor ever becomes, Photoshop is a bitmap program. It's unlikely that you are ever going to want to lay out all of your copy in it—the regular HTML text is more than sufficient for large bodies of work. But when it comes to headlines, banners and stand-out titles, Photoshop text and supporting tools rise to the occasion and combine to make some outstanding graphics—now more than ever before.

THE GREAT DEBATE: ALIAS VERSUS ANTI-ALIAS

Basically, anti-aliasing will blur the edges of the text slightly so that they lose the jagged quality that is common to bitmaps. Doing so will add colors to your image (and in turn increase your file size), but make your text much more readable and aesthetically pleasing. Turning off anti-aliasing (an option in the Text Editor) will cause your text to be jagged and rugged looking, usually displeasing to the eye.

The anti-alias option is not just for text. You will also see an anti-alias checkbox on many of the individual selection tool Option Palettes, particularly those that do not have straight edges.

A lot of Photoshop people love to go into long drawn-out explanations of the differences between alias and anti-alias text. Web designers especially will feel the necessity to tell you in long, mind-numbing detail the amount of colors that anti-alias text will contain, to properly prepare GIF images.

Here's the bottom line: I have been creating graphics and teaching graphic design for years, and have yet to find a reason why I would turn anti-aliasing off. Some say that anti-aliasing will make really, really small text look blurry, but my usual retort is that text has no business being that small. Anti-aliasing looks better, and for the scant few fractions of a second the extra colors will cost you in download time, it's a worthwhile investment.

Download the new version 5.0.2 from the Adobe Web site (see Chapter 1 for more info). Among other important features, this upgrade includes a new formula for anti-aliasing that creates more distinct and sharper text at smaller sizes.

Figure 5–1 shows the difference between aliasing and anti-aliasing.

WORKING WITH THE TEXT EDITOR

Before we go too deep into creating really cool text effects, it may be worthwhile to take a quick look at the Photoshop 5 Text Editor (a vast improvement from earlier versions). Figure 5–2 shows the Text Editor and it's components.

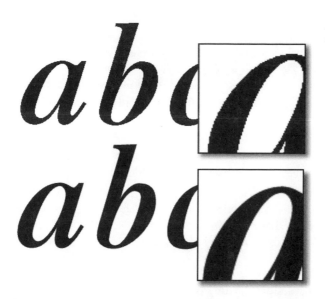

Figure 5–1: Aliasing is on top, anti-aliasing is on bottom

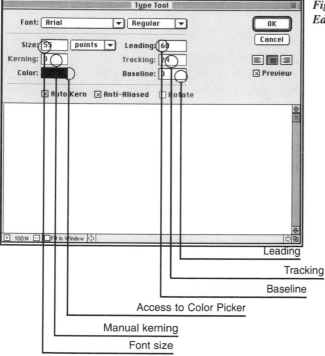

Figure 5–2: The new and improved Text Editor

Leading

Tracking

Baseline

Access to Color Picker

Manual kerning

Font size

The Text Editor interface is pretty straightforward—you can set your text, its size, leading, and, in an improvement from Photoshop 4.0, manually set the kerning, tracking, and baseline. Other improvements in the Text Editor include:

◆ Colors. Not only can you choose custom colors instead of just using the foreground color, but you can set more than one color within one text-writing session.

◆ Size and Measure. Just as with the colors, you can make text any number of sizes during one use.

◆ Preview. As you type, the text will appear in your canvas. Not only that, but you can move it around and place it on your canvas even with the Text Editor still open.

◆ Actual Editing. One of the coolest new additions is that for the first time, the Photoshop Text Editor actually does editing! Once you place your text, it automatically appears in a new layer that maintains the text attributes. If at any time you want to change something or fix a spelling error, just double click on the layer to edit what you've done.

There is no doubt that these are great improvements from previous versions of Photoshop. As we'll see in upcoming segments, some of these improvements will help us considerably in creating text effects for Web pages.

If you're using a colored or textured background in your Web page, it's best to use that same color or texture as the background on the canvas on which you will lay your text. That way it will lay seamlessly into your Web page and not be noticeable as a separate graphic.

GREAT WAYS TO COMBINE TEXT AND LAYER EFFECTS

Layer effects are some of the coolest new additions to Photoshop 5.0, allowing even the most untalented designers the opportunity to be the next Andy Warhol. Details on these effects and their properties are given in Chapter 1, "Photoshop Overview".

Although Layer Effects can be used for many applications, as we'll see in Chapter 6, "Navigation, Buttons, and Bullets", they really shine when used on text. They provide a quick and easy way to make your words pop off the page, adding dimension and depth to your overall image. Drop shadows, bevels, embosses, and other cool tricks can be applied with a minimum of work. However, as we'll see in the upcoming examples, the traditional (pre-version 5.0) method of creating some of these effects can still have a better, or at least different, result.

Readers who are still using earlier versions of Photoshop may want to skip the sections dealing with Layer Effects. If you create a graphic in Version 5.0 that uses Layer Effects, and then reopen it again in 4.0 or earlier, all of the effects will have disappeared and your graphics will look flat.

DROP SHADOW: CREATING DROP SHADOWS WITH LAYER EFFECTS

1. Open a new file, 360 pixels wide by 144 pixels high.

2. Select the Type tool and click anywhere on the canvas.

3. Within the Type Editor, choose a light color for your text, and, using either a bold Helvetica or Arial font, set your font size to 70 points. Make sure the "anti-aliased" option is clicked.

4. Type "Web Page" and manually position the words in the middle of the canvas, toward the top.

5. Push OK and your canvas looks something like Figure 5–3.

6. Choose Layer -> Effects -> Drop Shadow. You will get a dialog box similar to that in Figure 5–4.

7. Set your angle to 135 degrees, the distance to 5 pixels, and a blur of 7 pixels. You can see the drop shadow as it is being made. Before hitting OK, play around with some of the sliders and watch the different effects that each one has.

8. Hit OK, and your canvas will look something like the canvas in Figure 5–5.

Figure 5–3: The text is placed on the canvas

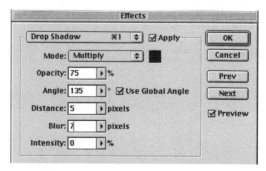

Figure 5–4: Layer Effects: Drop Shadow

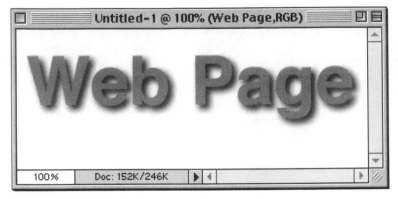

Figure 5–5: Drop shadow created with Layer Effects

And there you have it, easy as cake, instant drop shadow courtesy of Photoshop 5.0's idiot-proof drop shadow effects menu. The really cool part is that Photoshop 5.0 will preserve the filter effect and all of its settings, within the layer. If you ever want to change the drop shadow, all you have to do is double click the "F" on the right side of the layer to regain access to the "Drop Shadow" dialog box. Additionally, any new object you place on that layer will automatically be assigned the same filter effects.

If you move the text on your layer around your canvas, you'll notice that the drop shadow (like all the Layer Effects) will follow it around as if stuck by glue. Sometimes, though, it will be necessary to separate the effect from the original image, as illustrated in our next example.

1. Working off the previous example, make sure that the layer named "Web Page" is the active layer.

2. Choose Layer -> Effects -> Create Layer. Figure 5–6 shows the differences in the Layers Palette. Although you've gained an extra layer and can manipulate your drop shadow at will, that ability did not come without its price—namely that your text layer will no longer retain the Layer Effects information to apply to future objects, not is it editable anymore.

ADDING DIMENSION TO THE TEXT

An effect that is very easy, and quite effective in certain situations, is to add dimension to your text simply by doing the following:

1. Using the same document from the last section, add a layer between the shadow and the text.

2. Command + click (Ctrl + click in Windows) on the "Web Page" layer in the Layers Palette to get the selection of your text.

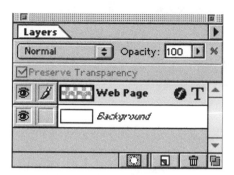 

Figure 5–6: The Layers Palette before and after separating effects. Notice the circled "I" is gone in the latter, and the drop shadow has its own layer.

Figure 5–7: Adding more depth

3. Push "m" to make the marquee the active tool and use the arrow keys to move your selection down and to the right by two pixels.

4. Fill your selection with black. You may want to reduce the opacity of your shadow a bit, and maybe drag your shadow further away from the text. The result is shown in Figure 5–7.

That was a super-easy illustration of an addition you can make by creating your drop shadow the traditional way. Here's another:

Skewing the Drop Shadow

1. Make the shadow layer your active layer by clicking on it.

2. Choose Edit -> Free Transform (in Photoshop 5.0, the Free Transform and Transform options are located in the "Edit" menu, as opposed to Photoshop 4.0, when they were located in the "Layer" menu).

Figure 5–8: Selecting Edit -> Transform

Figure 5–9: Dragging the shadow for a depth effect

3. Your shadow will now have a box around it with "handles" on the corners and the sides, as shown in Figure 5–8. Grab one of the bottom corner handles with your cursor, and, holding Command + Option (Ctrl + Alt in Windows), drag the corner inward and upward slightly. Continue dragging until your shadow looks like Figure 5–9. Get a distance effect by using a feathered, low-opacity eraser over the far end of the shadow.

EVEN MORE EXCITING LAYER EFFECTS

Drop shadows aren't the only popular feature that Photoshop 5.0 turned into a quick-and -easy Layer Effect. Other timeless design staples have also been incorporated, such as a wide array of bevel effects and various glows. On the plus side, each of the following effects will save you time and energy as you go about creating your Web site. On the down side, Layer Effects may bring a flood of glows, shadows, and bevels to the Web in even greater numbers then already exist. But whether you view the Layer

Effects glass to be half full or half empty, you still need to know how they work and what they offer just to keep up, if not move ahead of the pack. So that being said, here are some quick examples of the remainder of Photoshop 5.0's Layer Effects.

INNER SHADOW

The new Inner Shadow feature gives you an easy way of creating a really cool depth effect.

1. Lay out text.
2. Choose Layer -> Effects -> Inner Shadow.
3. Figure 5–10 shows the effect with the default setting, except the angle, which was changed to 135°.

This effect works best with larger, sans serif fonts.

Adding Additional Depth to an Inner Shadow

1. Choose Layer -> Effects -> Create Layer to separate the inner shadow into its own layer.
2. With the Inner Shadow layer active, push Command + T (Ctrl + T in Windows) to activate the Free Transform feature.
3. Hold down the Option key (Alt in Windows) and drag one of the corner handles in slightly. Next hold the Command + Option + Shift keys (Ctrl + Alt + Shift in Windows) to gain control over the perspective, and drag one of the top corner handle bars in slightly. If even more depth is desired, drag the top center handle bar down slightly. Figure 5–11 illustrates the process.

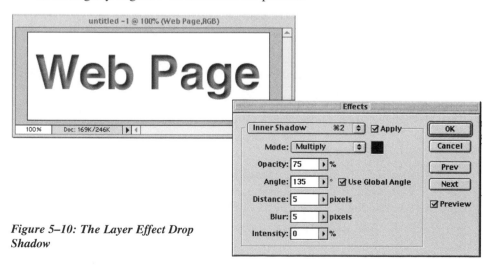

Figure 5–10: The Layer Effect Drop Shadow

Figure 5–11: Separating the Inner Shadow from the actual text allows you to manipulate it with the Free Transform feature, and to give the piece greater depth.

OUTER GLOW

Like the Drop Shadow, there may be instances that you find it's important to separate the Layer Effect into its own layer.

1. Lay out text.
2. Choose Layer -> Effects -> Outer Glow.
3. Figure 5–12 shows the effect with the Opacity set to 85%, the Blur to 18 pixels, and the Intensity to 352. I also changed my glow color to a bright yellow.

This effect looks the most natural using bright glow colors on darker backgrounds.

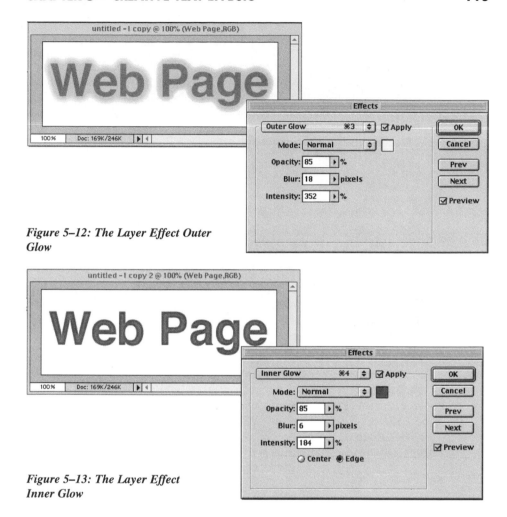

Figure 5–12: The Layer Effect Outer Glow

Figure 5–13: The Layer Effect Inner Glow

INNER GLOW

The least exciting of the new effects, Inner Glow puts a glow on the inside edges of your selection.

1. Lay out text.
2. Choose Layer -> Effects -> Inner Glow.
3. Figure 5–13 shows the effect with an Opacity setting of 85%, a Blur of 6 pixels, and an intensity of 184.

This effect works best with brighter glows within dark objects.

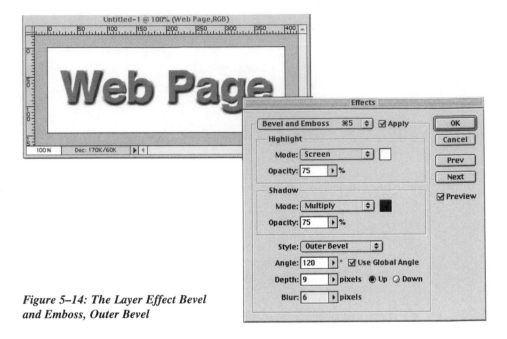

Figure 5–14: The Layer Effect Bevel and Emboss, Outer Bevel

BEVEL AND EMBOSS

This really cool feature all but negates any need for the "Emboss" filter found in the Filters menu. There are four separate Bevel and Emboss Effects for you to choose from:

Outer Bevel

1. Lay out text.
2. Choose Layer -> Effects -> Bevel and Emboss.
3. Choose Outer Bevel from the Style pull-down menu.
4. Figure 5–14 shows the effect with the default setting, except the Depth, which is set to 9, and the Blur, which is increased to 6.
5. Play around with the Opacity settings for both the highlight and the shadow to get a real clean, hammered-out effect for your text, especially when you have a photograph in your background.

Inner Bevel

1. Lay out text.
2. Choose Layer -> Effects -> Bevel and Emboss.

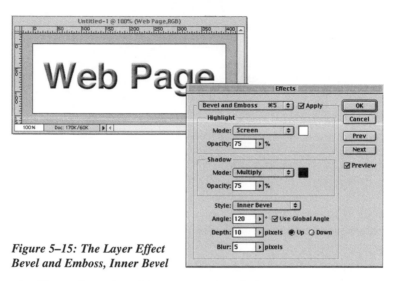

Figure 5–15: The Layer Effect Bevel and Emboss, Inner Bevel

3. Choose Inner Bevel from the Style pull-down menu.

4. Figure 5–15 shows the effect with the default settings, except the Depth, which is set to 10.

Emboss

1. Lay out text.

2. Choose Layer -> Effects -> Bevel and Emboss.

3. Choose Emboss from the Style pull-down menu.

4. Figure 5–16 shows the effect with the default for all settings. The result looks similar to the Inner Bevel Effect, with the addition of a slight drop shadow and highlight added.

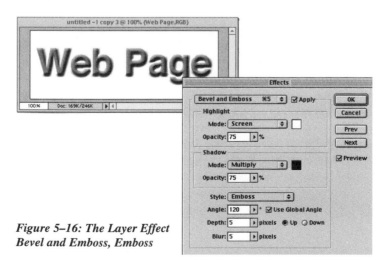

Figure 5–16: The Layer Effect Bevel and Emboss, Emboss

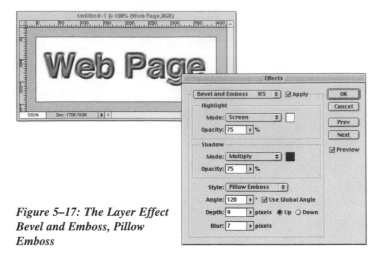

*Figure 5–17: The Layer Effect
Bevel and Emboss, Pillow
Emboss*

Pillow Emboss

1. Lay out text.
2. Choose Layer -> Effects -> Bevel and Emboss.
3. Choose Pillow Emboss from the Style pull-down menu.
4. Figure 5–17 shows the effect with the default for all settings except the Depth set to 9 and the Blur to 7.
5. Like the Outer Bevel Effect, experiment with the Opacity settings for your highlight and shadows as the key to getting a realistic look for your Pillow Emboss, especially on top of photographic backgrounds.

LAYER EFFECTS IN THE REAL WORLD

Although Photoshop 5.0's Layer Effects make developing certain design aspects rather simple, you're by no means limited to strictly filling in a dialog box to achieve your end result. Combinations of Layer Effects together, as well as other Photoshop tools, can put creativity back into the creation process.

Figure 5–18 shows the top portion of a Web site my agency is currently creating for a client, an osteologist who wants us to help them release information on the formation of bones and the human anatomy. The Figure also includes a magnification of the portion of the titlebar that utilizes the Layer Effects.

Although the subject matter is serious, our client wants the site to reflect his own personality, which is lighthearted and fun. Part of what we have done is to create the illusion in the titlebar of the words reflecting their meaning through imagery. In the full title of the site, "Bones & Your Body," a combination of Layer Effects, the Lighting Effects filter and the Paintbrush tool, was used to make the word Bones look as though it is made up of actual bones. The following shows the steps to take to create this effect:

1. Open a new file, 720 by 290 pixels. Create a new Layer, "Layer 1," to start your work on.

2. With the Type Mask tool, type "BONES" in a Helvetica or Arial font face, large enough to fit in the center of your canvas, as shown in Figure 5–19.

3. Feather your text selection by pushing Command + Option + D (Ctrl + Alt + D in Windows) and set the Feather Radius to 3. Hit OK.

4. Fill your selection with a light to medium gray color, as shown in Figure 5–20.

5. Choose Layer -> Effects -> Inner Shadow to access the dialog box. Change the settings to:

Opacity:	95%
Angle:	–48° (with "Use Global Angle" checked)
Distance:	5 pixels
Blur:	1 pixel
Intensity:	105%

Your image will look similar to Figure 5–21.

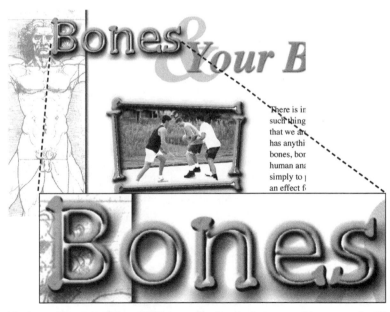

Figure 5–18: A combination of Layer Effects and other tools was used to create the illusion that the title in this upcoming Web site is made out of bones.

Figure 5–19: The Type Mask tool sets the selection marquee for the title.

Figure 5–20: After the selection is feathered and filled with color, the edges take on a soft edge.

Figure 5–21: The Layer Effects Inner Shadow, when used on a selection with a soft edge, creates an interesting "puffed up" effect.

Figure 5–22: The addition of the Outer Bevel from the Bevel and Emboss Layer Effects arsenal, accentuates the letters.

6. Before hitting OK, choose Bevel and Emboss from the main pull-down menu in the dialog box. Choose Outer Bevel from the subsequent Style pull-down menu. Keep the Highlight and Shadow options at their default options, and change the remaining settings to read:

Opacity:	95%
Angle:	–48° (with "Use Global Angle" checked)
Distance:	5 pixels
Blur:	1 pixel

   Hit OK and your image will now look similar to Figure 5–22.

7. If your image is no longer selected, select it now by holding down the Command button (Ctrl in Windows) and clicking Layer 1.

8. Choose Select -> Modify -> Contract and contract your image by 8 pixels.

9. Establish the selection as an Alpha Channel, by choosing Select -> Save Selection. Make sure that the Channel pull-down menu is set to New, and hit OK. The selection is now saved as an alpha channel and can be viewed in the Channels Palette.

10. Select Filter -> Render -> Lighting Effects to bring up the dialog box shown in Figure 5–23. In the Texture Channel pull-down menu, choose Alpha 1 and pull the Height selector over to Mountainous. Make sure the White is High checkbox is left unchecked and that the light source is coming from the North West direction as shown in Figure 5–23. Hit OK, and your image will look similar to Figure 5–24.

11. Deselect your selection by pushing Command + D (Ctrl + D in Windows).

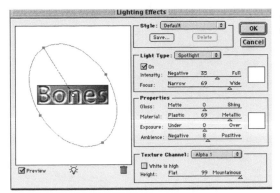

Figure 5–23: The Lighting Effects dialog box

Figure 5–24: The Lighting Effects filter on the Alpha Channel creates the inside of the bone frame.

Figure 5–25: Painting the end caps of the bone helps to develop its structure.

12. Add the cartoonish bone ends onto the letters to complete the effect. Do this by selecting the Paintbrush tool with a small, hard-edged brush, and paint the ends onto each letter. Because you're painting in Layer 1, which retains the Layer Effects settings, those same settings will apply to your newly painted additions. The final effect can be seen in the close-up provided in Figure 5–18, repeated in Figure 5–25.

Usually throughout this book, when a Web site that my agency has worked on is referenced for an example, I will provide the Web address for you to visit. At the time of this writing, however, the site referenced in this example is currently under production and is therefore not available for on-line review.

BEYOND LAYER EFFECTS: CREATIVE TEXT DESIGN

Although you can be endlessly creative with Photoshop 5.0's new Layer Effects, especially when they are used in combination with one another as shown in the preceding section, "Layer Effects in the Real World," don't forget that there's an entire world of design beyond Layer Effects. The next few pages will show how you can use combinations of tools and filters to create some really outstanding looks and special effects that will help your Web page come to life and stand out. Hammered Emboss plus great techniques for creating fire, ice, and 3D text are just the beginning of what Photoshop can do to enhance your Web sites.

CREATING A HAMMERED EMBOSS EFFECT

The preceding section touched on the power of the "Lighting Effects" filter. This example takes it a step further, making it the primary tool for creation, to give your text the illusion of having been hammered out from the other side of your canvas.

1. Open a new file 360 pixels wide by 144 pixels high.

2. Set your foreground to a rich shade of blue, and your background color to bright red.

3. With the Gradient tool, create a diagonal gradient from the top left corner to the bottom right, as shown in Figure 5–26.

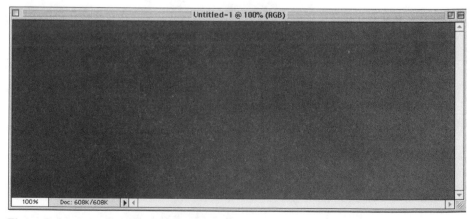

Figure 5–26: A gradient applied to the canvas

4. Choose the Type Mask tool and type "Text Fun" in a Helvetica or Arial type face at a font size of 75 points. (This effect tends to look better with sans serif fonts.) Click OK and center your type selection. Notice that while Photoshop 5.0 ordinarily places text on its own layer and preserves the components, this does not hold true for the selection text. Selection text is placed on the active layer and does not retain information for editing.

5. Choose Select -> Feather, and set the feather radius to 3. Hit OK. Your text selection now looks a little round at the edges.

6. Choose Select -> Save Selection to bring up the dialog box shown in Figure 5–27. For Channel, choose New and name it if you'd like. If you don't name it, it will automatically be called Alpha 1.

7. Choose Filter -> Render -> Lighting Effects. Figure 5–28 shows the Lighting Effects filter, one of the most interesting but more complex filters that Photoshop 5.0 provides for you.

8. With the Lighting Style set to "Default" and the light type set to "Spotlight," choose Alpha 1 as your texture channel. The preview window will show the emboss effect on your text.

9. Turn the light source so that the spotlight is shining down from a North West direction, giving your text a more universal shadow style. Make sure that the spotlight area is wide enough that none of your text is lost in dark shadows. Click OK. Your image now looks similar to Figure 5–29.

For a deeper emboss, go back to immediately after Step 6, and use the arrow keys to move your selection up about six spaces. The result will be similar to Figure 5–30 and adds some dimension to your image.

Figure 5–27: The Save Selection dialog box. Saving your selection created an Alpha channel.

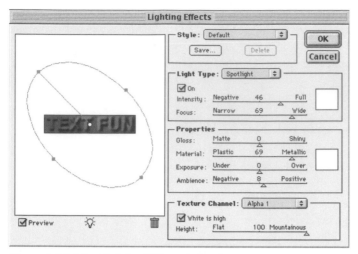

Figure 5–28: The Lighting Effects dialog box

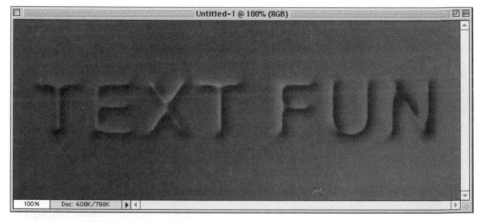

Figure 5–29: Final result when using a Lighting Effects filter on a saved feathered selection.

Figure 5–30: Moving your selection before using the Lighting Effects filter can create a deeper emboss effect.

CREATING BURNING, MELTING TEXT: TECHNIQUE ONE

This effect comes from a combination of artistic talent (yes, even though Photoshop makes some effects very simple, you still need some artistic ability!) and one of Photoshop's native filters.

1. Open a new file 360 pixels by 144 pixels.

2. Choose the Type Mask tool and type "Text Fun" in all caps, in a Helvetica or Arial type face, at a font size of 70 points, and in Bold. Click OK and center your type selection. Notice that while Photoshop 5.0 ordinarily places text on its own layer and preserves the components, this does not hold true for the selection text. Selection text is placed on the active layer and does not retain information for editing.

3. Create Layer 1 so that you are not working on the background layer.

4. Choose Select -> Save Selection and save your selection as an Alpha Channel.

5. Choose Select -> Feather and set the Feather Radius to 2.

6. Choose a bright red for your foreground color and a medium to dark orange for your background.

7. With the Gradient tool set to "foreground to background," hold the Shift key down for constraint and drag from the top of your selection to the bottom. Your canvas will look something like Figure 5–31.

8. Create a new layer over the currently active one.

9. Choose Select -> Load Selection. Figure 5–32 illustrates the Load Selection dialog box. Make sure that the "Channel" option is set to "Alpha 1" (or any other name you may have chosen for the selection you saved earlier).

Figure 5–31: A gradient (from red to orange) into a feathered text selection

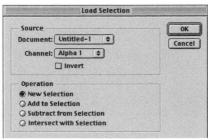

Figure 5–32: Load Selection dialog box

10. Make your foreground color white. Hit the "j" button to activate the Airbrush tool. (Notice that in Photoshop 5.0, the keyboard command for the Airbrush tool is "j" as opposed to the "a" of earlier versions.)

11. In the Airbrush Options Palette, set the Airbrush opacity to 30. (You can do this by pushing the "3" key or by using the palette's opacity slider.) The opacity slider is marked Pressure on the Options palette. Select a soft brush with a diameter of 100 pixels.

12. Swish through the selection so that various parts of your text will appear in a faint white, as shown in Figure 5–33. Deselect your selection when you are through.

13. Choose Filter -> Distort -> Ocean Ripple to pull up the dialog box illustrated in Figure 5–34. Use the default settings and hit OK. Your faded white letters will now be very curvy, as shown in Figure 5–35.

14. To create the fire and give the illusion that your text is melting, make layer 1 (your red to orange gradient) your active layer by clicking on it.

15. Choose the Smudge tool (located by scrolling through the choices under the Blur tool—see Chapter 1, "Overview to Photoshop"), and with a soft brush with a diameter of 27, drag the top of your gradient upward to smear the color. Do this over the top of all your letters. With a smaller brush, make the flame details by smearing up the gradient in smaller sections. Your image will look similar to Figure 5–36.

16. For a more authentic flame, try adding some yellow to the middle of your red-to-orange gradient.

Figure 5–33: After swishing through with white

Figure 5–34: Ocean Ripple

Figure 5–35: The effect of the Ocean Ripple filter

Figure 5–36: The final result after using the Smudge tool

CREATING BURNING, MELTING TEXT: TECHNIQUE TWO

This technique is a little more realistic looking, however it is also tough to get on a white background. It will take a little bit of work on your part to achieve a decent burn and have your text remain legible.

1. Open a new file 360 pixels wide by 360 pixels deep.
2. Fill the background with black.
3. Use the Type tool to place the word "TEXT" in the center of the canvas. Use white for the letters.
4. Flatten your image and choose Image -> Rotate Canvas -> 90° CW to turn your image 1/4 turn to the right.
5. Choose Filter -> Stylize -> Wind for the dialog box shown in Figure 5–37. Choose "Wind" for the method, and "From the Left" for the direction. Hit OK.
6. Hit Command + F (Ctrl + F in Windows) twice to exaggerate the effect of the filter.

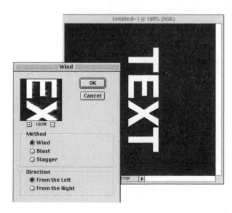

Figure 5–37: The Wind filter dialog box. Text has to be turned because Wind only goes left and right.

7. Rotate your canvas 90° CCW to its original position.

8. Select Filter -> Blur -> Motion Blur to bring up the dialog box shown in Figure 5–38. Set the angle to 59° with a blur of 4 pixels and hit OK.

9. Choose Filter -> Distort -> Ripple and maintain the default settings. Hit OK. Your canvas will look similar to Figure 5–39.

10. Add a new layer and fill it with a bright yellow. Change the layer mode to Overlay. Add another layer and fill it with bright red. Change this layer's mode also to Overlay. The final image is shown both in Figure 5–40 and in Color Figure 13.

Figure 5–38: Apply a Motion Blur filter

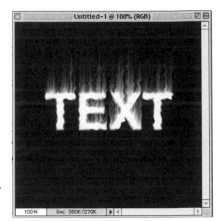

Figure 5–39: After the Ripple filter is applied

Figure 5–40: A realistic burning effect
See Color Figure 13.

CREATING ICY LETTERS

This is a pretty "cool" text effect (sorry, I couldn't resist).

1. Open a new file 360 pixels wide by 360 pixels deep.

2. Fill the background with black.

3. Use the Type tool to place the word "TEXT" in the center of the canvas. Choose an icy sky blue color for the letters.

4. Flatten your image, and choose Image -> Rotate Canvas -> 90° CW to turn your image 1/4 turn to the right.

5. Choose Filter -> Stylize -> Wind for the dialog box shown in Figure 5–41. Choose "Wind" for the method and "From the Right" for the direction. Hit OK.

6. With the wind effect, you're going to be placing your icicles, so hit Command + F (Ctrl + F in Windows) two or three more times until your icicles are as long as you'd like them.

7. Rotate your canvas 90° CCW to its original position.

8. Choose Filter -> Brush Strokes -> Accented Edges for the dialog box as shown in Figure 5–42. Set the Edge Width to 2, the Edge Brightness of 38 and a Smoothness of 5.

9. Create a new layer, and with the Airbrush tool brush randomly over the text, as shown in Figure 5–43. Make sure that you have white as your foreground color, and choose a brush size around 35 pixels. When through, set the layer mode to Overlay. Figure 5–44 and Color Figure 14 show the final image.

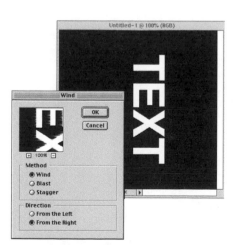

Figure 5–41: The Wind filter again gets us started

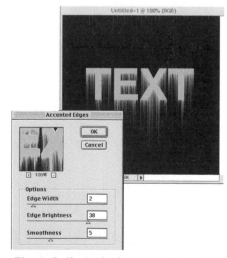

Figure 5–42: Apply the Accented Edges filter

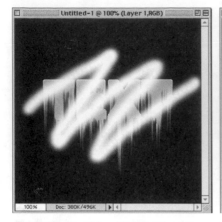
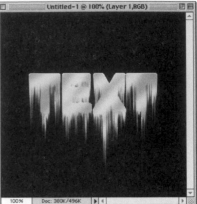

Figure 5–43: Airbrushing with white   *Figure 5–44: The final image.*
on a new layer set to Overlay will help
provide light hits on the ice.

CREATING DOTTED TEXT

For the person who is truly a skateboard junkie at heart, the dotted effect is a must (at least that's what advertising agencies seem to think).

1. Open a new file 504 pixels wide by 144 pixels deep.
2. With the Type Mask tool, place the words "Text Fun" in the center of your canvas.
3. Choose Select -> Feather and set the feather radius to 4. Fill the selection with any color you choose.
4. Deselect all.
5. Choose Filter -> Pixelate -> Color Halftone to bring up the dialog box. Lower the maximum radius to 4 and hit OK. Figure 5–45 and Color Figure 15 shows the result.

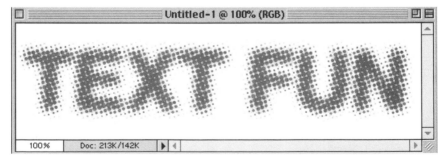

Figure 5–45: Dotted effect achieved by using the Color Halftone filter.

CREATING NEON TEXT

1. Open a new file 504 pixels wide by 144 pixels deep.
2. Use the Type Mask tool to write "TEXT FUN."
3. Choose Select -> Feather and set the feather radius to 3 to soften the edges.
4. Fill your selection with black. It will look similar to Figure 5–46. Deselect all.
5. With black and white as your foreground and background colors, choose Filter -> Render -> Difference Clouds. Your canvas will look like Figure 5–47.
6. Choose Image -> Adjust -> Invert.
7. Overlay any color and your image will look similar to Figure 5–48 and Color Figure 16.

Figure 5–46: Feathered text filled with black

Figure 5–47: Applying the Difference Clouds filter.

Figure 5–48: Invert the image for the neon result above.

CREATING QUICK 3D TEXT

1. Open a new file 576 pixels wide by 144 pixels deep.

2. With the Type tool, type "TEXT FUN" and center it on your canvas.

3. In Photoshop 5.0, text is put on a new layer that retains all of the text specifications for editing later. However, no luxury comes without its price. While the layer retains the settings, there will be certain things you cannot do to it, such as use traditional filters or change the perspective. To change this, Choose Layer -> Type -> Render Layer. This will turn your text into a regular graphic, giving you access to all of Photoshop's effects, but eliminating your ability to edit the text. (See? I told you everything had its price!)

4. Choose Edit -> Free Transform. (Notice that the Transform and Free Transform items are located under the Edit menu, as opposed to the Layer menu in version 4.0.)

5. Grab the bottom right corner handle and, holding the Shift + Option + Command buttons (Shift + Alt + Ctrl in Windows), drag outward. Drag one of the top corner handles and drag inward, until your text looks similar to Figure 5–49. Hit Return (Enter in Windows) or double click on the text to apply the transformation.

6. In the Layers Palette options menu, select Duplicate Layer to access the Duplicate Layer dialog box. Hit OK to accept the default setting and the new layer will appear just above your original. This new layer automatically becomes the active layer. Make the previous layer the active layer by clicking on it.

7. Choose Filter -> Blur -> Motion Blur and set your angle to 90°, and your distance to 75. Click OK.

8. With your Move tool, move the blur down until it fits below your letters and looks like Figure 5–50. You may have to play with the transform feature to fit it more exactly.

Figure 5–49: Text with a perspective transformation applied

Figure 5–50: Duplicating the layer and applying a motion blur creates a 3D effect.

CREATING BUBBLED TEXT

One of the coolest new toys in Photoshop 5.0 is the 3D Transform filter. Although it is a bit clunky (mark my words, future Photoshop versions will undoubtedly add improvements to this filter), it can still do some pretty amazing things. Mostly meant for changing perspectives of 2D images (such as a picture of a box of cereal or a soup can), this effect can manipulate text in some neat ways as well. (Other 3D Transform examples can be found in Chapter 8, "Animation.")

1. Open a new file 576 pixels wide by 144 pixels deep.
2. With the Type tool, type "TEXT FUN" and center it on your canvas.
3. Choose Layer -> Type -> Render Layer.
4. Select the letters by Command + clicking (Ctrl + clicking in Windows) on the text layer in the Layer Palette. Save your selection as a channel.
5. Deselect all and choose Filter -> Render -> 3D Transform to access the palette shown in Figure 5–51.

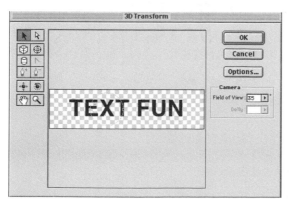

Figure 5–51: The cool new 3D Transform filter

Erase
bottom of
spere

Figure 5–52: The effect of the 3D Transform filter on the text.

Figure 5–53: The final effect after the bottom ring is erased and a drop shadow is placed.

6. Using the sphere tool, create a sphere around part of the letters. Use the trackball tool and rotate the sphere upward just a bit as shown in Figure 5–52. Hit OK.

7. Erase the bottom of the sphere.

8. Create a new layer in between the background and your text layer. Load the Alpha Channel you created earlier.

9. Choose Select -> Feather and feather your image by 4 pixels. Fill it with black.

10. Lower the opacity on your layer to around 30% and move your shadow just a little off center. The final image is shown in Figure 5–53.

FILLING PART OF YOUR TEXT WITH AN IMAGE (WORKING WITH MASKS)

1. Open a new file 576 pixels wide by 144 pixels deep.

2. With a Type tool, type "TEXT FUN" and center it on your canvas.

3. Choose Layer -> Type -> Render Layer.

4. Command + click (Ctrl + click in Windows) the text layer to grab the selection and save the selection as a channel named "Alpha 1."

5. In the Channels Palette, shown in Figure 5–54, click on the channel marked Alpha 1. You'll notice that your canvas has changed—your background is now black and your text is white to show where your selection is.

6. You'll also notice that no matter what colors were in your color palette, they are black and white now. That is because by selecting the channel Alpha 1, you have turned off the other channels that hold the color values. With the Gradient tool, hold the Shift key for constraint and make a gradient from top to bottom, white to black. Your canvas looks like Figure 5–55.

7. Choose Select -> Load Selection, and choose Alpha 1. Hit OK. You'll see that only the upper half (the white half) of your text is selected now. Click on the channel marked RGB to load the selection into the color channel. Your canvas and color palette go back to normal.

8. Open an image on a separate canvas. In this example, I used the image of an island resort (where I'll be writing my next book...) shown in Figure 5–56. Copy the image to your pasteboard.

9. Back in your original canvas, the top of your text is still selected. Use the Paste Into command to paste your image into your selection. You'll see that, as in Figure 5–57, your image is 100% opaque on top and gradually fades to 0% as it goes down your text. As long as the channel that you loaded is selected, the same effect will happen to any effect you use.

Figure 5–54: The Channels Palette

Figure 5–55: Setting a gradient within the channel selection.

Figure 5–56: The image I will use to partially fill my text selection.

Figure 5–57: The final text after being partially filled.

SUMMARY

Text in Photoshop, long a thorn in the side and a source of frustration for graphic and Web designers, has made a stunning transformation in version 5.0. Now Web designers can combine these improvements with Photoshop's other features to make text just as much a part of the artwork on a Web site as the art itself. This chapter should give you more than what you need to take your already developed Photoshop skills and crank out some extraordinary visual copy effects that command your visitor's attention.

chapter 6

NAVIGATION, BUTTONS, AND BULLETS

In just one word, how would you describe the most widely accepted reason that the Web has become so popular so quickly? Here's a hint: it has nothing to do with the fact that insecure guys can shamelessly lie to faceless women.

That reason came in second.

No, the real reason the Web has grown so quickly is *hyperlinks*. Hyperlinks have allowed the virtual library to penetrate our everyday lives and make gathering information both simple and enjoyable. Rather than having to run to a card catalog every time you need to research a new reference, the Web puts all information just a click or two away.

As Web users began to realize the potential and convenience of the Internet, the importance of establishing effective navigation systems became evident to Web designers. Graphic artists have come to take advantage of Photoshop for button and navigation tasks, and today button art has almost become an industry all its own. Sites will often be judged more on their ease of navigation than on their aesthetic design, and the truly successful designers will combine creativity of shape, color, and texture with logic of layout and a well thought-out site map.

In this chapter, you'll learn how and why buttons have become so important, quicker Photoshop methods for creating certain navigation staples, and exciting techniques for designing more interesting button and bullet styles.

THE IMPORTANCE OF BUTTONS

It's pretty standard by now that blue underlined text indicates that those particular words will give you access to a new page of information. But as modem speeds have gotten faster, and people have come to expect more from the Web in terms of graphics and design, it is no longer enough to link each page with just text. Designing buttons and navigation devices has become an artform unto itself, and creating them can be some of the most fun and creative things you'll do with Photoshop for the Web.

Because the buttons are going to give your user access to every part of your site, it is important to make sure you set up your navigation system long before you even open Photoshop.

Oftentimes mapping out your site on paper is the best way to attack the navigational aspect of your site. To make your site successful, map it in such a way that the user has to hit the browser's "back" button as little as possible. This is especially true for large sites, where it may be easy to get lost among the pages. For example, check out a site that my agency worked on for the Automatic Switch Company, at www.asco.com. One of the product pages is shown in Figure 6–1.

Although it is light on really intense graphics (Asco markets the site toward engineers, who were determined to be largely disinterested in graphic design), we did pay a lot of attention to the navigation system for the 300+ page site. There is practically no page that is not within two clicks of any other page, and the user almost never has to use the "back" button.

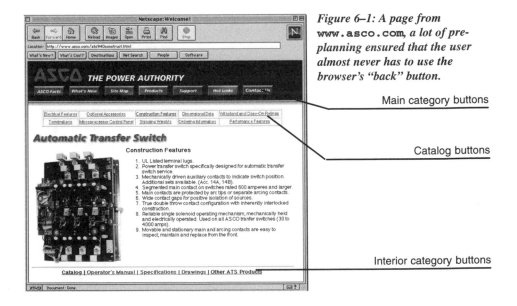

Figure 6–1: A page from www.asco.com, a lot of pre-planning ensured that the user almost never has to use the browser's "back" button.

Main category buttons

Catalog buttons

Interior category buttons

I know that you're anxious to get back to the Photoshop part of all this, but the design of your buttons is just as important as how the pages are set up. Like backgrounds, the buttons you choose should add to the overall design of your site, not detract or work to confuse the reader. It is easy to get carried away and make the buttons the focal point of your site, affecting download time or distracting your audience from giving proper attention to the real information provided on your site (unless your site is titled "Various Types of Buttons for the Web," in which case just ignore this whole paragraph).

CREATING BEVELED BUTTONS

Beveled buttons are some of the more popular buttons on the Web, and Photoshop 5.0 makes it easier than ever. Easier is not always best, though, and as you'll see, version 5's Emboss and Bevel Command is limited relative to what you can do with Channels and the Lighting Effects filter.

USING SIMPLE BEVELS TO CREATE BUTTONS

1. Open a new file, 216 pixels by 72 pixels (yes, these are a bit big for buttons, but for this example, I'd like you to *see* what you're doing—we can resize later).
2. Create Layer 1 and make that the active layer (note: the new Effects features will not work on the background layer).
3. Choose a light shade of blue to fill your canvas with.
4. Choose Layer -> Effects -> Bevel and Emboss to get the dialog box shown in Figure 6–2.

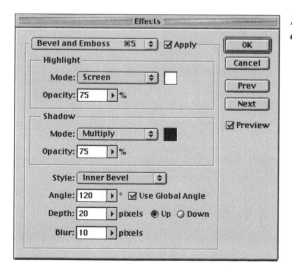

Figure 6–2: The Layer Effects Bevel and Emboss dialog box

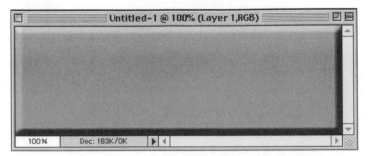

Figure 6–3: Inner Bevel applied of Depth 20 pixels, Blur 10 pixels

5. From the Style pull-down menu, choose Inner Bevel.

6. For this example, set the Angle to 120 degrees, the Depth to the maximum 20 pixels, and the Blur to 10. Come back to this later and experiment with the different settings.

7. Hit OK and your canvas will look similar to Figure 6–3. Notice that the bevel is slight, even though the bevel is at its maximum depth of 20. We could make it appear deeper by increasing the blur, but that will diminish the look of the sloped sides.

CREATING BUTTONS WITH DUAL BEVEL

1. Working off the previous example, use the Rectangular Marquee tool to make a selection of the solid blue area in your button.

 You may wonder why I'd suggest using the Rectangular Marquee tool instead of, say, the Magic Wand with a low tolerance. The answer is that Layer Effects will still read the entire layer as your shade of blue, and not distinguish the shadow or the light.

2. Choose Select -> Modify -> Contract and choose a setting of 3. This will make sure that your selection is not interfering with the beveled edge you created. It will look similar to Figure 6–4.

3. We're going to put a new bevel on this selection. Since Layer Effects always apply to the entire layer, the fact that you have one particular portion selected won't matter much. Hit Command + C (Ctrl + C in Windows) to copy your selection, and then Command + V (Ctrl + V in Windows) to paste it in the same spot but on a new layer.

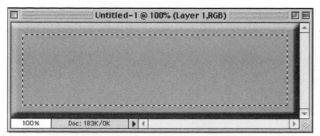

Figure 6–4: Part of the main field was selected, copied, and pasted onto a new layer, so a new layer effect can be applied.

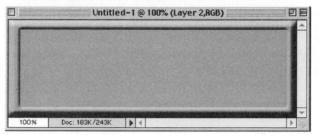

Figure 6–5: A bevel effect applied to the new layer, this time beveling downward instead of upward. The result is a ridge around the edge.

4. Choose Layer -> Effects -> Bevel and Emboss and, keeping the angle and the depth the same, push the radio button for "down" instead of "up," and lower the blur to 2. Your button will look like the button in Figure 6–5.

USING TRADITIONAL METHODS FOR BEVELS

Depending on what you're looking for, you may want to use more traditional methods of creating a beveled button, which tend to be less limited.

1. Open a new file 216 pixels by 72 pixels.

2. Choose a color to fill your canvas with.

3. Select All, choose Select -> Modify -> Border, and choose a border setting of 12.

4. Choose Select -> Save Selection, and choose New in the Channel pull-down menu (if you do not name them, channels will automatically default to "Alpha 1," "Alpha 2," and so on in your Channels Palette). All color dissapears, and even the foreground and background colors are now black and white. The Channel Palette is shown in Figure 6–6.

5. Deselect all and choose Filter -> Render -> Lighting Effects to bring up the dialog box shown in Figure 6–7. In the Texture Channel pull-down menu, select Alpha 1. Set the direction of your light to be similar to that of the Figure.

6. Click OK and your image will look like Figure 6–8.

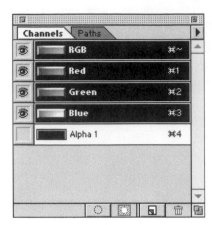

Figure 6–6: The Channels Palette. Alpha 1 is our selection.

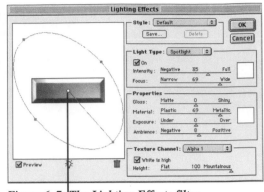

Figure 6–7: The Lighting Effects filter

Light direction and distance

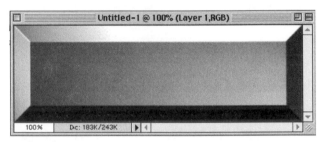

Figure 6–8: The simple bevel created with the Lighting Effects filter.

CREATING TRADITIONAL DUAL BEVEL

1. Still working from the previous example, open the Channels Palette. Make Alpha 1 the active channel by clicking on it. Select All by pressing Command + A (Ctrl + A in Windows). Choose Select -> Modify -> Border and set the Border to 24 (twice what our original border was).

2. Choose Select -> Save Selection. This time your new channel is automatically named Alpha 2. Make Alpha 2 the active layer by clicking on it.

3. Hit Command + L (Ctrl + L in Windows) to open up the Levels dialog box, as shown in Figure 6–9. The Levels dialog box allows you to adjust both the input and output levels of your image or selection. While Input Levels allow you to increase the Shadows and Highlights and adjust the Midtones, the Output Levels let you decrease the Shadows and Highlights.

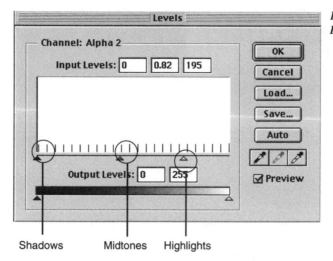

Figure 6–9: The Levels Dialog Box

Shadows   Midtones   Highlights

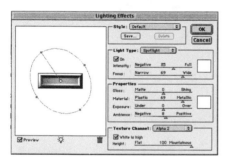

Figure 6–10: The Lighting Effects dialog box

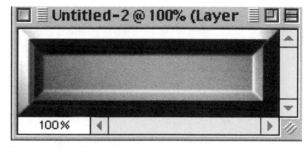

Figure 6–11: The final result shows a deep outer ridge.

Increase the Highlights in the Input Levels by moving the right slider to the left until it has a reading of 195. Adjust the Midtones slider, in the center, over to the right, for a reading of 0.85. This will make the neutral areas in your button darker, and the highlighted areas brighter.

4. Hit Command + D (Ctrl + D in Windows) to deselect all.

5. Click the RGB channel to make your color channels active again.

6. Go back to the Lighting Effects filter and this time make sure that the Texture pull-down menu is on Alpha 2 and no longer on Alpha 1. Play around with the light until it looks like the light shown in Figure 6–10.

7. Click OK and your image will be similar to that shown in Figure 6–11.

CREATING CIRCULAR BEVELS

Another popular type of button is a circular one, and again, the addition of a bevel can help add to the depth and realism of your buttons.

CREATING A SIMPLE CIRCULAR BEVEL

1. Open a new file, 216 pixels by 216 pixels. You can reduce the size of the button later.

2. Create a new layer so that you start your button on Layer 1. We'll be using some of Photoshop's Layer Effects later, which don't work on the background layer.

3. Using the Elliptical Marquee tool, hold down the Shift key for constraint and drag to create a circle in the middle of the canvas, like in Figure 6–12.

4. Set the background color to black and choose some light shade of blue for your foreground color. Using the Gradient tool, with the options set to Foreground to Background, drag a gradient from the North West position of your circle to the South East position. This is illustrated in Figure 6–13.

5. Make sure the circle is selected and hit Command + C (Ctrl + C in Windows) to copy it to your clipboard. Hit Command + V (Ctrl + V in Windows) to paste it back again. It will automatically appear in its own separate layer.

6. Choose Edit -> Transform -> Rotate 180 degrees.

7. Choose Edit -> Transform -> Numeric to access the dialog box shown in Figure 6–14. Make sure that Scale is checked, and reduce your selection to 80% on both axes. Hit OK. The result will be similar to Figure 6–15.

Figure 6–12: A perfect circular selection, made by holding the Shift key while dragging with the Circle Marquee tool.

Figure 6–13: The gradient has been added.

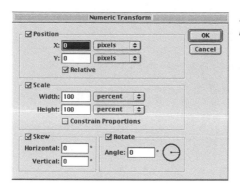

Figure 6–14: The Numeric Transform dialog box

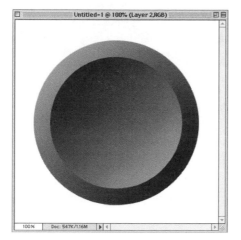

Figure 6–15: An indent appears when the original gradient is made smaller and flipped.

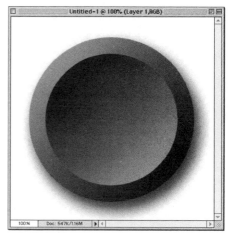

Figure 6–16: The button gains depth with the drop shadow.

8. Add a shadow to the button by making Layer 1 the active layer again, and choose Layer -> Effects -> Drop Shadow.

9. In the dialog box, select a distance of 10 and a blur of 20. Hit OK and the drop shadow will appear as in Figure 6–16.

This seems to be as good a place as any to mention that any of the butttons shown here, especially the circular shaped ones, can be used as bullets as well. The truth is, except for their size, many buttons and bullets are interchangeable—even the rectanglar buttons described earlier in this chapter can be made into bullets if they are narrowed into squares instead of rectangles.

CREATING A PUSHED-IN "COAT" BUTTON

You know those big round buttons your grandmother was forever sewing onto something? Well, this exercise will make grandma's job a little bit easier...

1. Follow Steps 1–3 from Simple Circular Bevel earlier in this chapter.

2. Fill your selection with a light shade of blue.

3. With your circle still selected, choose Select -> Save Selection, and save your selection as Alpha 1.

4. Within your Channels Palette, make Alpha 1 your active channel.

5. If your rulers are not already showing, click Command + R (Ctrl + R in Windows) and pull a horizontal and vertical line from each ruler (by placing your cursor over the left ruler and dragging to the right) to establish a middle point on the circle, as in Figure 6–17. If you're still using Photoshop 3.0, you'll have to place guides by opening a new layer and using the line tool.

6. With the Radial Gradient tool selected, and the gradient range set to Foreground to Background in the options palette, drag a gradient from your center point to the edge of your circle.

7. Hit Command + L (Ctrl + L in Windows) to access the Levels dialog box. Set the Shadows level to 32, and the Highlights level to 235. You'll see that your gradient is no longer as smooth as it once was.

8. Make the RGB channel active again by clicking on it. Note that you can see the color in your image again.

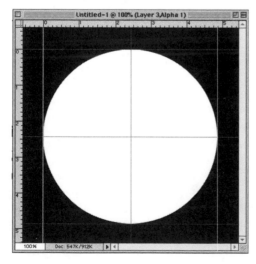

Figure 6–17: Midpoint of the circle is located by using both the horizontal and vertical rulers.

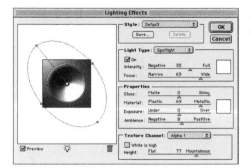

Figure 6–18: The Lighting Effects dialog box previews the button.

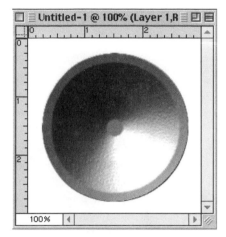

Figure 6–19: Final product after setting lighting effects

9. Choose Filter -> Render -> Lighting Effects to access the Lighting Effects dialog box shown in Figure 6–18. Set your light type to "spotlight" and move the direction to be coming from the northwest. Make sure that the "White is high" option is clicked, and set your Texture Channel to Alpha 1. Click OK.

10. Your button will look like the one shown in Figure 6–19.

CREATING A PILL-SHAPED BUTTON

Pill-shaped buttons are a great effect that give you the personality of a round button, the rigidity of a rectangular one, but leave enough space to write on. They're fairly easy to make and very functional.

1. Open a new file, 432 pixels by 216 pixels. This is too large for a button, but for the example, I'd like for you to see what you're doing—you can reduce the size later.

2. Open a new layer and, using the Elliptical Marquee tool, hold the Shift key down and make a circle toward the left side of your canvas.

3. Select the Paint Bucket tool and fill your circle with a light shade of blue.

 Make sure that Anti-aliased is clicked off in the Paint Bucket Options palette. Leaving it on can lead to an unwanted haloing effect.

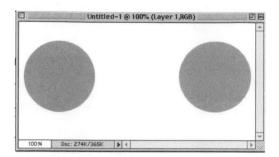

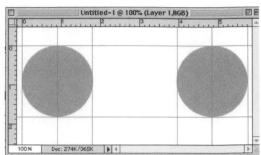

Figure 6–20: Two identical circles will become the ends of the pill button.

Figure 6–21: Use the rulers to build the body of the button.

4. Hit the V key to select your Move tool, and, holding the Option + Shift (Alt + Shift in Windows) keys down, drag a copy of the circle to the other side of the canvas. The option key is what activates the copy function, while the shift key restricts you to dragging in a perfectly straight line. Your canvas will look like Figure 6–20.

5. If your rulers are not already visible, hit Command + R (Ctrl + R in Windows) to make them visable. Drag down two horizontal rules, one at the top and one at the bottom of your circles, and drag over vertical lines to pinpoint the center diameter of both circles, like Figure 6–21.

6. Select View -> Snap to Guides to make sure that your next selection will hug the rules you just made.

7. With the Rectangular Marquee tool, make a selection from the top left corner of your rules to the bottom right corner. Fill your new selection with the same color that you used to fill the circles. Your image should look similar to the image in Figure 6–22.

8. Hold down the Command key (Ctrl in Windows) and click on Layer 1 to select your entire image. Start a new layer so that we don't disturb the pill you just created.

9. Choose the Reflected Gradient as your tool and hit the d key to change the foreground and background colors to black and white. Hit the x key to switch the foreground and background colors. Starting from the middle of your selection, drag a gradient downward and just slightly to the right to create the diagonal gradient that you see in Figure 6–23.

10. In the Layers Palette, select "soft light" for your mode. This will make the gradient blend in with the blue on Layer 1, making it seem as if there were a light going through it.

11. With Layer 2 still the active layer, choose Layer -> Effects -> Bevel and Emboss.

12. In the Bevel and Emboss dialog box, select Emboss as your style. Figure 6–24 shows the pill button with different Depth and Blur amounts.

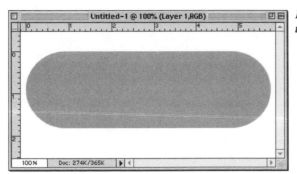

Figure 6–22: Fill the body with the same color as the circles.

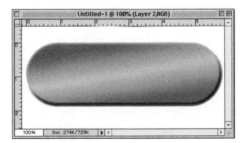

Figure 6–23: Use the striped gradient tool to create a black to white to black gradient over the pill button. Choosing "soft light" as your layer mode will make your button appear to have a light hit on it.

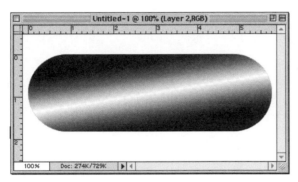

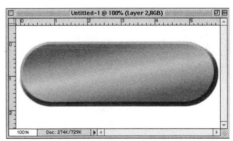

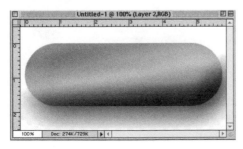

Figure 6–24: Various Layer Effects settings:

Top Left: Inner Bevel, Depth = 5, Blur = 5
Top Right: Inner Bevel, Depth = 20, Blur = 10
Bottom Left: Inner Bevel, Depth = 20, Blur = 40

One More Cool Thing with This Example

I cannot think up a good title for what this is, so I'll just say it's a cool thing that you can do to add flavor to the previous example.

1. Make Layer 1 the active layer and select the pill button on it by Command (Ctrl in Windows) clicking on Layer 1.

2. Choose Select -> Modify -> Contract and enter 16, which is the maximum.

3. Choose Select -> Modify -> Border and choose a border of 10.

4. Choose Select -> Feather and feather your selection by 2.

5. Choose Select -> Save Selection and save your selection as Alpha 2.

6. Choose Filter -> Render -> Lighting Effects.

7. Set the Texture Channel to Alpha 2, and the direction of the light as shown in Figure 6–25. Click OK and your image should look like the image in Figure 6–26, only cooler because yours is in color.

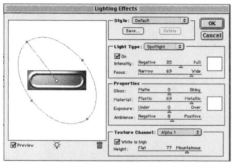

Figure 6–25: Using the Lighting Effects on the pill button to create a stark ridge toward the edge.

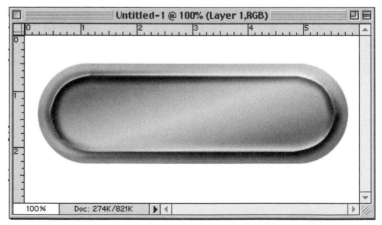

Figure 6–26: An inner ridge gives the button increased depth

CREATING BUTTONS WITH TEXTURE ADDED

Once you have gotten the hang of beveled buttons, you're probably going to want to put some texture on them, depending on the look or theme of the Web site. The following are just some of the great textures that you can create in Photoshop 5.0. After that are some text effects to work with the texture we're creating.

CREATING BUTTONS WITH A BRUSHED METAL TEXTURE

The brushed metal effect can be a cool texture for a button, but is probably a good technique to learn for other projects, too. Personally, even though you can do this particular effect at 72 ppi like all the others, I think it comes out nicer if you create the texture at 150-200 ppi and then scale it down.

1. Open a new file, 432 pixels by 216 pixels, 200 ppi. You can scale it down to proper size later.

2. Create a new layer to start your work on.

3. Make white your background color and a medium to dark gray your foreground color.

4. Open the Gradient tool palette by double clicking on the Gradient tool. Push the Edit button to access the Gradient Editor, as shown in Figure 6–27. (This palette is described in detail in Chapter 5, "Creative Text Effects".)

5. Create a gradient as shown in Figure 6–27 by alternating between the foreground color and the background color to simulate stripes. Click OK to leave the Gradient Editor when you're finished.

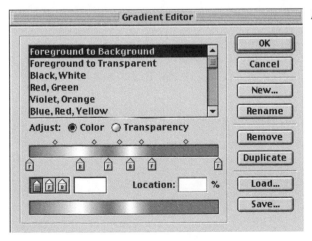

Figure 6–27: Gradient Editor

6. Drag the Gradient tool crosshairs from the top left corner to set your gradient.

7. Your canvas should look as though there is light reflecting off of it.

If the stripes are too well defined, choose Filter -> Gaussian Blur and move the slider outward until the stripes are blended better.

The result will look like Figure 6–28.

8. Choose Filter -> Noise -> Add Noise to access the dialog box shown in Figure 6–29. Set the noise Amount to 50, using a uniform distribution. Click OK.

9. Choose Filter -> Blur -> Motion Blur. Set the angle to match the direction that your light hits are going. Set the Blur Distance to 110, and hit OK.

10. Choose Image -> Adjust -> Color Balance to bring up the dialog box shown in Figure 6–30.

11. In the midtones, move the top slider closer to Cyan until the first numeric color level reads -16. Move the bottom slider closer to Blue until the last number color level reads +28. Hit OK.

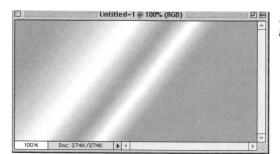

Figure 6–28: The gradient placed into the selection

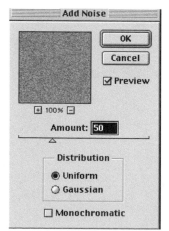

Figure 6–29: The Add Noise filter

12. Select Image -> Image Size and reduce your image to 72 ppi.

13. Bevel the button with one of the methods described earlier. (You may have to make your canvas a bit larger to get a decent bevel effect. If so, do this by choosing Image -> Canvas Size, and making each dimension just a bit larger.) I chose to use Layer Effects, with an inner bevel 20 pixels deep and 8 pixels blurred, as seen in Figure 6–31.

14. Using the Type Mask tool, open the text editor and Type "HOME" in large letters and hit OK. You'll notice that the selection text resides on Layer 1 and does not automatically start a new layer as regular text does.

15. We're going to use the Layer Effects options for our text. Because the effects options automatically apply to everything on the layer and not just what you've selected, we're going to have to work on a different layer. Move your text selection where you want it and push Command + C (Ctrl + C in Windows) to copy that part of the image to the pasteboard. Now hit Command + V (Ctrl + V in Windows) to paste it back. You'll see that it pastes into a new layer.

16. Choose Layer -> Effects -> Bevel and Emboss. Figure 6–32 and Color Figure 17 show how some different settings can look, each nicely complementing the brushed steel effect.

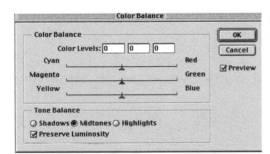

Figure 6–30: The Color Balance dialog box

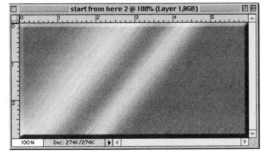

Figure 6–31: The final product resembles a button made of steel.

Figure 6-32: Various Text Effects

Top Left: Outer Bevel, Depth =5, Blur = 5
Middle Left: Emboss, Depth = 20, Blur = 7
Bottom Left: Outer Bevel, Depth = 20,
             Blur = 6 Plus Inner Shadow,
             Default Settings
Top Right: Inner Shadow, Distance = 10
             Blur = 3

CREATING WATER PUDDLE BUTTONS

This button design will help you make a splash on your Web site (sorry—sometimes I cannot resist the really cheesy jokes). Instead of each button having a hard edge, the Water Puddle button takes advantage of a variance in shape and texture to create its effect.

1. Open a new file, 600 pixels by 400 pixels, 200 ppi. You can scale it down to proper size later.

2. Create a new layer, Layer 1, to start your work on.

3. Use your Free Form Lasso tool to make a wavy, elliptical selection, as shown in Figure 6–33 to create the outlines of your puddle.

4. Make white your foreground color and select a light shade of blue for your background color.

5. Choose the Radial Gradient tool and, starting from the center of the selection, create a gradient from white to light blue, as illustrated in Figure 6–34.

6. Press Command + D (Ctrl + D in Windows) to deselect your selection.

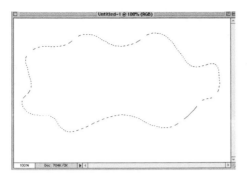

Figure 6–33: A wavy, elliptical selection

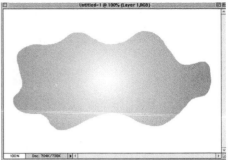

Figure 6–34: Selection filled with white to blue gradient

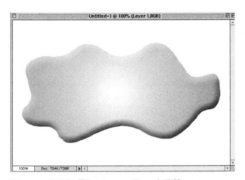

Figure 6–35: The Inner Bevel Effect

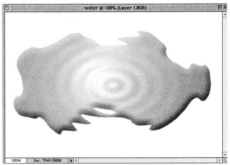

Figure 6–36: The Zig Zag filter provides a pond-like ripple.

7. Choose Layer -> Effects -> Bevel and Emboss. From the Style pull-down menu, choose Inner Bevel.

8. Set the Depth to 10 pixels, and the Blur to 20 pixels. Click OK and the result will look similar to Figure 6–35.

9. Choose Filter -> Distort -> Zig Zag to access the dialog box. Set the Amount to 34% and the Ridges to 7%. Hit OK and your image will look similar to Figure 6–36.

10. Add a slight shadow by choosing Layer -> Effects -> Drop Shadow. Set the Opacity to 40%, the Distance to 3, and the Blur to 4. Hit OK.

11. Place the button name on your puddle with the Text Editor, as shown in Figure 6–37.

12. The text will need to be fluid as well and not as harsh as it currently appears. Before applying a filter, choose Layer -> Type -> Render Layer.

13. Applying the same amount of the Zig Zag filter would distort the text too much and make it illegible. Instead, select Filter -> Distort -> Ripple and set the Ripple amount to 115% and the Size to Medium.

Figure 6–37: Straight Text is too harsh

Figure 6–38: The Ripple filter makes the text blend in better with the button.

Figure 6–39: Add a few extra drops on the fringe to make the puddle more realistic.

14. Press OK and your final button will look similar to Figure 6–38. Don't forget to reduce the resolution to 72 ppi before using on your Web site.

For a more realistic puddle effect, add a few droplets around your button, as shown in Figure 6–39 and Color Figure 18.

OTHER TYPES OF BUTTONS

There are a lot of buttons you can make with the examples given in this chapter. Of course, not all buttons are limited to rectangles, circles, and pills with bevels and embosses. There are plenty of other types of buttons that you can use, including image icons, tabs, and others. The following pages show just a couple examples that have been used in different sites.

TABBED BUTTONS

Creating folder tabs are a clever way to help your user navigate through a Web site. By using various intensities of shadows and/or various tab shapes, you can have the tabs come forward or backward to show which page the viewer is seeing.

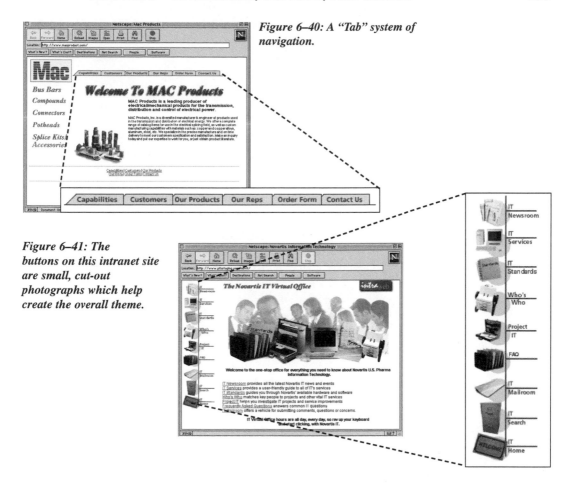

Figure 6–40: A "Tab" system of navigation.

Figure 6–41: The buttons on this intranet site are small, cut-out photographs which help create the overall theme.

In Figure 6–40 and Color Figure 19, I created a tab navigation system for Mac Products' Web site (www.macproduct.com). Each tab appears to come forward as the user clicks on a different topic.

BUTTONS MADE FROM IMAGES

Buttons don't always have to conform to the traditional expectation of what a button should look like. Sometimes the button can be small pictures—icon sized—to help add to an overall theme. Figure 6–41 and Color Figure 20 show a home page my agency created for a Novartis intranet. They wanted to go with an office theme throughout the intranet site. To enhance the imagery, especially in the lower-tier pages where graphics gave way to text, we created office-oriented pictures for each of the buttons. Rolodexes, briefcases, file cabinets, and other photographs played a part in not only the navigation, but in tying the concept together.

CREATING COMPLEX NAVIGATION TOOLS

There is no Web law that states all buttons have to be free-standing images, rectangular or square, fitting a certain image. While those type of buttons certainly make up a large part of navigation on the Web, and will certainly show up in your Web pages at most points, there are other times when it is necessary to be a little more creative in your design, and a little more advanced in your programming. Image maps and rollovers are a couple of the ideas you can use to both ease your navigation and help jazz up your site's appeal.

IMAGE MAPS

It wasn't too long ago that image maps were significantly more difficult to create, needing CGI scripts to make them function properly. But that was back in the good old days, when people churned their own butter, a thirty-mile drive took two days by horseback, and people were satisfied with a 9800 speed modem.

Okay, maybe I'm overplaying this just a bit, but you know what I'm saying. The Web changes fast, and one of the more recent changes for the better are easy-to-execute image maps that you can design in Photoshop and program in simple HTML.

If you've read this far into this chapter, you know the importance of navigational elements. Without the proper tools, users can quickly get lost in your site or even find it too confusing to bother with. Sometimes, buttons alone are enough to create a good navigation system. Sometimes, it takes a bit more.

Image maps allow you to create links to different pages through one graphic. The example in Figure 6–42 is an image map that I created for the Automatic Switch

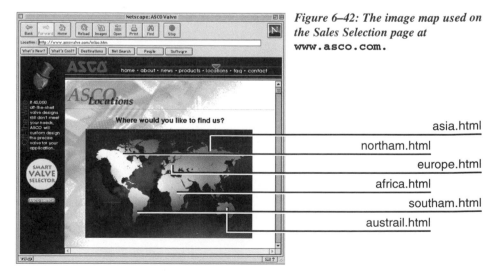

Figure 6–42: The image map used on the Sales Selection page at www.asco.com.

Company's valve division Web site (www.asco.com). Besides wanting their "locations" page to be attractive, I also needed for it to be functional. A list of continent names would have worked, however that would have been boring, and not in sync with the rest of the site.

Creating an Image Map. Step One: Graphic Navigation

Any graphic can be used to make an image map. Although the example given in Figure 6–42 uses a picture of the world map, you are not limited to geographical references. Practically any image you'd like can contain multiple hot spots.

Another popular use for image maps would be in designing navigation bars in place of separate individual buttons.

1. Open a new file, 432 pixels by 72 pixels.

2. Choose a color from the Color Picker or the Swatches Palette, and fill the canvas with that color.

3. Click the default colors button on the toolbar or hit the D key to make your foreground color black again.

4. Choose the Type tool, and place the following words on your canvas:

   Home • About Us • Service • Products • Contact Us.

   Make sure that the words are centered on the canvas. On a Mac system, you can create the bullets by typing Option + 8. Windows users type Alt + 0149 for the bullet. Your canvas should look like the one shown in Figure 6–43. What you're building is a very basic, no frills navigation bar.

5. Index your image by choosing Image -> Index and select Adaptive from the pulldown menu. Hit OK and save your image as navbar.gif.

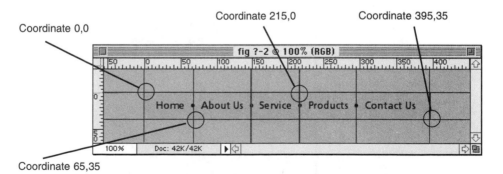

Figure 6–43: How the coordinates are determined and measured in a simple image map.

Creating an Image Map. Step Two: Measuring Coordinates

Once you have designed your simple navigation bar, you're ready to begin bisecting it into clickable rectangles. The rectangles in an image map—each of which will hyperlink to a different Web page—are defined by the coordinates of the top left corner and the coordinates of the bottom right corner.

Figure 6–44 shows how these coordinates are measured. If you remember your high school geometry classes, we measure coordinates on a grid by plotting the X axis first and then the Y axis. (See—and you spent all your time in geometry class wondering why you needed to learn all that stuff!)

Plotting points here will differ a little from your average geometry problem since, as shown in Figure 6–44, an ordinary grid has the bottom right quadrant being a positive number on the x axis, and a negative number on the y axis.

The grid in your Photoshop canvas, however, which is essentially a blow-up of the bottom right quadrant, measures both the x and y axes as positive numbers. As long as you remember this, the rest will be easy.

Figure 6–43 shows the coordinates for various points on the navigation bar. The rectangle with the word "Home" in the center is defined by the two sets of coordinates as shown: 0,0 for the top left corner, and 65,35 for the lower right corner.

1. Turn the rulers on (View -> Show Rulers). Make sure they are measuring in Pixels. If they are not, change them to pixel units by opening the Info Palette. The bottom left quadrant has a cross-hair with a small triangle next to it. Click the triangle and choose "Pixels" from the resulting pop-up menu.

2. Note that the top left corner of your canvas is set to 0,0 on the rulers.

3. Place a vertical guideline in between each word on your canvas. Place horizontal guidelines at the very top and bottom of your canvas. Your canvas should look like the sample provided in Figure 6–43.

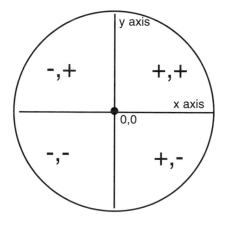

Figure 6–44: Geometry classes teach graphing with negative numbers in 3 of 4 quadrants. Image Maps for Web sites keep all quadrants as positive numbers.

4. Measure the corners in a similar fashion for all the rectangles on your navigation bar. In most instances, it is easier and acceptable to round to the nearest 5 (if the coordinate is 68, for example, rounding up to 70 is fine).

5. Write down the measurements on a separate sheet of paper.

The coordinates for each of the rectangles shown in the Figure are:

	Top left corner	Bottom right corner
Home:	0,0	65,35
About Us:	65,0	150,35
Service:	150,0	215,35
Products:	215,0	295,35
Contact Us:	295,0	395,35

Creating an Image Map. Step Three: Referencing in Your HTML Document

Once you have a graphic and have measured it for the coordinates, you're going to need to write the proper codes in your HTML document to make it work.

1. Begin your HTML document, which would contain your navigation bar, on a white background. The coding for your document should look something like the following:

```
<HTML>
<HEAD>
<TITLE>Web Navigation</TITLE>
</HEAD>
<BODY BGCOLOR=#FFFFFF>

<IMG SRC="navbar.gif">

</BODY>
</HTML>
```

2. Within your <HEAD> </HEAD> tags, create some extra space to add more text.

3. You'll write your map commands between the <HEAD> </HEAD> tags. The additions to your HTML document are written and explained as follows:

```
MAP NAME="navigationmap">
<AREA SHAPE="rect" COORDS="0,0,65,35" HREF="home.html">
<AREA SHAPE="rect" COORDS="65,0,150,35" HREF="about.html">
<AREA SHAPE="rect" COORDS="150,0,215,35"
HREF="service.html">
```

```
<AREA SHAPE="rect" COORDS="215,0,295,35"
HREF="products.html">
<AREA SHAPE="rect" COORDS="295,0,395,35"
HREF="contact.html">
</MAP>
```

`<MAP>`	Opens the command that will hold the information about your image map. Giving it a name will allow you to reference it later.
`<AREA>`	Defines the exact measurements of your map.
`SHAPE="rect"`	Defines it first as a rectangle (other options are "circ" for circle, and "poly" for polygon).
`COORDS="X,Y,X,Y"`	The coordinates for each rectangle that you wrote down earlier (see Creating an Image Map Step Two: Measuring Coordinates ealier in this chapter).
`HREF="pagename.html"`	Tells the browser which page to link to when the image within the specified coordinates is clicked on.
`</MAP>`	Ends your <MAP> command.

4. To tell the browser that your image will act as your map, add the USEMAP command and reference the MAP name given earlier:

```
<IMG SRC="navbar.gif" USEMAP=#navigationmap>
```

As you roll over each word on your navigation bar in the browser, you will notice that your cursor changes to show that it is clickable, and that the name of the page to link to shows up at the bottom of the browser (if it doesn't, check to make sure that you measured your rectangles correctly).

5. Get rid of the blue border around your image by inserting the BORDER=0 command:

```
<IMG SRC="filename.gif" USEMAP=#navigationmap BORDER=0>
```

ROLLOVER BUTTONS

Because my company is a creative advertising agency, we have some liberty to be more wild and expressive than we can be for some of our clients. At the same time, we are looking to attract corporate clients, so we cannot be too outrageous.

On our site, the home page, shown in Figure 6–45, introduces the user to the navigation tools for moving throughout the site. Each circle that you see is a rollover—as you move the mouse over each circle, the name of the button appears at the top of the

Figure 7–45: My agency's home page located at www.pfsnewmedia.com.

screen. A smaller version of the image is on every page in the site, allowing for easy navigation. The various rollovers are shown in Figure 6–46 and Color Figure 21.

Valery Feeny, Director of Web Development at PFS New Media, wrote the HTML coding and JavaScript necessary to make the rollovers work. "I knew that our site had to be dynamic—it had to show creativity as well as prove functionality," explains Valery. "Our future clients would be judging us on our site. Although we had the means to go really out of control with graphics and programming, our clients are typically more mainstream and corporate/conservative. So from a marketing standpoint, I decided that sleek, elegant, and interesting would be better than flashy and outrageous. I decided on rollover buttons for the navigation bar to show both creativity and programming ability, since rollovers are becoming one of the really popular features on the Web lately."

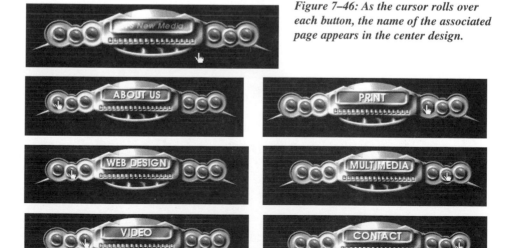

Figure 7–46: As the cursor rolls over each button, the name of the associated page appears in the center design.

The following is the partial HTML and JavaScript that Valerie wrote for the navigation on our home page. Although this is not a Photoshop technique and therefore not explored or explained, it is a helpful script to have as a reference.

```
<HTML>
<HEAD>
<TITLE>PFS New Media</TITLE>

<SCRIPT LANGUAGE="JavaScript">
// define rollover variables and load top rollover images

        if(document.images)
        {       text0=new Image()
                text1=new Image()
                text2=new Image()
                text3=new Image()
                text4=new Image()
                text5=new Image()
                text6=new Image()
                text7=new Image()

                text0.src="images/mid2.gif"
                text1.src=text0.src
                text2.src=text0.src
                text3.src=text0.src
                text4.src=text0.src
                text5.src=text0.src
                text6.src=text0.src
                text7.src=text0.src
        }

// load descriptive rollover images

        function initialize()
        {       if(document.images)
                {       text1.src="fields/about.gif"
                        text2.src="fields/Web.gif"
                        text3.src="fields/video.gif"
                        text4.src="fields/home.gif"
                        text5.src="fields/print.gif"
                        text6.src="fields/multi.gif"
                        text7.src="fields/contact.gif"
                }
```

```
                    }


// display rollovers

        function display(num)
        {       if(document.images)
                {       if (num=="0")
document.holder.src=text0.src
                        if (num=="1")
document.holder.src=text1.src
                        if (num=="2")
document.holder.src=text2.src
                        if (num=="3")
document.holder.src=text3.src
                        if (num=="4")
document.holder.src=text4.src
                        if (num=="5")
document.holder.src=text5.src
                        if (num=="6")
document.holder.src=text6.src
                        if (num=="7")
document.holder.src=text7.src
                }
        }

</SCRIPT>

<MAP NAME="navmap">
<AREA SHAPE="rect" COORDS="30,25,55,55" HREF="about.html"
onmouseover="display(1)" onmouseout="display(0)"
ALT="About Us">
<AREA SHAPE="rect" COORDS="55,25,80,55" HREF="Web.html"
onmouseover="display(2)" onmouseout="display(0)" ALT="Web
Design">
<AREA SHAPE="rect" COORDS="80,25,105,55" HREF="video.html"
onmouseover="display(3)" onmouseout="display(0)"
ALT="Video">
</MAP>

<MAP NAME="navmap2">
<AREA SHAPE="rect" COORDS="0,20,25,60" HREF="print.html"
onmouseover="display(5)" onmouseout="display(0)"
```

```
ALT="Print">
<AREA SHAPE="rect" COORDS="25,20,50,60" HREF="multi.html"
onmouseover="display(6)" onmouseout="display(0)"
ALT="Multimedia">
<AREA SHAPE="rect" COORDS="50,20,80,60" HREF="contact.html"
onmouseover="display(7)" onmouseout="display(0)"
ALT="Contact">
</MAP>


</HEAD>

<BODY BGCOLOR=#000000 BACKGROUND="Webbg.gif" onload="ini-
tialize()">
<CENTER>

<TABLE CELLPADDING=0 CELLSPACING=0 BORDER=0>
<TR>
<TD><IMG SRC="images/left.gif" BORDER=0
USEMAP=#navmap></TD>
<TD><A HREF="home.html"><IMG SRC="images/mid.gif"
NAME="holder" BORDER=0></A></TD>
<TD><IMG SRC="images/right.gif" BORDER=0
USEMAP=#navmap2></TD>
</TR>
</TABLE>
<BR>
<TABLE>
```

To find out more about JAVA and JavaScript, please visit the Web site that accompanies this book at http://www.phptr.com/togo.

SUMMARY

Buttons and navigation are what give people the ability to find their way through the Web. If a navigation set-up is attractive and functional, it will not only become a major part of your site's overall appearance, but it will open up all of the other pages to your users. Poorly planned and designed navigation tools will hinder the user's ability to find sought-after information. Paying special attention to how you establish your buttons, image maps and rollovers will prove worthwhile as people will extend their visits and really have the opportunity to find the information you have available.

chapter 7

INLINE GRAPHICS:

IMAGE IS

EVERYTHING

More and more often, Web designers are relying on graphic elements rather than text to get their message across to potential visitors. As speeds of modems increase and users become more sophisticated, the images that are used in your site will play a more important role in presenting information. These images can be as simple as a photograph or an illustration, and as complex as a multiphotographic collage.

This chapter will briefly explore some of the available methods of getting images into Photoshop and techniques for retouching scanned, damaged, or otherwise problematic images. We'll then take a detailed journey into some of the Photoshop features—some tried and true, some brand new—that have helped turn good Web sites into great Web sites.

GETTING IMAGES INTO PHOTOSHOP

Your Web site is all laid out in your head, and you've got a stack of family vacation pictures that you are dying to put on line. So how do you do it? You can try to fold them up and shove them into your disk drive, but that rarely works. There are better ways, though, that are far more effective.

PERSONAL SCANNERS

There are many scanners on the market that do a great job of getting photographs into Photoshop. If you're not sure which scanner to buy, you might want to check out the following Web sites that offer reviews and descriptions:

- www.byte.com
- www.zdnet.com/pcmag/features/scanners/_open.htm
- www.inconference.com/digicam/scanners.html
- www.scanshop.com/scanner

Some of the above Web sites also give some useful inside tips to better scanning, so they're worth a quick glance.

Once your scanner is hooked up and all the necessary software has been installed into your system, you'll have to let Photoshop know that the scanner is there before you begin to scan. For this example, I am going to be using the HP 4C. Other scanners will have a different interface, and may function differently, but the basic theory will remain the same.

1. Choose File -> Import -> Twain Select and choose the scanner that you installed. (Note: you will only have to do this once.)

2. In the scanner interface shown in Figure 7–1, the object that you are scanning will appear in the preview area. Create a marquee around the object or part of the object that you wish to scan.

3. From the Type pull-down menu, choose what type of scan you would like to make. In most instances, I usually choose "Sharp Millions of Colors." That way I get the most out of the image and can reduce colors later. Although most scanners have tools in them that you can use to manipulate your image, you're better off concentrating your efforts on getting a clean, raw scan and manipulating it in Photoshop.

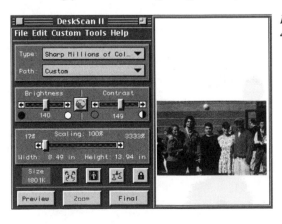

Figure 7–1: The interface of the HP 4C ScanJet desktop scanner

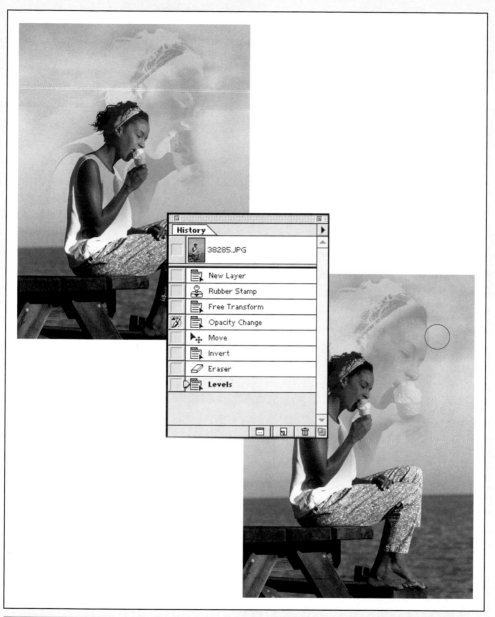

Color Figure 1

The History Brush, shown as the large circle in the lower picture, reverts just a portion of the picture to the point in the palette marked by the icon.

JPEG Compression Setting 10 92K (91,415 bytes)

Adaptive 8-bit Dithered 68K (67,150 bytes)

JPEG Compression Setting 5 28K (26,433 bytes)

Adaptive 8-bit No Dithering 58K (57,915 bytes)

JPEG Compression Setting 0 18K (16,813 bytes)

Adaptive Web Dithering 56K (54,104 bytes)

Photographic image: gradient color in background

COLOR FIGURE 2

File sizes and quality of images as JPEGs and GIFs. The size as measured in "K" is somewhat unreliable—look at the byte size for a more accurate measure.

JPEG Compression Setting 10
76K (76,937 bytes)

Adaptive 8-bit Dithered
58K (58,162 bytes)

JPEG Compression Setting 5
24K (23,002 bytes)

Adaptive 8-bit No Dithering
44K (44,313 bytes)

JPEG Compression Setting 0
16K (15,008 bytes)

Adaptive Web Dithering
50K (15,008 bytes)

Photographic image: flat color in background

COLOR FIGURE 2 *(Continued)*

JPEG Compression Setting 10 100K (100,431 bytes)

Adaptive 8-bit Dithered 72K (70,535 bytes)

JPEG Compression Setting 5 34K (32,537 bytes)

Adaptive 8-bit No Dithering 64K (61,655 bytes)

JPEG Compression Setting 0 22K (20,209 bytes)

Adaptive Web Dithering 58K (57,289 bytes)

Photographic image: many colors and contrasts

COLOR FIGURE 2   *(Continued)*

JPEG Compression Setting 10 62K (60,164 bytes)

Adaptive 8-bit Dithered 36K (33,257 bytes)

JPEG Compression Setting 5 36K (33,594 bytes)

Adaptive 4-bit color 18K (15,703 bytes)

JPEG Compression Setting 0 30K (27,868 bytes)

Adaptive Web Dithering 24K (22,131 bytes)

Illustrative image: line drawing with color fills.

COLOR FIGURE 2 *(Continued)*

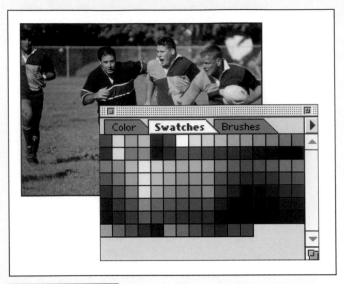

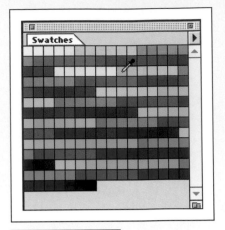

Color Figure 3
The Swatches Palettes hold colors for you to use repeatedly in your image.

Color Figure 4
Put your cursor in the Swatches Palette to access the eyedropper tool, and select your desired color. Swatches shown above indicate web-safe colors.

Color Figure 5
Your photographic images could appear with horrific results on 8-bit monitors.

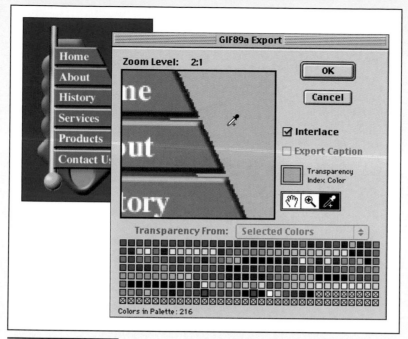

COLOR FIGURE 6

The background was turned to red, since that color wasn't used anywhere in the image. But a red halo is left around the fringe.

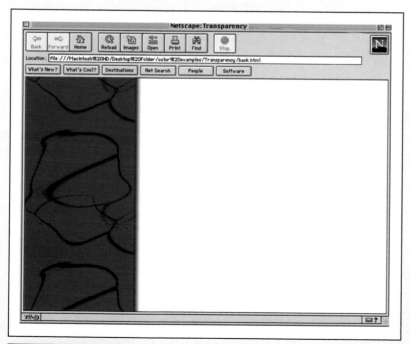

COLOR FIGURE 7

The background on this mock site will be an obstacle for transparent elements because of the black lines through it.

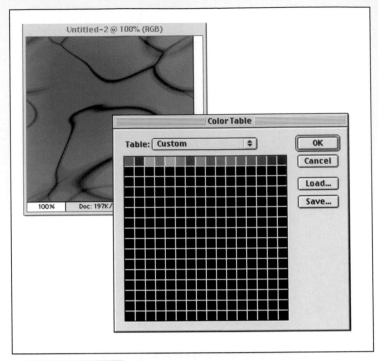

COLOR FIGURE 8
The Custom Table will help find the average of colors in the background to aid in transparency.

COLOR FIGURE 9
By filling the background of the navigation bar with the average color of the border, there is a reduced halo around the navigation bar.

COLOR FIGURE 10
The final mock site, with different elements made transparent. Portions were made trasparent from their individual layers.

white	lavendar	blanchalmond
snow	lavendarblush	bisque
seashell	mistyrose	moccasin
floralwhite	mintcream	bisque
oldlace	honeydew	moccasin
linen	beige	wheat
ghostwhite	cornsilk	navajowhite
whitesmoke	antiquewhite	peachpuff
gainsboro	papayawhip	lightsteelblue
lightgray	ivory	lightblue
silver	lightyellow	skyblue
darkgray	lightgoldenrod	lightskyblue
lightcyan	lemonchiffon	deepskyblue
azure	palegoldenrod	dodgerblue
aliceblue	khaki	cornflowerblue

Color Figure 11

All of the following colors can be referenced in HTML by their name, instead of their Hexidecimal code.

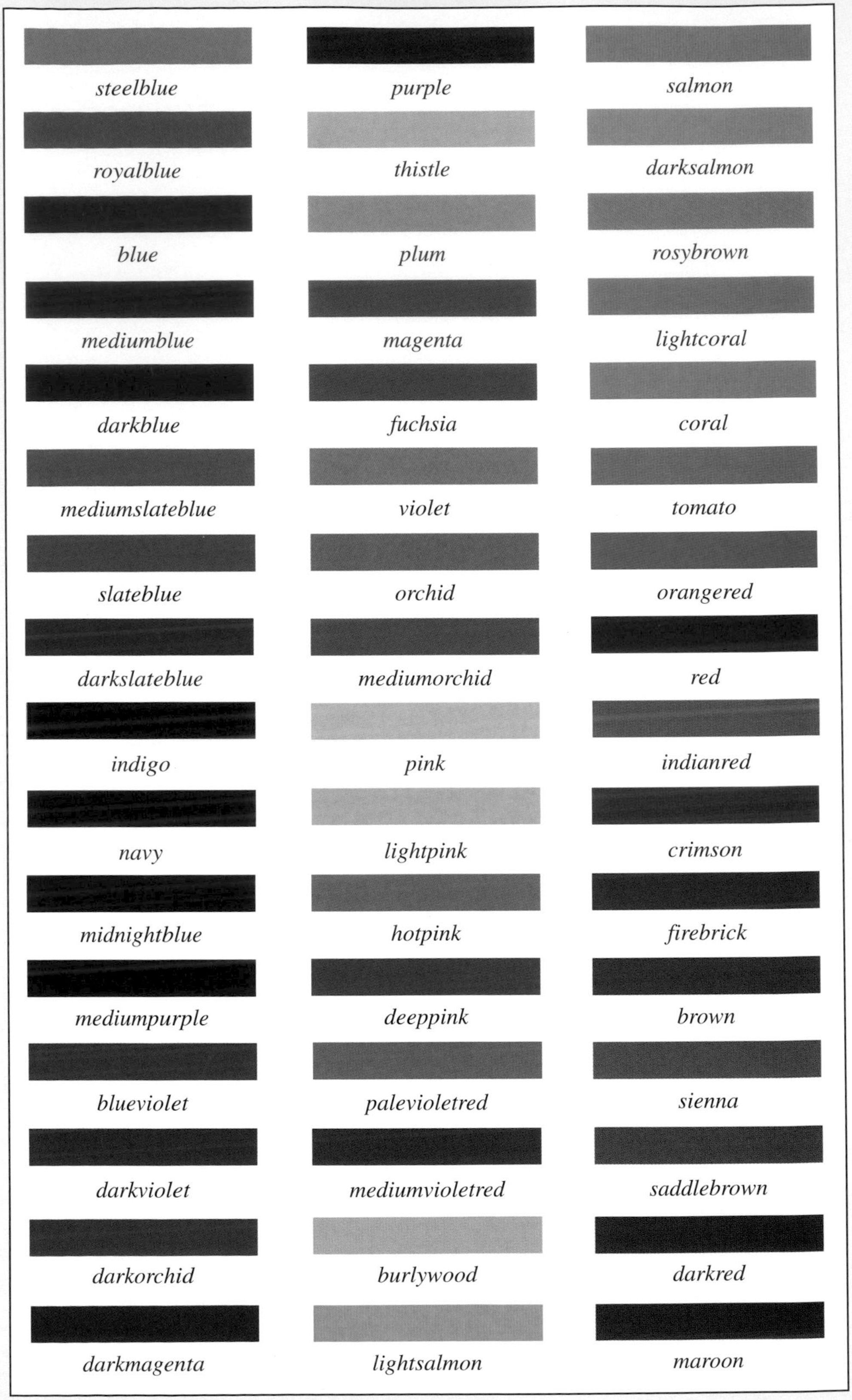

steelblue	purple	salmon
royalblue	thistle	darksalmon
blue	plum	rosybrown
mediumblue	magenta	lightcoral
darkblue	fuchsia	coral
mediumslateblue	violet	tomato
slateblue	orchid	orangered
darkslateblue	mediumorchid	red
indigo	pink	indianred
navy	lightpink	crimson
midnightblue	hotpink	firebrick
mediumpurple	deeppink	brown
blueviolet	palevioletred	sienna
darkviolet	mediumvioletred	saddlebrown
darkorchid	burlywood	darkred
darkmagenta	lightsalmon	maroon

COLOR FIGURE 11 *(Continued)*

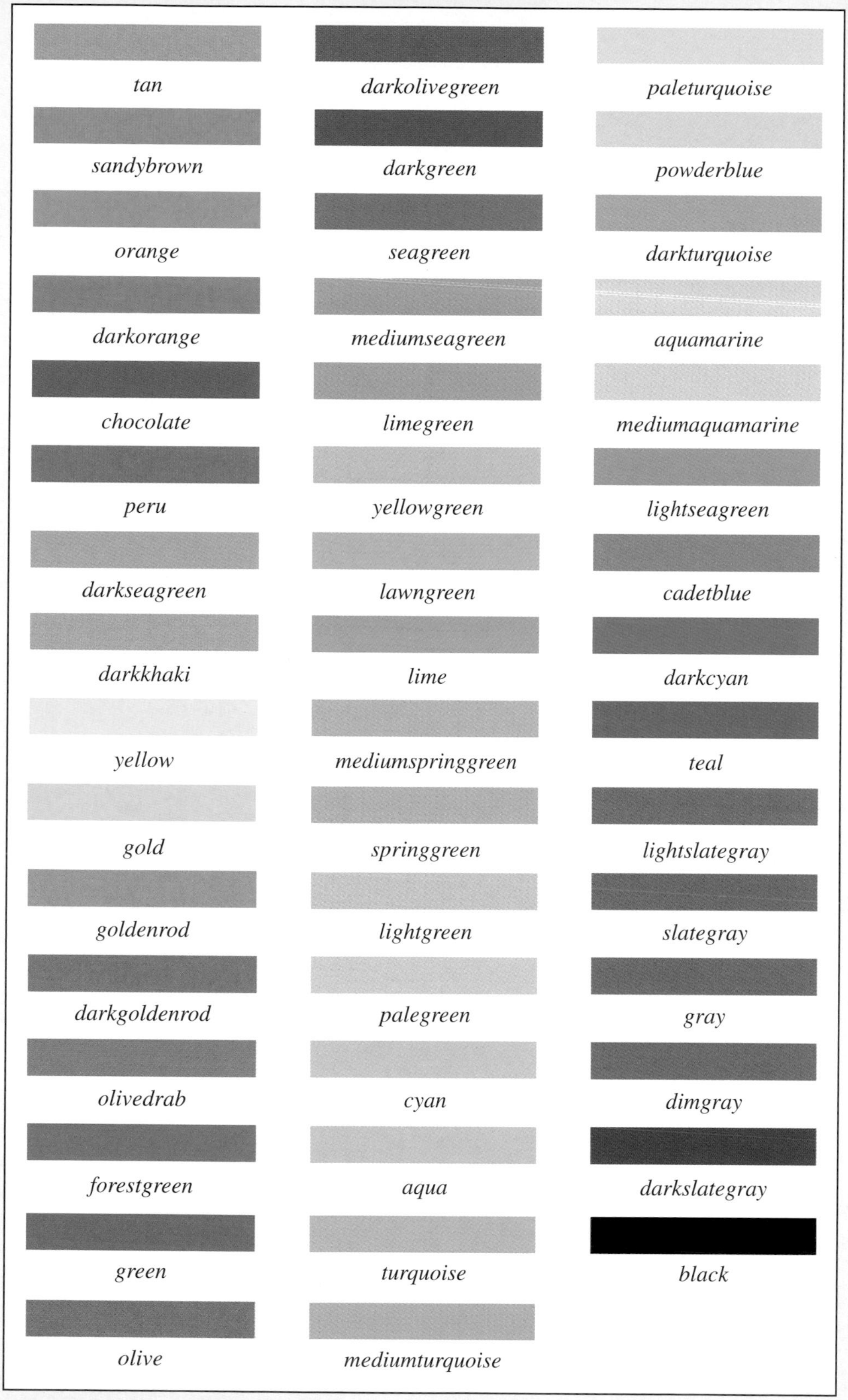

tan	darkolivegreen	paleturquoise
sandybrown	darkgreen	powderblue
orange	seagreen	darkturquoise
darkorange	mediumseagreen	aquamarine
chocolate	limegreen	mediumaquamarine
peru	yellowgreen	lightseagreen
darkseagreen	lawngreen	cadetblue
darkkhaki	lime	darkcyan
yellow	mediumspringgreen	teal
gold	springgreen	lightslategray
goldenrod	lightgreen	slategray
darkgoldenrod	palegreen	gray
olivedrab	cyan	dimgray
forestgreen	aqua	darkslategray
green	turquoise	black
olive	mediumturquoise	

COLOR FIGURE 11 (*Continued*)

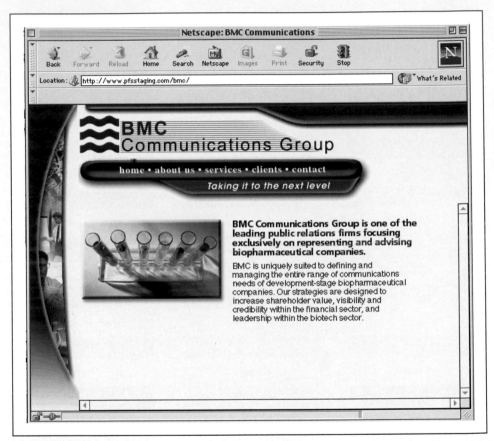

COLOR FIGURE 12
This site we created for BMC Communications. To make all the elements fit in properly, and to reduce download time, the site was broken up into 4 frames.

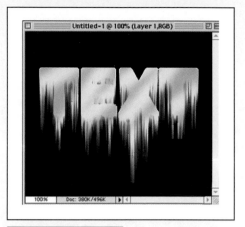

COLOR FIGURE 13
Fire effect

COLOR FIGURE 14
Ice effect

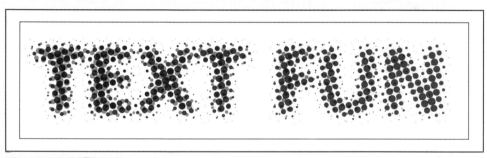

COLOR FIGURE 15
I used a gradient of blue to red before applying the Color Halftone filter. Try this same effect in the Channels Palette to create an effect of large dots to small dots.

COLOR FIGURE 16
Neon text

COLOR FIGURE 17
Buttons with a steel texture and layer effects

COLOR FIGURE 18
Buttons don't have to take a traditional shape, as displayed with this puddle-shaped button.

COLOR FIGURE 19

This web site for Mac Products (www.macproduct.com)
utilizes tab graphics for its navigation.

COLOR FIGURE 20

Buttons don't need to have any particular shape, as demonstrated by
the image buttons in this Novartis intranet site.

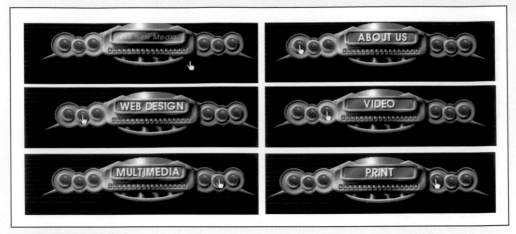

COLOR FIGURE 21
Various states of a roll-over button

COLOR FIGURE 22
This picture of my friend, Michali, came out washed out when I scanned it.

COLOR FIGURE 23
After using the Color Balance adjustment, I was able to add red and yellow to her highlights, midtones, and shadows to give her picture more vibrancy.

COLOR FIGURE 24
Changes to the color of the buttons after adjusting the hue and saturation.

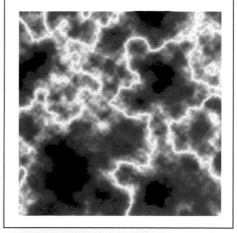

COLOR FIGURE 25 *(left)*
Lightning effect with lens flare.

COLOR FIGURE 26 *(right)*
The lightning effect with the Difference Clouds filter.

COLOR FIGURE 27

The lightning effect is part of the PFS logo, and a central part of our home page.

COLOR FIGURE 28

This sales sheet incorporates various collage techniques.

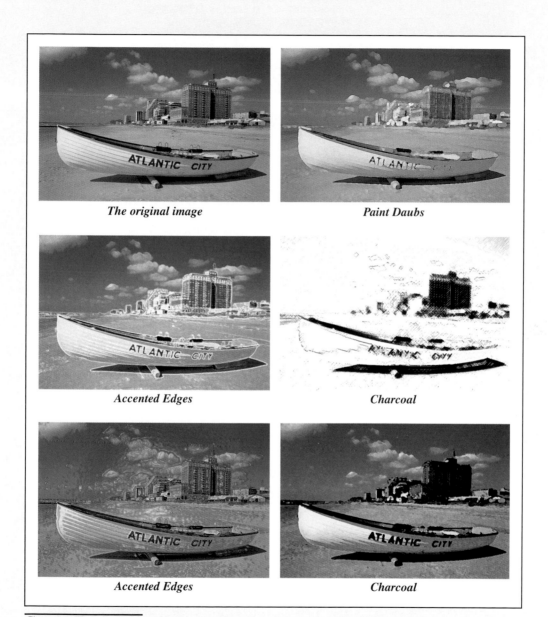

The original image

Paint Daubs

Accented Edges

Charcoal

Accented Edges

Charcoal

COLOR FIGURE 29
Various changes using the Gallery Effects

COLOR FIGURE 30

This splash graphic for Future Media Concepts involves multiple animations, and was assembled with tables. It can be found at www.fmctraining.com.

COLOR FIGURE 31

The Metrolpolitan Electric League Website (www.electroleague.org) laid out in Photoshop.

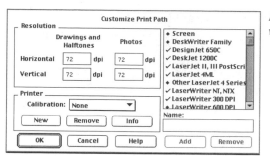

Figure 7–2: The Print Size dialog box will change the resolution of the scan.

4. Because Web graphics don't need to be greater than 72 ppi, I change the scan resolutions by choosing Image -> Print Size to access the dialog box shown in Figure 7–2, changing all the variables to 72 ppi.

5. Use the slider to increase or decrease image size and hit Final or Scan.

The image will appear in a new canvas in Photoshop, ready to be manipulated.

Scanning at higher resolutions will give you more detail in your image, but you may wind up scanning the actual texture of the original paper at higher resolutions. Later in this chapter I'll discuss how to fix these problems with the Gaussian Blur filter.

Each scanner model will be different from other models let alone models of other manufacturers. Interfaces, troubleshooting solutions and work-arounds will also vary—too much, in fact to really get into it in a book on Photoshop for the Web. Check out this book's Web site at http://www.phptr.com/togo for further details, or pick up Robert Gann's book, *Desktop Scanners*, also published by Prentice Hall, for a really in-depth scanner discussion.

Unless you take extra good care of both your original image and the bed of your scanner, you'll almost definitely have a fair amount of dust particles on your scanned image. Later in this chapter I'll discuss how to get rid of these.

Photo CDs

Today it's easier than ever to get your photos on a CD. CD-ROM drives are standard issue on most computers, and having your images on a photo CD can be helpful when creating your Web images. Some of the benefits of having your pictures on a photo CD include:

◆ You don't have to do your own scanning—professionals do it for you!

◆ A small additional price per image will give you a number of resolutions, so you can use them for anything from Web design to printing.

◆ The CD will act as storage so you can use a minimal amount of hard drive space.

◆ Printed icons of the images on the back of the CD case will help catalog your images for future use.

◆ The first time you get a photo CD, there's something just kinda...cool about it.

To get your photos on a CD, simply bring them to any service bureau, or even to most one-hour photo developing shops. Depending on the place you bring them to, the average wait for your CD can range anywhere between 24 hours and one week. Prices, as of the time of this writing, usually fall between $2.00–$4.50 per picture depending on the desired resolution, plus $20.00–$25.00 for the CD-ROM.

You can usually avoid the CD-ROM fee by supplying your own CD-ROM. If you'e already gotten your photos on a CD-ROM, and you're getting more, just have them put the new images on the old CD, if there's still room.

Don't confuse the floppy disk that sometimes comes with your film for the Photo CD. The disks usually just contain icons of your photos, to make it easy to reorder—not hi-res images that are suitable for printing.

STOCK PHOTO CDs

If you don't have any of your own photographs to scan or put on a CD, there are many companies who do all the work for you. Collectively, stock photo companies have millions of images that you can use in your designs, usually broken up into convenient categories for simple reference. Collections such as "Business Today," "Vacations and Leisure" and "North American Locations" provide you with both generic and specific images to choose from.

The following companies are some of the ones that I use often, when I need a picture but don't feel like dusting off the camera:

◆ Photodisc   `www.photodisc.com`

◆ Eyewire   `www.eyewire.com`

◆ Corel   `www.corel.com`

◆ Comstock   `www.comstock.com`

- ◆ Adobe Image Library   `www.adobe.com/newsfeatures/imagelib`
- ◆ Artville   `www.artville.com`
- ◆ Digital Stock   `www.digitalstock.com`

Stock images are usually sold in one of two ways:

- ◆ You can purchase one CD that contains multiple images, any of which you have the right to use for one predetermined price per CD. (Different categories will have different prices.)
- ◆ You can choose a picture or set of pictures from a catalog or CD sampler and negotiate a price with the stock house. They will supply you with a transparency, negative, etc. Price is based on usage, distribution, etc.
- ◆ Low-res images can also be downloaded directly from the Web.

Make sure you read the disclaimers and copyright material carefully for each company. Although you will have the rights to the photos you purchase, there may still be limitations on their usage.

DIGITAL CAMERAS

Digital cameras have roared onto the scene and are continuing to gain popularity quickly. Although still a bit pricey, digitals allow you to skip the film aspect of photography altogether and send your image directly to your computer. Even more exciting is that digital cameras that come with a view screen allow you to check out your picture after you take it and decide to either save it or delete it.

Price ranges for digital cameras tend to vary, however the lower-priced units (under $1000) do not really supply a high enough resolution for quality commercial printing. They are ideal for use on the Web, though, and are an increasingly popular source for Internet photography.

Because the features, prices, and abilities of digital cameras change too rapidly for me to write their specifications in this book, you may want to visit the following Web sites for articles and reviews:

- ◆ `www.zdnet.com/familypc/content/9706/fthw/index.html`
- ◆ `www.dcresource.com`
- ◆ `www.computers.com/cdoor/0,1,0-21-2,00.html?st.cn.re.story.co`

RESIZING AND RESAMPLING IMAGES

When you bring an image into Photoshop, you're not obligated to keep it at its original size or resolution. In fact, as I will explain later, when scanning images for the Web, changing the size and the resolution will be necessary in achieving an optimal image quality: file size ratio.

Although you can make size and resolution changes in a few different ways (see "Cropping Image Edges" later in this chapter), the best way is to do the following:

1. With an open image, choose Image -> Image Size to access the dialog box shown in Figure 7–3 (7–3 shows the *resize* dialog box, Figure 7–4 displays the options used to *resample*). The top portion of the dialog box displays your image in pixel size (the default setting), as well as providing information on the file size. The bottom portion of the dialog box shows the size in terms of inches, or other desired measurements including percent, points, and picas.

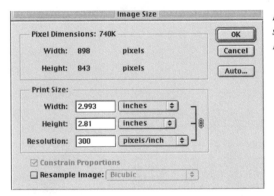

Figure 7–3: The Image Size dialog box, set to Resize the image (with the Resample box unchecked).

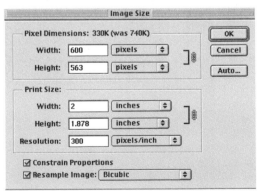

Figure 7–4: The Image Size dialog box, set to Resample the image (with the Resample box checked).

2. Decide how you want to change your image:

Resizing your image generally implies changing its physical size without changing the number of pixels. To do this, make sure that the Resample Image checkbox is left unchecked. The dialog box will look like Figure 7–4. You'll notice that the Width and Height dimensions in the Pixel information section stay static—they cannot be manipulated. Beyond that, the Contrain Proportions checkbox, reflected in the chain link in the Print size section links the Width, Height, and Resolution.

Change the size of your image by manipulating any one of the available variables. If you reduce the Resolution, the Width and Height will increase proportionately. Alternately, if you increase the Resolution, the Width and Height will decrease. This practice holds true, too, if you increase or decrease either the Width or Height. In the end, the following mathematical equations will always hold true:

Width (Print Size) x Resolution = Width (Pixel Dimensions)

Height (Print Size) x Resolution = Height (Pixel Dimensions)

The file size of your image will not change, no matter what dimensions you decide upon. Figure 7–5 shows an example of a resized image and its file size, before and after.

Resampling will actually change the number of pixels in your image and can be done by checking the Resample Image. As shown in Figure 7–4, the dialog box differs from the dialog box for resizing your image in a few distinct ways:

Original Picture
7.707 inches x 5.087 inches
2312 pixels x 1520 pixels
300 ppi resolution
3.37M

Resized Picture
4 inches x 2.64 inches
2312 pixels x 1520 pixels
578 ppi resolution
3.37M

Figure 7–5: The resized image. Notice that the pixels and file size stay the same, but the resolution and physical size change. The screen display, however, does not change, as the small physical size in the revised picture has a higher resolution.

◆ The Width and Height in pixels can be changed.

◆ The chain in the Print Size info section only links the Width and Height.

◆ A new chain appears in the Pixel Dimensions info section linking the Width and Height

◆ The Constrain Proportions checkbox is made active (when unchecked, the chain links disappear).

◆ A pull-down menu for how you want to resample your image is made active.

Regardless of what you change in your image, the file size and the Pixel Dimensions will be affected. You will also have three choices as to how to resample your image, with each choice accessible through the Resample Image pull-down menu:

◆ *Bicubic* is the smoothest, but also the slowest.

◆ *Bilinear* is faster but not quite as smooth.

◆ *Nearest Neighbor* will cause Photoshop to throw away or duplicate pixels as necessary.

You'll most often want to use the Bicubic option, even if it takes a few seconds longer. The quality increase is worth the almost insignificant wait. Figure 7–6 shows an image that has been resampled.

Original Picture
7.707 inches x 5.087 inches
2312 pixels x 1520 pixels
300 ppi resolution
3.37M

Resampled Picture (Bicubic)
4 inches x 2.64 inches
1200 pixels x 792 pixels
300 ppi resolution
929K

Figure 7–6: The resampled image. Notice that the pixels and file size both change.

Resampling up is usually not such a great idea and rarely has a use-able effect. When you increase either the resolution or the physical size independent of each other, Photoshop is forced to add pixels to the image where there were none. Because Photoshop does not have any information as to what to put in these new pixels, an image that is resampled up usually looks blurry or pixilated (see Figure 7–7).

Resampling down, though, is a good idea, especially when creating Web sites. To make sure that scanned images have the maximum quality, scan each image in at 300 ppi (even 600 ppi depending on the details in your image). Then resample down to the 72 ppi resolution level. The number of pixels and the file size will both be smaller, but your image will have the best chance of retaining decent quality this way.

Figure 7–7: The top image is 72 ppi, shown at 200%. The botttom image shows the same picture resampled up to 600 ppi, also shown at 200%. So much information has been forced into the picture that it is blurred almost beyond recognition.

PHOTO RETOUCHING TECHNIQUES

No matter what medium you're designing for, whenever you scan or otherwise import original photography into Photoshop, you'll most likely have to do at least a little bit of retouching. Retouching can include cropping a picture's edges, removing dust and scratches, or fixing the colors. Depending on your train of thought, retouching can either be painfully dull or one of the most exciting parts of Photoshop—some companies have even developed their retouching talents to such an extent that that's all they do, and they make tons of money doing it.

CROPPING IMAGE EDGES (SAY THAT 3 TIMES FAST!)

Sometimes it may be tough to scan a picture without also scanning some unwanted edges. It is even more difficult to place a picture on the scan bed perfectly straight and have it stay that way after you close the top of the scanner.

There are other reasons for cropping images besides bad scanning. These include cropping to reduce file size for faster uploading of Web pages and cropping one image or a series of images to match the dimensions of another image. Whatever your reasons are, it is important to understand the various techniques you can use to crop in Photoshop.

Using the Crop Tool

1. Choose the Crop tool from the toolbar. It's hidden under the Marquee tools.

2. Drag a selection around the portion of your image that you wish to keep. If you make a mistake, use the handles on the corners and sides of the crop selection to make changes. Holding the Shift key down while dragging will constrain the proportions.

3. Outside the selection, your cursor will look like a curved line with arrowheads at either end. Drag your mouse in the direction of either arrow to crop at the appropriate angle. Figure 7–8 illustrates this.

   To change the center of rotation, drag the point of origin (the center crosshair in the crop marquee) to another area of the image.

4. Hit the Return/Enter button to crop your selection, or the esc button to cancel your selection.

Figure 7–8: You can rotate the Crop tool for diagonal scans or shots before making your final cut.

Using the Marquee to Crop

1. Use the Rectangular Marquee to make a selection around the area you wish to keep.

2. From the menu options, choose Image -> Crop. (Easy, huh?)

Changing the Canvas Size to Crop an Image

1. Decide the portion of your image that you wish to crop away. Figure 7–9 shows an image with the guides marking off the areas I wish to crop away and the areas I wish to keep.

 You don't need to use the ruler or the guides to crop with this method, but it helps for accuracy.

2. Choose Image -> Canvas Size to access the dialog box shown in Figure 7–10. The information toward the top of the dialog box shows the Current Size (file size), as well as the current Width and Height. Below that is the area in which you can change the size of your canvas. If you increase the Width and Height, Photoshop will add pixels to your canvas, filling them in with your background color.

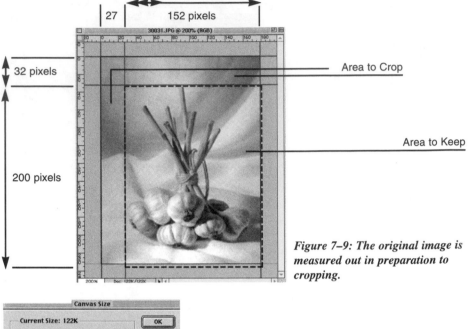

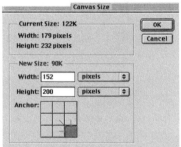

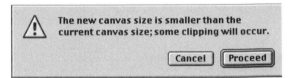

Figure 7–9: The original image is measured out in preparation to cropping.

Figure 7–11: The Warning reminds you that your image will crop.

Figure 7–10: The Canvas Size dialog box

For this example, reduce the Width and Height by the amount that was measured out in Step 1.

3. The Anchor point in the dialog box represents the full image in nine separate squares. If you click the middle square (which is the default), the image canvas will increase or decrease around that portion of your image. Because in this example the entire portion of the image that you want to keep is in the lower right corner, click on the lower right box in the Anchor grid. Hit OK.

A warning box (shown in Figure 7–11) will appear to let you know that the dimensions you have entered will cause your image to be cropped. Click Proceed. Your image will be cropped as shown in Figure 7–12.

Figure 7–12: The cropped image.

Cropping to Make Sizes Match

This will prove especially helpful when you are trying to turn images into buttons that need to be the same size.

1. In the Crop options palette (double click on the Crop tool to access it), check the Fixed Target Size box, and enter the desired dimensions for Width, Height, and Resolution. As you crop each image, your Crop marquee will resize your image to these dimensions.

or

1. Copy and paste one image into the canvas of another.
2. Choose Edit -> Free Transform, and drag one of the corner handlebars in or out until the posted image is the desired size.

REMOVING DUST AND SCRATCHES

Figure 7–13 is a close-up of the corner of an image scanned from a personal flatbed scanner. You can see that there are dust, scratches, and rips on it, either from the original photograph itself or from the glass on the scan bed. Although they may seem minor, you'll want to get rid of these things, especially if you are working on a site for a client.

There are a number of different ways that you can get rid of dust, scratches, even rips in your photographs when working in Photoshop.

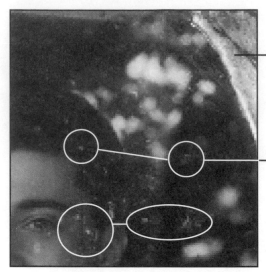

Folded & ripped corner

Dust specs

Figure 7–13: Rips and dust litter this picture. Although this image is blown up to see the specs better, they still detract from the picture even at normal size.

For photos with a significant number of specs, dots, and dust

1. Use the Dust & Scratches filter. From the menu options, choose Filter -> Noise -> Dust and Scratches. You'll see the dialog box shown in Figure 7–14. Personally, I'm not crazy about this tool, but a lot of people like it, and who am I to editorialize?

2. Use the Radius slider to establish the extent to which the filter will seek out random pixels or noise within your image. You'll want to experiment with this, depending both upon your image and the number and severity of unwanted noise: a higher Radius number will cause the image to be more blurry.

3. The second slider is to set the Threshold, setting the amount of tonal difference between the affected pixels.

**For just a few specs and dust particles, or
as a follow-up to using the Dust & Scratches filter**

1. Select the Rubber Stamp tool.

2. Zoom in on your image to 200% or 300% and take a quick glance over the entire image. Figure 7–15 shows the difference in the photo before and after using the Rubber Stamp tool.

3. Suck up a part of the image that has a similar color tone or pattern, use a soft-edged, small brush, and clone acceptable parts of your image over the dust and scratches.

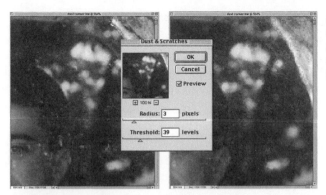

Figure 7–14: Before and after shots using the Dust & Scratches filter. Obviously the rip in the corner is largely unaffected.

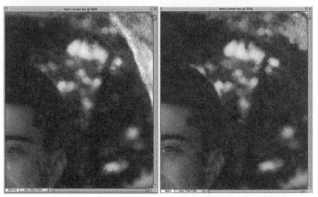

Figure 7–15: Before and after shots using the Rubber Stamp tool. Notice the rip in the corner has been fixed, replaced by the trees from the image background.

Try not to clone from an area too geographically close to the area you are correcting. Oftentimes a pattern will emerge that could look worse than the original dust and scratches.

REMOVING NOISE FROM AN IMAGE

There are any number of ways to remove large problems like noise from an image. In truth, the ability to bring photographs from a state of disrepair back to useable form again is one of the more remarkable aspects of Photoshop. There is, in fact, such a variety of methods for cleaning up an image, especially when it comes to removing noise, that I could dedicate an entire chapter to the topic. But, since we only have a few pages to spare, I'll quit babbling and illustrate a few of the more popular and more effective techniques:

Using the Despeckle Filter

Choose Filter -> Noise -> Despeckle to activate this tool. Unlike many other filters, this one does not have a dialog box associated with it. The Despeckle filter finds the edges of your image and preserves them, while blurring the rest of your image. A sample of the Despeckle filter is shown in Figure 7–16.

Using the Median Filter

Choose Filter -> Noise -> Median to access the dialog box shown in Figure 7–17. The dialog box offers you the option of selecting a radius value between 1 and 16. As Figure 7–17 shows, the greater the radius value, the more severe the final effect will be on your image.

When you enter a value in the radius selector, the Median filter will, for every pixel in your image (or specified selection), take an average of the colors of all the pixels that fall within the desired radius. It will ignore any extreme pixels that could tend to throw an accurate average off and apply the average color to the starting pixel. It will do this for every pixel in your image (or selection).

Figure 7–16: Using the Despeckle filter.

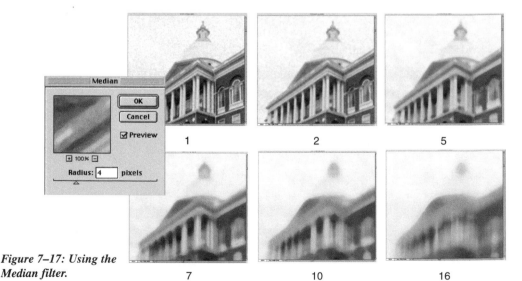

Figure 7–17: Using the Median filter.

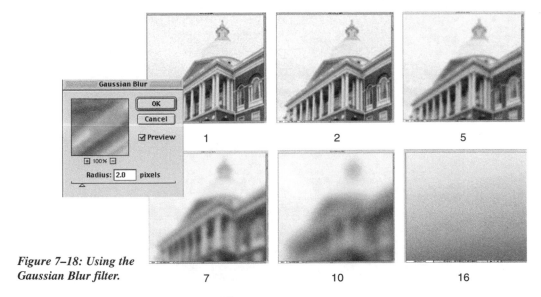

*Figure 7–18: Using the
Gaussian Blur filter.*

Using the Gaussian Blur Filter

This tool is widely considered the most powerful and most useful of the Blur filters, as well as the most effective when it comes to eradicating noise from an image. You can access the dialog box (shown in Figure 7–18) by choosing Filter -> Blur -> Gaussian Blur. Like the Median filter, there is only one form of control, a radius slider, with which you can control the amount of blur you desire (from a minimum of 0.1 to a maximum of 250). As you can see in Figure 7–18, the higher the Blur Radius, the more severe the effect it will have on your image.

The Gaussian blur filter works by blurring the number of pixels in the established Radius selector, following an internally devised Gaussian distribution curve. Although the higher end values will blur your image beyond recognition (hardly the solution for reducing noise), they are often useful in creating other effects.

SHARPENING BLURRED PHOTOGRAPHS

Quick editorial: the Sharpen tool bites. That's just my opinion, of course, and others may disagree, but I've rarely found it useful. There are effective ways, however, to sharpen a blurred photograph. As it often does in other instances, the Photoshop Filter menu comes to the rescue, providing the necessary tools to keep you from thinking that you need thicker glasses.

Within the Filter -> Sharpen submenu, there are four filters: Sharpen, Sharpen Edges, Sharpen More, and Unsharp Mask. Each of these filters works by affecting the contrast between the target pixel and the neighboring pixels. The first three do not have a dialog box or any customizable options. Try each out on a blurry photograph and test the results. Figure 7–19 shows the original blurry photograph, while Figures 7–20 to 7–22 show the results of each of the first three filters.

Figure 7–19: The original blurry image before being manipulated.

Figure 7–20: Sharpen filter   *Figure 7–21: Sharpen Edges Filter*   *Figure 7–22: Sharpen More Filter*

To really get a good sharpening effect, it's the fourth Sharpen filter that you'll want to master: Unsharp Mask. This filter yields the power of each of the other filters, in that it works to sharpen the entire image (Sharpen and Sharpen More), as well as the edges (Sharpen Edges), plus gives more flexibility and control. So by now you're asking: if that's true, then why bother with the other Sharpen filters at all? Well, the answer is you don't have to. In that case, you'll ask, why did Photoshop put them there in the first place? The answer to that, my friend, is I don't know—but at least it helped fill up a half page of text for this book.

The Unsharp Mask filter brings up the dialog box shown in Figure 7–23. The three sliders offered in the dialog box offer you a vast amount of control over how you sharpen your image:

◆ Set the *Amount* to the percentage (1 to 500) you would like to sharpen your image. As you may expect, the higher the percentage, the more severe the sharpen effect.

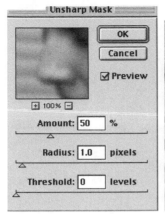

Figure 7–23: Unsharp Mask dialog box   *Figure 7–24: Unsharp Mask filter, correct adjustment.*   *Figure 7–25: Unsharp Mask filter, extreme adjustment.*

◆ The *Radius* slider, measured in pixels, allows you to set the thickness of the edges that are sharpened. Again, the higher the value, the more drastic the effect, with greater contrast in your image as a result.

◆ The *Threshold* slider works a bit differently from the other sliders, in that the greater effect on the image is realized when you have a lower value. As you set the level of the Threshold, you will determine the difference between the target pixel and its neighbor pixel that must exist before Photoshop sharpens those pixels.

The Unsharp Mask filter, because it has three separate control values, is difficult to master. You'll have to experiment with it to see how much adjustment you'll need to sharpen any given image. Keep changes to the sliders slight for images that are just a little out of focus, as the image in Figure 7–19 is. Figures 7–24 and 7–25 show the results of two different Unsharp Mask settings, one with an extreme effect and one that sharpens the image correctly.

COLOR CORRECTION TOOLS AND TECHNIQUES

Because of differences in scanner settings and other variables, the colors in your scanned image may not look like your original photo. One of the scan results I've regularly come across is a slight grayish film over the image, or a lack of sharpness in the shadows and highlights. Other times your photograph might scan exactly as planned, but the original picture may need some color enhancements.

Figure 7–26 shows how flat the photograph of my office looks after I scan it in. You can see that it lacks depth and seems flat. There are a couple of methods that I'll use to go about correcting this:

◆ By choosing Image -> Adjust -> Levels, I bring up the dialog box shown in Figure 7–27. This will let me manipulate the photograph and add necessary depth. This histogram in the center shows how the dark and light areas are distributed throughout the picture. The left slider adjusts the shadows, the middle slider adjusts the midtones, and the right slider adjusts the highlights.

As the histogram shows, there is a lack of shadow and highlight in my photograph. By moving the left and right slider in towards the edges of the histogram, I'll distribute the levels more evenly throughout the image. Figure 7-28 shows the after effects of adjusting levels.

◆ For more precise tonal correction, choose Image -> Adjust -> Curves. This tool is more complex than Levels, but also more accurate. The Curves dialog box shown in Figure 7–29 displays a full tonal range graph of your image. Unlike the limited Levels command discussed above, which allows you control over only three ranges (shadows, midtones and highlights), Curves will let you make adjustments at any point along the 255-point range.

Although a full explanation of how Curves works is beyond the scope of this book, the ultra-basic rule of thumb is that as you pull points on the diagonal downward, parts of your image will become darker, while dragging points higher than the diagonal will make the image lighter. Experimenting with levels can bring about some pretty surprising results! Figure 7–30 shows the curves associated with some final images.

Figure 7–26: My office photograph came through the scanner with a gray film over it, leaving it looking washed out.

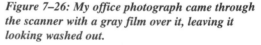

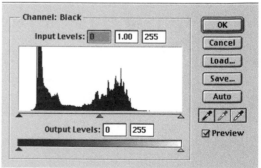

Figure 7–27: Adjusting the levels for brighter highlights and darker depth.

The Levels Palette before adjustments

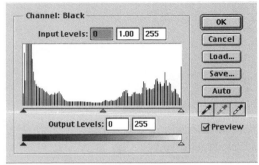

The Levels Palette after adjustments creates a more dispersed histogram.

Figure 7–28: The image gains definition and sharpness after Levels adjustments.

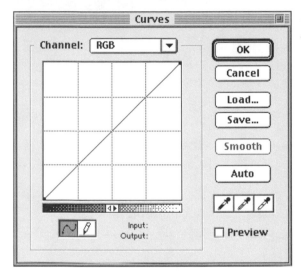

Figure 7–29: The Curves feature gives you greater control than Levels.

 In the Layers Palette, choose New Adjustment Layer and make your desired adjustment from there. The changes will happen on a separate "adjustment layer" so that you can make further changes later on, or even eliminate their effects completely.

Figure 7–31 (Color Figure 22) shows a picture of Michali, a friend of mine. Although always beautiful, this picture washed her out after scanning, leaving her in need of some color. I'll use Photoshop to tint the picture a bit and give her a tan. Because there is good contrast between her and the background, I chose to use the Magnetic Lasso to select her.

Figure 7–30: Manipulating the curves can cause some pretty drastic results. The first of the three curves is the proper correction—the remaining two are great special effects.

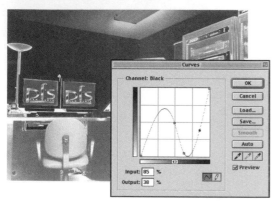

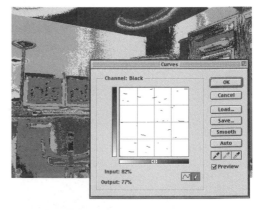

The Magnetic Lasso tool is a new feature to Photoshop 5.0—if you're using an older version, try using the Free-form Lasso and a steady hand.

The Magnetic Lasso tool, added in version 5.0 as a way to save time when making selections, will discriminate between colors and find the edge, creating a fairly accurate selection. You can make the Magnetic Lasso tool more or less sensitive and accurate by manipulating the controls in the Options dialog box (Figure 7–31.)

◆ **Lasso Width** will establish how sensitive the tool is to color differences in your image. The higher the number, the more sensitive and discriminatory the tool will be in its selection, so even shades of the same color will be separated.

◆ **Frequency** will set the number of points, or anchors, to be placed as your cursor changes direction as you move it around your image. These can help you in the event of a mistake, or an accidental wrong turn—simply retrace your steps to a previous point and click on it. You'll be able to resume making your selection in the proper direction.

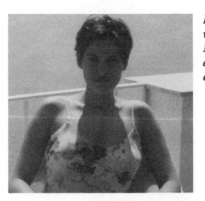

Figure 7–31: The picture of my friend, Michali, lacks vibrancy of color. Her face is selected by using the Magnetic Lasso tool. The dialog box offers setting adjustments to make the tool more or less sensitive to color.

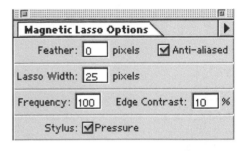

◆ **Edge Contrast** will determine how drastically different surrounding and adjoining colors have to be in order for the Magnetic Lasso to include them. Use a high percentage if you have very stark color transitions.

Once the selection has been made, soften the edges by choosing Select -> Feather. Since my image is low-res, I'll choose a radius setting of 1 (I'd have chosen a higher number for a higher-res image). By doing this, I reduce the chance that my color correction will have a very hard edge and look unnatural.

You may wonder why I would do it this way rather than just set the Feather Radius within the Magnetic Lasso's options palette. Although this is a perfectly acceptable alternative, if you feather your selection separately, you can undo it without losing your selection, should you decide that your feather radius was too much or too little.

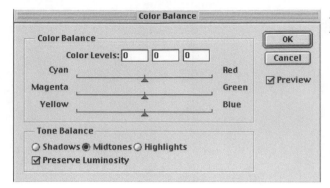

Figure 7–32: The Color Balance dialog box

To give Michali her color back there are a couple of steps that I can take:

◆ Choose Image -> Adjust -> Color Balance to access the dialog box shown in Figure 7–32. There are three adjustment sliders that I can control, each allowing me to add colors to and simultaneously subtract colors from my image. With the radio buttons, I can do this for each of three tonal ranges: shadows, midtones, and highlights.

To make her more tan, I'm going to want to add both red and yellow by moving the sliders in those directions. As I do this, I will also be subtracting cyan and blue, respectively. I'll do this for all tonal ranges and experiment with the amounts of colors that I want to add until I achieve a color that I am happy with. (I also increased the shadows in the level adjustment.) Color Figure 23 shows the result.

◆ Another way that I can give her some color would be to use the modes in the Layers Palette. In my Color Picker, I've chosen a color that I think would be great for her tan or even a little darker than I would like. I'm going to add a new layer and, with my selection still active around her face, I'll fill the selection with my chosen color. In the Mode pull-down menu on the front of the Layers Palette, I choose Overlay, which combines my chosen color with the underlying photograph and increases the color intensity in her skin while not losing the defining features in her face.

Adjusting Color with Hue/Saturation

Although there are many ways to use the Hue/Saturation adjustment mechanism in your photography, I'll demonstrate this instead on buttons that you might create for your Web site (See Chapter 6 for more about creating buttons.)

Figure 7–33 shows a few quick buttons that I made, and Color Figure 24 shows that they are a rich blue. Oftentimes when I create a site, I will make all of the buttons one color except for the one for the page that the user is on, which will be an obviously different color. For example, if the user is on the Products page of a certain Web site, all

Figure 7–33: Simple blue buttons I created for a Web site.

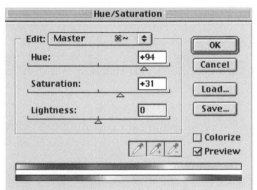

Figure 7–34: The Hue/Saturation dialog box

of the buttons might be blue except for the "Products" button, which would stand out as red. By standing apart from the others, your Web user will know immediately which page he or she is on.

Instead of recreating all of the buttons over again, I'm going to choose Image -> Adjust -> Hue/Saturation to bring up the dialog box shown in Figure 7–34. An improvement over the older controls found in Photoshop 4.0, the dialog box lets you change the color as well as its saturation and light/darkness. Use the top slider (Hue) to change the color completely, the center slider (Saturation) to add or subtract richness from the color, and the bottom slider (Lightness) to add highlights or shadows.

Color Figure 24 shows the change in the dialog box and the subsequent result.

COOL AND USEFUL EFFECTS FOR INLINE IMAGES

Whether or not you decide to use actual photography in your Web site construction, Photoshop offers unlimited potential to design and create cool effects. This section will offer recipes for creating and manipulating elements for photographic collages, picture frames and borders, as well as some Photoshop-original work, such as various techniques for creating lightning and clouds and using both native and third-party filters.

Figure 7–35 offers a glance at how some of the techniques you will see in this section have been used to enhance Web site design. Even though the subjects of many of the sites I have worked on (and shown here) are more corporate in nature and often do not leave room for elaborate design, there are ways you can manipulate and harness your imagination to make room for creativity.

Keep in mind as well that the techniques in this chapter (and throughout this book, for that matter), are not necessarily confined to the examples shown here—it is the underlying technique that is important, not the framework for the example. Take the lessons from this chapter, practice them, change some of the variables here and there, and apply them in different ways. Once you learn the basic framework, all doors are open.

COOL LIGHTNING EFFECTS

There are a number of different ways to make lightning. I'll demonstrate two of them, as each can have a very different effect from the other.

Lightning Effect: Technique One

1. Open a new file, 360 by 360 pixels, with a black background.
2. Create two new layers immediately, and make sure Layer 2 is your active layer.
3. Use white as your foreground color and make your Paintbrush the active tool.
4. From the Brushes Palette, choose a brush that is 4 pixels in diameter with a soft edge. Begin drawing a jagged line from the top of your canvas toward the bottom, creating the main current in what will be an electrical storm. Use a smaller brush, 2 pixels in diameter, to create the "arms" of your current. Allow them to wander in crazy directions, as they might in a real storm.

Not all of the brushes you'll need are provided in the default brush palette. To create a new brush, choose New Brush from the palette menu, or click once on the empty part of the palette. To resize an existing brush, choose Brush Options from the palette menu, or double click on your desired brush.

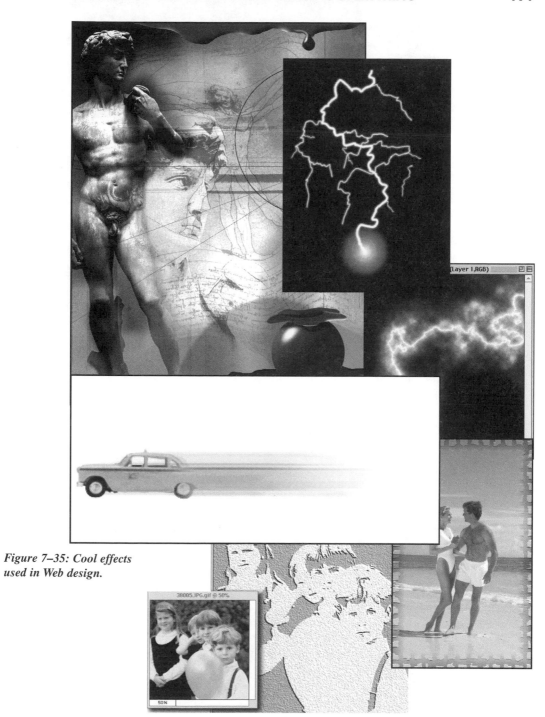

Figure 7–35: Cool effects used in Web design.

5. Change brushes once more to one with a diameter of 1. These will be the faintest currents, which have either died out or are striking farther away. Figure 7–36 illustrates Steps 1 through 5.

6. Once you have your lightning bolts where you want them, make Layer 1 your active layer. Hold the Command button (Ctrl in Windows) while clicking Layer 2 in the Layers Palette, to load the selection of your lightning.

7. Choose Select -> Modify -> Expand and expand all the pixels by 1.

8. Choose Select -> Feather, and set your feather radius to 1 to make the edges softer.

9. Fill your selection with a bright yellow to give your lightning a glow. Lower the layer opacity to 50%. Filling your selection with purple instead of white can create a nice effect, too.

10. As a final touch, we'll put a light flash where the lightning may have struck. In the Layers Palette, choose New Layer (instead of clicking the "New Layer" icon at the bottom of the palette). You will see the dialog box presented in Figure 7–37.

11. Under the Mode pull-down menu, choose Screen and check off the box marked "Fill with screen neutral black." The black that exists there will be invisible to you, yet it will exist to make certain filters possible to work with.

12. With the Circle Marquee tool, make a circle around the bottom of your main current and feather it with a radius of 4.

13. Choose Filter -> Render -> Lens Flare to access the dialog box shown in Figure 7–38. Set the Flare to 155, directly centered and hit OK.

14. Use the Move tool to move your flare around if necessary. Figure 7–39 provides an example of a completed piece (Color Figure 25).

Lightning Effect: Technique Two

Figure 7–40 shows my agency's logo, which uses this lightning technique as the main graphic feature. This particular technique is best designed over a black background, and creates a significantly more realistic lightning bolt than in the previous technique. The down side, however, is that the lightning here is more random, and not as easily manipulated.

1. Open a new file 360 by 360 pixels.

2. Make sure that your background and foreground colors are set to black and white.

3. Create a gradient from the top left corner to the bottom right.

4. Choose Filter -> Render -> Difference Clouds to fill your canvas with a cloud texture. The first time you do this you may not get a particularly great effect, so hit Command + Z (Ctrl + Z in Windows) and then Command + F (Ctrl + F in Windows) to redo the filter until you get clouds with high contrasts, such as in Figure 7–41.

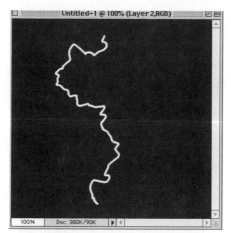

Figure 7–36: Creating lightning

Create the main arm of your lightning in white on black or dark blue background.

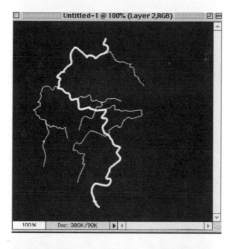

Use a smaller brush to create the arms of the lightning.

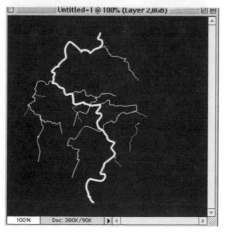

Your final, smaller brush will create the faintest arms, those in the background or that have already faded.

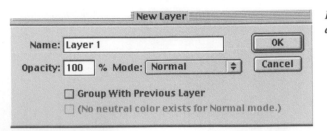

Figure 7–37: The New Layer dialog box

Figure 7–38: The Lens Flare filter dialog box will provide a spark of light in your selection.

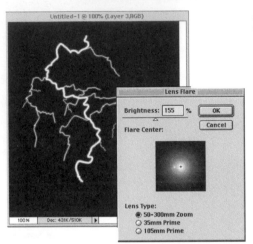

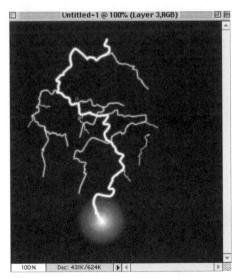

Figure 7–39: The final image with the lens flare.

Figure 7–40: My agency's logo uses the lightning effect as its main design feature.

Figure 7–41: The canvas filled with clouds from the Difference Clouds filter.

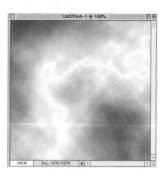

Figure 7–42: Inverting the clouds clearly shows where the lightning will be created.

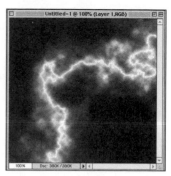

Figure 7–43: The final image, after adjusting the Levels. Color Figure 26 shows the lightning with color added.

Figure 7–44: PFS Web site with lightning effect.

5. Hit Command + I (Ctrl + I in Windows) to invert the colors. You will start to see where the lightning is on the canvas, as in Figure 7–42.

6. Open the Levels dialog box, and pull the Shadow arrow over to the right. Continue to pull it until the background gets darker, and the lightning becomes the focal point of your canvas.

7. On a new layer, fill the canvas with a dark blue. Set the color mode to Soft Light. The final outcome is shown in Figure 7–43 (Color figure 26)

Figure 7–44 (Color Figure 27) shows the home page of the PFS Web site (www.pfsnewmedia.com) which features the logo prominently. The lightning takes center stage and establishes the tone for the rest of the site.

CREATING COOL COLLAGE EFFECTS

Remember back in fourth grade, sitting at your desk with a smock on, carefully cutting and over-pasting magazine pictures to a piece of construction paper, vaguely wondering why you were bothering? Well, thanks to a few forward-thinking teachers, you are now well prepared to move on from construction paper to today's high-tech collages.

But to safeguard against creating the electronic equivalent of a fourth-grade collage, there are few things you should be aware of and take into consideration before you create your collage, especially for the Web:

◆ Make sure your images relate to each other. Throwing together a random conglomeration of images will most likely not produce the effect you desire. Try and collect images that will somehow have the same theme, or at least the same media. Sometimes combining photography with illustrations can work, but more often than not they will tend to look like a scattered mess.

◆ Map out your collage on paper first. Even though Photoshop's layers will allow you to move images easily from one place to another, knowing in advance where each should go will save you time and energy in the long run.

◆ Collages work best when there is a central image. If there is not a main subject to focus on, the collage will look jumbled and the eye will not have any clear route to follow.

◆ Blended edges work better with blended edges. Similarly, hard edges work well with other hard edges. Rarely, however, do they combine well.

◆ When creating a collage for the Web, remember that you have limited space in which to place the completed image. Because of this, you'll often be better off not creating collages with too much detail. Fine detail will often be lost on the viewer when seen on a monitor as opposed to a printed page.

◆ As you'll undoubtedly see throughout this book, quality of an image is often the trade-off in achieving a lower file size. Collages are likely to have a number of transitions throughout them, which will use a large number of colors. These colors may dither poorly when you reduce the file into a GIF for color reduction. Try to either create your images without multiple blends or use the browser-safe Web palette from the beginning. See Chapter 2 for more information on the Web palette.

Of course, none of the above rules are set in stone, nor do I mean to imply that they hold true in every case. But these and other tips that you'll discover as you practice are a solid set of guidelines that could prove to be the difference between your collage looking like a professional project and a fourth-grade homework assignment.

Figure 7–45 and Color Figure 28 show a collage that I did for one of my agency's brochure sell sheets. This collage, used in part of our Web site as well, combines both soft, blending collage effects with stark, hard-edged contrasts. The photo of

Figure 7–45: A collage created for one of my agency's brochure sell sheets.

Michangleo's David appears on the side of the image area, while a ghostly blow-up of his face from the same picture fades off over it. A wavy page of one of Da Vinci's most famous works, a depiction of the human form, provides a subtle, detailed background. A liquid blob of my own creation is melting in the foreground, as liquid from the top of the image drips and splashes on it.

1. Open two photographs to make your collage. Make sure that one of them has an obvious subject or object—like a family member or some other main feature. For this example, I will be using the two photographs shown in Figure 7–46, called Picture One and Picture Two. My pictures are currently 200 ppi (pixels/inch)—too large for the Web, but necessary for some of the effects I will use. We can reduce the size later for use on the Web.

If you don't have two different photographs, or any that have a main subject as I have in my picture of the Statue of David, you can download the pictures I am using at the Web site that accompanies this book at `http://www.phptr.com/togo`.

Figure 7–46: The two photos that will be used to create my collage.

2. With the Marquee tool, make a selection around a portion of the main subject in Picture One. Press Command + C (Ctrl + C in Windows) to copy the selection to your pasteboard.

3. Press Command + D (Ctrl + D in Windows) to deselect your selection.

4. Press Command + V (Ctrl + V in Windows) to paste the image from your clipboard back into Picture One. Notice that it pastes into its own layer, name "Layer 1" by default.

5. Choose Edit -> Free Transform and manipulate the size by dragging one of the corner handles outward. Hold the Shift button while dragging to constrain the proportions. Drag it out until the image is nearly three times its original size. Press Return (Enter in Windows) to activate the transformation.

6. Drag the Opacity Slider on the Layers Palette down to 40% for a more ghostly effect. Figure 7–47 shows the progress to this point.

7. Remove some of the color from the image on Layer 1 by pressing Command + L (Ctrl + L in Windows) to access the Levels dialog box. Manipulate the Input Highlights by dragging the slider on the right out to the left, until you begin to lose tone and detail in the image. Do the same with the Output Highlight slider. Press OK when through. Figure 7–48 shows the effect of this.

8. Make the Background layer active by clicking on it. By doing this, any new layer that you create will appear between your background and Layer 1.

9. We're now going to add Picture Two to the collage. You don't need to copy and paste to do this—instead simply choose the Move tool, and drag the entire image in Picture Two onto the canvas in Picture One. You'll notice that it appears on its own layer, "Layer 2."

Figure 7–47: The image on Layer 2, enlarged and only 40% opaque

Figure 7–48: The same image, made more ghostly by manipulating the input and output Levels.

10. Create a mask of your image on Layer 2 (which should now be the active layer). Do this by dragging Layer 2 down to the Create Mask icon at the bottom of the Layers Palette (the first icon on the left). Doing this has caused a number of things to happen:

   ◆ A new icon has appeared to the right of the image icon on Layer 2 in the Layers Palette. This icon shows the mask as white (image area) surrounded by black (transparent area).

   ◆ There is a chain link in between the image icon and the mask icon. When the link is present, you can move the image and the mask at the same time anywhere on your canvas. Turn the link off by clicking on it and the mask remains permanent. Your image will be limited to moving within the mask only.

   ◆ Your brush icon in the Layers Palette, which used to indicate that the layer was both active and ready for manipulation, has changed to the mask icon. Brushes and other tools won't work the same when in this mode, as we'll soon illustrate. You can return to Standard Mode by clicking on the icon of your image on Layer 2 in the Layers Palette. Figure 7–49 illustrates the changes in the Layers Palette.

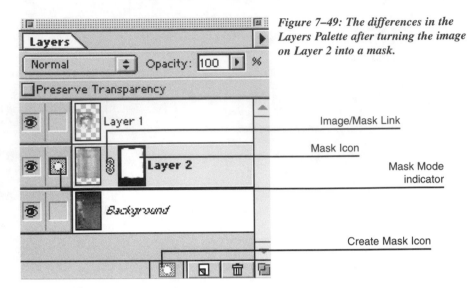

Figure 7–49: The differences in the Layers Palette after turning the image on Layer 2 into a mask.

◆ Foreground and Background colors in your toolbar have changed to black and white while in Mask Mode, to represent transparency and solid area, respectively. Your original colors will return as soon as your image is returned to Standard Mode.

11. While still in Mask Mode, activate the Linear Gradient tool. Create a gradient from black to white, left to right over the entire image in Layer 2. Hold the Shift key down to ensure that your gradient stays straight and is not made at an angle. You'll see that instead of coloring your image black and white as you may expect, the portion of your image that was covered in black has disappeared gradually as the gradient became more intense. Figure 7–50 illustrates this.

12. Reduce the Layer 2 opacity to 15% so that your image acts more like an underlying force.

13. Erase portions of your image on all layers as necessary so that your image looks complete without hard edges. Use theTransform function also, if your image needs some perspective.

14. For the final touch, choose Image -> Image Size and change your resolution from 200 to 72 ppi (more suited for the Web). Hit OK. The completed image is shown in Figure 7–51 (it is basically a recreation of the sales sheet shown in Figure 7–46, but without the melting sphere in the foreground).

Depending on the subject matter, you may benefit from keeping your collage faint in the background and offsetting stark images in the foreground. Figure 7–52 shows a situation where I did just that for Automatic Switch Company's Web site to add "pop" to a few of their products.

Figure 7–50: The Gradient tool while in Mask Mode causes the areas in black to become transparent.

Figure 7–51: My final collage, after a little tweaking.

Figure 7–52: This collage created for Automatic Switch Company (www.asco.com) uses stark images against a faded collage background.

Other Collage Tips: Defringing and Removing Mattes

In certain cases, you may be cutting and pasting images from one canvas onto another without feathering the selections first. Oftentimes there will be a faint halo around your image, where your selection picked up the background. If you experience this haloing, choose Layer -> Matting -> Defringe and choose a width that will be enough to remove the halo. If your halo came from a white or a black background, choose Remove White Matte or Remove Black Matte, respectively.

TURNING A 2D IMAGE INTO A 3D IMAGE

Although it's kind of hidden and lost in the crowd of all the other filters, the 3D Transform function is probably the most fun of Photoshop 5.0. You can use this filter to take any flat surface, and turn it into a 3D cube (cereal box?), cylinder, or sphere. Once you learn the basics of this new feature, your Web graphics will take on a whole new... dimension.

1. Open or create a 2D image, similar to that shown in Figure 7–53. The Compuburger Instant Meal in the Figure was developed by Jurges Cortina, one of the designers at my agency, using a combination of Infini-D 3D modeling software and Photoshop. Make sure that you have plenty of blank canvas around your image (you'll need it to get a good 3D effect without the edges getting cut off).

2. Choose Filter -> Render -> 3D Transform to access the dialog box shown in Figure 7–54.

3. The second set of tools in the 3D Transform toolbar makes up the shapes and methods to turn your flat image into a 2D object. Choose the first of these tools— the cube.

4. In the preview window, drag from the top left corner to the bottom right corner of your image. A 3D wireframe cube will appear, as shown in Figure 7–55.

Figure 7–53: The original image created in Photoshop.

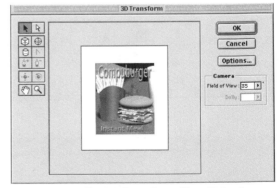

Figure 7–54: The 3D Transform filter dialog box

Figure 7–55: Wireframe around the image

Figure 7–56: Wireframe molded around the image

Figure 7–57: After the image is rotated, hit OK to accept the changes.

Figure 7–58: The final image after the background is removed.

5. You'll want the right face of the of the wire cube to fit snugly over your image. Use the Direct Selection tool (the white arrow in the upper right of the toolbar) and drag the lower right handle on the wireframe to the bottom right corner of your image. Drag the lower center handle to the bottom left corner of your image. The rest of the wireframe will be adjusting as well. Continue manipulating the wireframe until it looks similar to Figure 7–56.

6. The third set of tools in the 3D Transform box toolbar allow you to move your selection. Click on the Trackball tool (the circular one on the right), and drag your selection to the right and downward, enough so that your image displays three sides, creating the illusion of 3D.

7. Click OK to render your image and it will look similar to Figure 7–57.

8. The annoying part of this filter is that instead of simply rendering the image, it makes a copy of it, so that the 3D image is directly above the original 2D image. Unfortunately, it's still on the same layer, so you'll have to use some selection technique to grab the 3D box (try the polygon lasso, clicking on all corners of your 3D image). Cut and paste, and dispose of the layer containing the original image. The final result will be similar to Figure 7–58.

You can remove the background from the piece while still in the 3D Transform filter by pushing the Option button and turning off the Display Background command. But beware: turning this command off will turn your background black—probably not the effect you are looking for.

CREATING THE ILLUSION OF SPEED

A fairly easy trick, this effect will give the impression of a car (or anything else) moving quickly.

1. Open a picture of a car, or anything else that would look natural if it were moving fast. I chose the picture of the car (just something from a Photodisc that I had in my image library). Make sure that the subject of your image is on its own layer—not the background layer.

2. Move your main subject to one of the sides of your canvas to give yourself enough room to play, as shown in Figure 7–59

3. Copy your image and paste it so that your copy appears on a new, higher layer. Make sure that your copy is lined up horizontally with the original image.

4. Lower the opacity of the layer with the original image to around 50%.

5. Choose Filter -> Blur -> Motion Blur. This is the filter that will give us the moving effect. In the Motion Blur dialog box (shown in Figure 7–60) set the angle to 0°. With the preview box checked, move the distance slider to the right until you get the motion distance that you like. Hit OK.

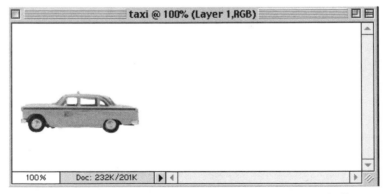

Figure 7–59: The car image I'm using to demonstrate the speed effect. Move the object to one side to leave room for the motion trail.

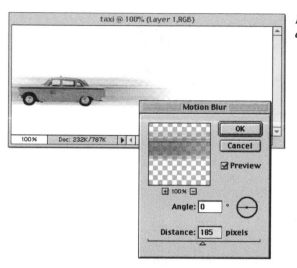

Figure 7–60: The Motion Blur dialog box

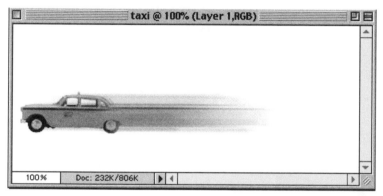

Figure 7–61: The final image makes the car look like it's moving quickly.

6. Your final image will look similar to the one in Figure 7–61. If necessary, take an eraser to the back end of the solid image on the topmost layer, as well as to the motion tail, to fade it out more if necessary, and your image will have the illusion of speed.

This type of effect practically begs to be turned into an animated GIF. Whether your subject is a car driving, a person running, or an airplane flying, you can easily create this effect in a number of different frames and create a small but eye-catching animation with it. See Chapter 2 for more information on creating animated GIF's.

METHODS FOR FRAMING IMAGES

The next few examples illustrate and briefly explain a number of techniques that you can use for creating cool framing effects for pictures. Most of the following take advantage of Photoshop's native filters, both alone and in combination with each other. Other effects will use third-party filters, which you have to buy separately from Photoshop. Some of these third-party filters are described in the next section.

DROP SHADOWS

1. Hit Command + A (Ctrl + A in Windows) to select all of your image.
2. Copy and paste the image so that it's on a new layer.
3. If necessary, increase the size of the canvas, keeping your image in the upper left.
4. Chose Layers -> Effects -> Drop Shadow and play with the settings. It will preview in real time, so you will know when you need to continue changing the setting. Figure 7–62 shows the final result.

Figure 7–62: Drop Shadow

CURVED CORNERS

1. In the Channels Palette, create a new channel, Alpha 1, by clicking the New Channel icon at the bottom of the palette.

2. Create a selection near the center using the Rectangular Marquee tool.

3. Feather your selection by choosing Select -> Feather and set the radius to 5.

4. Deselect your selection and open the Levels dialog box. Adjust the Highlights slider to 40, and the Midtones to 1. Hit OK.

5. Choose Select -> Load Selection and choose Alpha 1 from the Channel pull-down menu. Hit OK. Click on the RGB channel.

6. With any of the selection tools, place your marquee where you would like it in the image.

7. Choose Edit -> Stroke and set your Stroke Width to 3 pixels, and the Location to Inside.

8. Invert your selection by hitting Command + Shift + I (Ctrl + Shift + I in Windows) and press Delete to remove the excess background. Figure 7–63 illustrates this process.

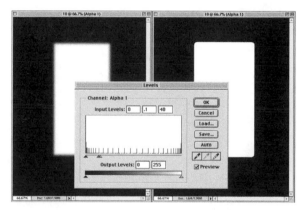

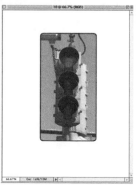

Figure 7–63: Create a selection with corners by feathering a rectangular marquee in the Channels Palette, and using the Levels dialog box. Switch to RGB mode and erase the excess image.

You can also try using this process to create cool buttons with rounded edges, perhaps a combination of the rectangular and pill-shaped buttons that you'll find in Chapter 6, "Navigation, Buttons, and Bullets".

USING FILTERS TO CREATE PICTURE BORDERS

Following are some of the results of using various filters on the edges of photographs. These are merely representational border designs—experiment with other filters and combinations of filters using the simple recipes that follow.

Mosaic Tile Border

1. Hit Command + A to select all of your image.
2. Choose Select -> Modify -> Border and set the border Width to 20.
3. Select Filter -> Texture -> Mosaic Tile. Figure 7–64 illustrates.

Cloud Border

1. Hit Command + A to select all of your image.
2. Choose Select -> Modify -> Border and set the border Width to 20.
3. Select Filter -> Render -> Clouds. Figure 7–65 illustrates.

Polka Dot Border

1. Hit Command + A to select all of your image.
2. Choose Select -> Modify -> Border and set the border Width to 20.
3. Select Filter -> Pixelate -> Color Halftone. Figure 7–66 illustrates.

Brick Border

1. Hit Command + A to select all of your image
2. Choose Select -> Modify -> Border and set the border Width to 20
3. Select Filter -> Texturizer and choose Brick texture. Figure 7–67 illustrates.

Figure 7–64: Mosaic tile border

Figure 7–65: Cloud border

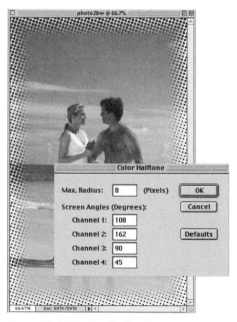

Figure 7–66: Polka dot border

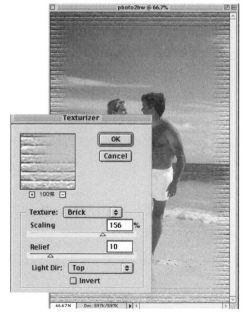

Figure 7–67: Brick border

USING THIRD-PARTY FILTERS FOR IMAGE EFFECTS

Photoshop's filters are arguably the feature of the program that makes it so much fun. But while its native filters offer so much in terms of enhancements and effects, some of the most exciting filters are made by outside companies. These are referred to as third-party filters, and can be purchased separately for various prices depending upon the manufacturer.

To install third-party filters, simply place them into your Plug-ins folder in your Photoshop 5.0 folder.

While there are a number of third-party filters, each with their own benefit, the following are some of my favorite as well as some of the most popular of the filters out there.

KAI'S POWER TOOLS

Besides being some of the most widely used and exciting filters on the market, KPT 3.0 has one of the coolest interfaces around. There are many different filters in the KPT bundle, including the following:

◆ **KPT Gradient Designer**

The Gradient Designer, shown in Figure 7–68 is far more powerful and easy to use than the gradient editor in Photoshop's Gradient tool.

Giving you access to numerous spectrums as well as literally hundreds of presets, the Gradient Designer doesn't use the clunky foreground/background/unique color markers that Photoshop does. Instead it provides the color spectrum directly below your gradient mix and a nifty bracket system for transitions of one color to another. In addition, there are a number of Mode, Loop, and Repeat options, as well as the ability to adjust the hue, saturation and others.

◆ **KPT Texture Explorer**

A great tool for making backgrounds, bumpmaps, or just adding texture to a photograph, the Texture Explorer allows you to start from loads of preset textures and manipulate from there. Adjust color, even shift pixels to randomly create your own texture. This filter is worth the price of the filter kit alone. Figure 7–69 shows the interface.

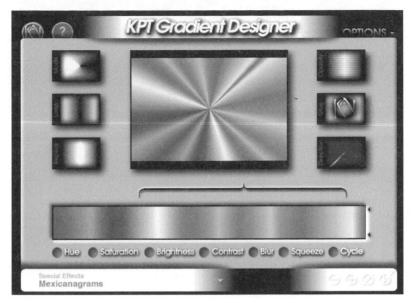

Figure 7–68: KPT Gradient Designer

Figure 7–69: KPT Texture Explorer

◆ **KPT Seamless Welder**

Remember the part of Chapter 5 that discussed how to make a seamless background? Well, this tool, shown in Figure 7–70 does the job without making you use the Rubber Stamp or Blur tools. Simply make a selection that leaves at least 10% of your selection size around the edges, and let this filter do the work for you.

◆ **KPT Vortex Tiling**

Want your picture to have that 3D, "come from a distant far-off-point-in-space" look? This is your tool (Figure 7–71). There's really nothing much to say about it, besides that it is really, really cool.

◆ **KPT Page Curl**

Although it's a bit overused, the KPT Page Curl is a really neat filter that creates a realistic illusion. Easier to use than in earlier versions of KPT Power Tools, the Page Curl filter allows you to easily manipulate the amount of curl, as well as choose which corner and which direction the curl takes place. Figure 7–72 shows an example.

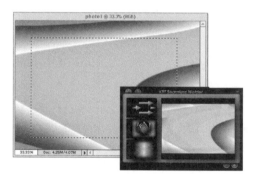

Figure 7–70: KPT Seamless Welder

Figure 7–71: KPT Vortex Tiling

Figure 7–72: KPT Page Curl

Other KPT filters that are worth mentioning:

- ◆ Spheroid Designer
- ◆ Planar Tiling

- ◆ Glass Lens
- ◆ Video Feedback

For more information on KPT 3.0 check out their Website at www.metacreations.com.

GALLERY EFFECTS VOLUME 1: CLASSIC ART

A multitude of filters, each one has a use for more artistic effects. Some of them are purely original, and some of them are simply a repeat of the filters that Photoshop already provides—but even these are in many ways more powerful than the native Photoshop version.

Since the interface for these filters is unappealing and even a bit clunky (you have to hit "Preview" each time you want to see how a setting will affect your image) the Figures provided here will show the result rather than the interface of various filters.

◆ **GE Chrome**

This filter allows you to take a standard image and give a polished chrome look, as shown in Figure 7–73.

◆ **GE Plastic Wrap**

A bizzare filter, this will make it seem as though you are looking at your image or selection through a Zip-Loc bag. (Figure 7–74)

◆ **GE Notepaper**

I haven't quite figured out why they called this one "Notepaper," but as you can see in Figure 7–75, it's a pretty neat effect.

◆ **GE Watercolor**

If Da Vinci only had a computer! I know people who make tons of money just turning his clients' photographs into watercolor painting using this filter (Figure 7–76)

Figure 7–74: Gallery Effects Plastic Wrap

Figure 7–73: Gallery Effects Chrome

Figure 7–75: Gallery Effects Notepaper

Figure 7–76: Gallery Effects Watercolor

Other GE filters that are noteworthy:

- ◆ Torn Edges
- ◆ Chalk & Charcoal
- ◆ Glass

- ◆ Glowing Edges
- ◆ Water Paper
- ◆ Rough Pastels

See Color Figure 29 for color renditions of these and other Gallery Effects filters.

For more information on Gallery Effects, check out the Adobe Web site at www.adobe.com. You'll have to hunt around a bit—the information is a little hidden. But the Adobe site has a nice keyword search engine that should help.

Other cool third-party filters include:

- ◆ Andromedia Series   www.andromeda.com
- ◆ Eye Candy (by Alien Skin)   www.alienskin.com
- ◆ Wacom (bundled with the tablet)   www.wacom.com

SUMMARY

By now your brain should be racing with ideas, your pen busily scribbling the new filters you want for next Christmas, and your ability to retouch artwork and create graphics from scratch expertly honed. The new Photoshop version 5.0, along with the already amazing features from previous versions and your own expertise to this point should combine to help you create advanced Web sites that are bound to attract and keep 'em coming back!

ANIMATION

By now, if you are familiar with the Web, you're familiar with Web animation. Spinning logos, bouncing balls, blinking lights... they've all become as tired and boring as watching a congressional debate on C-Span. But like tired and boring congressional debates, spinning Web logos are here to stay. And until technology improves, and download time and plug-in support are no longer a factor, many of your clients and your Web site visitors will expect you to have something moving somewhere on your page.

This chapter will help you to understand some of the animation options that are available to you. We'll begin with a review of the basics in case you are unfamiliar with how to create animated GIFs, and move into creating killer banner ads—still a main source of building traffic to a Web site. You'll also learn how to use Photoshop and the handy Actions Palette for previewing your animations before assembling everything in separate programs.

ANIMATION BASICS

There a number of different types of animations on the Web, including Java and Java applets, Macromedia Flash applications, and others. The most common, though, are animated GIFs. Unlike the JPEG format (please read Chapter 2, "Preparing Images for the Web"), GIFs allow you to bundle a number of frames (or GIF images) into one file. Each "frame" will play in rapid succession to give the appearance that it is moving, much like a flipbook.

Because GIF animations work like this, you need to keep in mind that each frame will be loaded into the browser individually—depending on your file, this could significantly affect the download time.

◆ **Keep the number of colors down to a minimum. This will make each individual frame easier to manage and download.**

◆ **If possible, don't make an animation larger than 12–15 frames.**

◆ **If you want to have animations on each page of your site, try to create ones that you can recycle. This way they will load from the cache instantaneously, rather than having to download a whole new animation for each page.**

The other thing that is important to remember is that even though you may technically be able to make colors of a GIF animation transparent, in most cases it will have a poor effect. Instead of seeing just your browser window behind the image, you'll be able to see all the other frames as well. If you're confused by that, don't worry—I'll go into it again later in this chapter.

While you'll make your individual frames in Photoshop, the program does not currently have a way for you to assemble them into an animated GIF. Instead, Macintosh users probably will use a popular freeware program called GifBuilder and Windows users will work in a program called GIF Movie Gear.

For the sake of these examples, I will be using the Mac-based program GifBuilder. Windows users can still gain insight by reading this chapter, as the PC-based GIF Movie Gear is not drastically different from its Mac-based counter part. In addition, a very brief overview of GIF Movie Gear follows toward the end of this section.

GIF ANIMATION VERSUS OTHER ANIMATION TECHNIQUES

Although still somewhat small and choppy, the animated GIFs are widely used because it is easy to make and virtualy every system and browser can download them with little effort. That does not mean that there aren't other acceptable alternatives on the market, though. Among the growing field of programs that can create Web content beyond the abilities of animated GIFs are Macromedia's Flash and Director programs. Each offers viable options to designers and clients who seek more than just the broken frame movement of GIF animation, and both are poised to become a staple in the Web animation forum. Currently, though, neither is without its limitations.

MACROMEDIA FLASH

Flash is a terrific vector-based program that allows designers to create intricate keyframed animations with interactive rollovers and zoom-in/out capabilities. Because it is a vector and not a bitmapped program, the file sizes for Flash files are usually extremely low and will load into a user's browser very quickly. Flash offers a bare-bones tweening animation technique as well, which allows you to set the beginning and ending frames, while the program figures out what has to happen in between.

The downside of Flash is that because it is vector based, the graphics will often look cartoonish, much like you might expect to find in Adobe Illustrator. An even worse detriment is that not everyone will be able to see your Flash document unless they have the Flash plug-in instsalled in their browser's plug-in folder.

MACROMEDIA DIRECTOR (SHOCKWAVE)

Director can do far more than animation—you can house your entire Web site within this program! Director applications for the Web can include full-blown animations, rollovers, audio files, the ability to ensure proper spacing for all of your elements, slicker layouts, and even interactive games. Although it's already making its presence felt on the Web, watch for this program to play a much larger role in the way sites are developed. For more information, check out *Director To Go*, by Dennis Chominsky.

Director applications are compressed and made ready for Web use by Shockwave, which creates a .dcr file. The negative to Shockwave and Director for Web use is the same as for Flash—people cannot see it unless they have the Shockwave plug-in in their browser's plug-in folder. It's an easy plug-in to download, but like the Flash plug-in, the user will have to quit their browser to install it. The other negative is that at current modem speeds (28.8 is the average as of the writing of this book), really involved Shockwave applications can take a while to download. Many people get around this by offering two sites—a Shocked site and an HTML site.

EXAMPLE: MAKING A BALL BOUNCE

Okay, okay, so it's overused. You've all seen a ball bouncing on the Web before. But this chapter is not about design style, it's about how to make animations. So for the purposes of temporary illustration, this will do the trick.

The basic concept is that we will create an animation in which a ball seems to bounce up and down while the shadow underneath gets lighter and darker.

1. Open a new file, 72 by 216 pixels and immediately create two new layers. We'll begin working on Layer 2, at the top of the Layers Palette.

Figure 8–1: The original circle filled with color with a shadow cast below.

2. With your Elliptical Marquee tool, hold the Shift key for constraint and make a circle toward the bottom of your canvas and fill it with a bright red color.

3. Create a new layer and, within the circular selection, use your airbrush to put a shadow on the bottom and a small highlight on the top. You may need to adjust the layer opacity to get the proper shadow/highlight depth. Figure 8–1 gives an example of what your picture should look like.

4. From the Layers Palette, choose Merge Down to combine the shadow/highlight with the red circle. Rename the layer "Ball 1."

5. On Layer 1, use your Elliptical Marquee to make an oval beneath your red ball. Choose Select -> Feather with a feather radius of 5 to soften the edges. Click OK.

6. Fill your selection with black to create a shadow similar to that shown in Figure 8–1. Rename the layer "Shadow."

7. Reactivate the "Ball 1" layer, and choose Duplicate Layer from the palette pull-down menu. Name the new, duplicated layer "Ball 2," and hit OK. Do this four times for a total of five separate balls. Name each successive layer "Ball 2," "Ball 3," and so forth.

8. On each duplicated layer, move the ball upward with the Move tool. Hold down the Shift key for constraint. When you're through, each individual layer will look like the balls shown in Figure 8–2. Each of these layers will later become individual frames for your animation. As you can see from the Figure, as you move the ball upward, you should also diminish the shadow opacity.

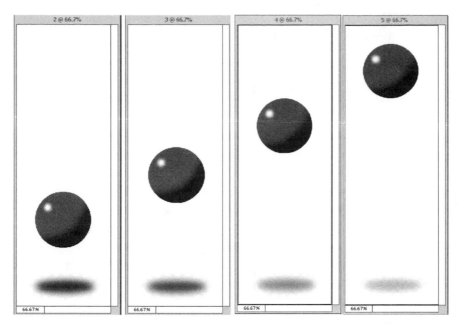

Figure 8–2: The duplicates will become the frames for the animation. Each one saw in increase in the height of the ball, and a decrease in the opacity of the shadow. To make sure the animation is smooth, the changes were made in equal percentages.

VIEWING AN ANIMATION WITH THE ACTIONS PALETTE

You can save yourself some time by using Photoshop's Actions Palette to view the animation. Although it may seem like an annoyance to set up the Action, it is far better than having to create separate frames, import them into an animation program, and run the animation only to find that you need to change something and go back to Photoshop.

1. Make the "Shadow" layer active in the Layers Palette.
2. Make all layers invisible except "Shadow" and "Ball 1." You can make a layer invisible by clicking the Eyeball icon next to it.
3. From the Actions Palette pull-down menu, choose New Action. Name the Action "Ball Animation." The Record button will be activated with the creation of your new Action.
4. Make "Ball 1" invisible—this will become the first command in the "Ball Animation" Action.

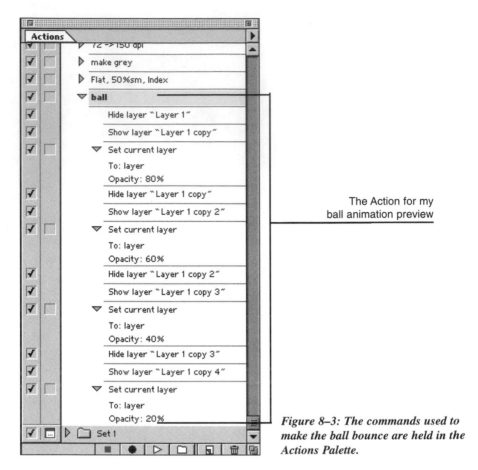

Figure 8–3: The commands used to make the ball bounce are held in the Actions Palette.

5. Make "Ball 2" visible—this will become the second command in your Action.

6. Push the number 8 on your keyboard to reduce the opacity of the active layer ("Shadow") to 80%.

7. Make "Ball 2" invisible.

8. Make "Ball 3" visible.

9. Push the number 6 on your keyboard to reduce the opacity of the active layer ("Shadow") to 60%.

10. Continue doing this for all layers.

11. When you're through, push the Stop button at the bottom of the Actions Palette. Figure 8–3 shows the full Action as it has been recorded.

12. You can play the Action by pressing the Play button at the bottom of the Actions Palette, but you won't see much of a change. To see the Action change the layer visibility, choose Playback Options from the palette pull-down menu.

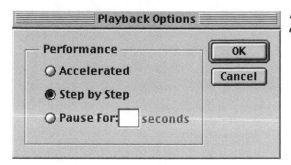

Figure 8–4: The Playback Options dialog box.

13. In the dialog box shown in Figure 8–4, choose Step by Step, and press OK.

14. Play your Action. It won't run as smoothly or as quickly as it will when it is a completed animation, but it will run well enough to give you an idea as to whether or not you have changes to make before leaving Photoshop.

WORKING IN GIFBUILDER

One of the most popular programs for creating animated GIFs on the Macintosh platform is GifBuilder. Very easy to use, you can find GifBuilder at any number of places on the Web and download it for free. No one site is really better than any other to download it from, but you can grab GifBuilder from the To Go Web site, at `http://www.phptr.com/togo`.

To create an animation in GifBuilder, you would first separate the various layers in Photoshop (assume we're still building off the bouncing ball animation established earlier) into five individual files or frames. From that point:

1. Open GifBuilder. From the Windows menu open the frames, preview, and color windows.

2. Choose File -> Open and open the first frame you created in Photoshop.

 In Photoshop, save each ball layer as a separate file to import each as an individual frame.

3. Choose File -> Add Frame and add the next picture you created. Do this for all the images. When you finish, GifBuilder will look similar to Figure 8–5.

4. At this point, you have a five-frame animation of your ball going from its lowest position to its highest. To make it come back down again, continue to add frames, this time in reverse order. As you'll see later, there is no need to add the original first frame again. The result is illustrated in Figure 8–6.

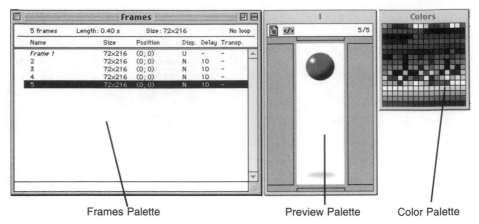

Frames Palette   Preview Palette   Color Palette

Figure 8–5: GifBuilder after placing 5 frames

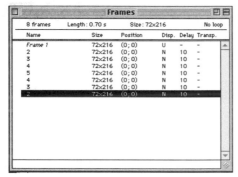

Figure 8–6: The Frames Palette after adding the remaining frames

5. Hit Command + A (Ctrl + A in Windows) to select all of your frames. Choose Options -> Colors -> Best Palette to ensure that your animation will have a proper color palette on all platforms.

6. Choose Options -> Loop to access the palette shown in Figure 8–7. Choose "Forever" and hit OK.

7. With all frames still selected, choose Options -> Interframe Delay for the palette shown in Figure 8–8. Set the delay to 25/100 of a second, so that the frames will change once every quarter of a second. Hit OK.

8. To see your animation work, choose Animation -> Play.

9. Save your file using an original name.

10. You can place your animation in your Web page using the <IMG SRC> tag, as you would any other image.

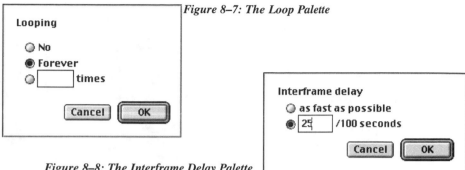

Figure 8-7: The Loop Palette

Figure 8-8: The Interframe Delay Palette

OTHER FEATURES OF GIFBUILDER

The preceding example showed the basics of how to create an animation. In most cases, that's the way you'll create your animations. There are other features of GifBuilder that you'll use from time to time as well. The following will provide a brief explanation of some of the other features of GifBuilder.

◆ **Edit -> Copy HTML Tag**

This will actually write the necessary HTML code to place your animation. Automatically copied to your clipboard, all you have to do is paste it into your HTML.

◆ **Option -> Transparent Background**

This option will allow you to designate a color in your animation to take on transparent qualities. Choosing this will help reduce file size for quicker downloading of the animation. However, transparent animations are not always good things. In our previous example of the bouncing ball, allowing the white background to be transparent would not let the browser background show through, but rather would allow all the frames in your animation to show through at the same time.

◆ **Option -> Frame Size**

This is a tricky feature, as you may expect that changing the frame size would scale down your animation image. It doesn't, however. Instead, it just squeezes or expands the canvas size of your animation so that making the frame size smaller would just crop the edges of the image in each frame.

Filters

GifBuilder has a number of different filters to create various effects, each of which can help improve your animation. Figures 8-9 to 8-11 illustrate the different filters in GifBuilder and how they can add to your animation.

Figure 8–9: The Dissolve filter

Figure 8–10: The Slide filter

Figure 8–11: The Tile filter

Although there are many filters in GifBuilder, the ones that tend to work the best are the Transitions filters, especially the Dissolve, Slide, and Push. Figure 8–12 shows the four frames of a simple but effective banner ad that we created for the ASCO Web site. The ad utilizes the Dissolve filter to get the message across, and the interframe delay allows the dissolve to happen quickly, while the two anchor frames each remain on screen for 1.5 seconds each. The banner ad loops forever.

Figure 8–12: The ASCO banner ad uses the Dissolve filter to display a simple but effecive message.

MOVIE GEAR FOR THE PC

GifBuilder, as of the time of this writing, is strictly for Macs. For PCs, you might want to check out GIF Movie Gear, a popular program that you can download from many sites and use to create GIF animations on your PC. You can download Movie Gear at `http://www.ptrph.com/togo`

Movie Gear has a simple, easy-to-use interface. The toolbar that spans the top basically provides icon shortcuts for the menu bar options, while the lower bar displays information on both the individual frames and the animation as a whole.

To create an animation in Movie Gear:

1. Choose File -> Insert Frame and select the image you want to load. Do this for every frame that will appear in your animation.

2. Set the time delay between frames by clicking on each frame individually and selecting Edit -> Frame Properties.

Play the animation by pressing the universal Play triangle on the top toolbar.

ADOBE IMAGEREADY

Seasoned designers of Web graphics have undoubtedly heard the name ImageReady floating around in discussions of Adobe, Photoshop, and the Internet. New designers probably jumped on the bandwagon in time to get a copy of ImageReady bundled with their purchase of Photoshop. Either way, though, get ready to hear a lot more of it.

ImageReady is Adobe's answer to providing tools and functions specifically geared toward Web users. While Photoshop is still the program of choicc for designing graphics, ImageReady does offer some exciting features that Photoshop doesn't, such as the ability to easily create a tiled background and manage a divided picture to be reassembled in HTML (See Chapter 9 for more details). But the function that really grabs attention and is propelling ImageReady to stardom is the Animation Palette. By working directly from Photoshop's Layers Palette, ImageReady makes creating animations far simpler than it is using other programs.

To create an animation in ImageReady:

1. From within ImageReady, choose Windows -> Show Animation from the upper menu bar.

2. Open an animation that you've created in Layers in Photoshop. In this instance, use the Ball animation that we used in the previous examples. However this time, rather than keeping the shadow on its own layer, put a shadow on each layer with a ball.

3. From the Animation Palette pull-down menu, choose New Frame. Do this to create a total of 8 separate frames (5 frames for the ball to go up, and then three for the ball to go down—you don't need to duplicate the uppermost and lowermost ball in the animation).

4. Make a connection for each frame with a layer in your animation Layers palette. Click on the first frame in the Animation Palette, and then hide all but the "Ball 1" layer in the Layer palette. For the second frame, hide all layers except "Ball 2." Continue this for each frame in the animation.

5. Choose Play options from the Animation Palette pull-down menu and set how often you want the animation to loop.

6. Click on the Optimized tab in the Animation Palette and choose File -> Preview In -> and choose your desired browser. Your chosen browser will launch, and display not only the animation, but also the HTML code for you to copy and paste into your own HTML document.

7. Change the speed of the animation if necessary by setting a value for Delay in the Animation Palette.

SUMMARY

As the Web becomes more a part of our everyday lives, audiences will come to expect more dynamic elements in the Web pages they view. Static images alone will not be sufficient to retain viewers and assure return visitors. While animation alone is not enough to turn an ineffective Web site into an effective one, the movement and interest it can generate can play an important part in taking advantage of this expanding technology.

Macintosh GifBuilder as well as the PC equivalent GIF Movie Gear, are great tools for creating animated GIFs. Although nothing more than a flashback to the old flip-book style of making things move, they each offer simple means of creating animations. Now that you understand how these applications work, the only thing that's left to gain is the patience it takes in Photoshop to make the various frames that you'll need.

chapter 9

REAL LIFE

EXAMPLE:

A COMPLETE

WALK THROUGH

You've paid your dues—you read through that really boring chapter about JPEGs and GIFs, you suffered through as many bevel effects as you can stand, and now you're ready for some fun. You're ready to do something just a little bit different that combines most of the elements this book has taught you and get the full use of Photoshop for the Web.

The techniques in this chapter combine aspects of Photoshop with HTML tables. By using tables, you can give the illusion of a very large single image that incorporates detailed graphics and multiple animations with relatively low download times. Done properly, it will allow you to test the extent of your creativity for both Photoshop graphics and the Web.

Without sounding intimidating, I would recommend that you know a bit of HTML before diving into this chapter. However, as the main graphic in this chapter gets built, I'll provide the HTML code for building a table as well as a fairly detailed explanation of what each tag means and how it is used.

LEARNING BY EXAMPLE

Future Media Concepts, New York City's only certified Adobe and Avid training center (where I teach on occasion) asked my company to build their official Web site. Because they deal with people in the design and technology industries, the site (www.fmc-training.com) had to possess two main ingredients:

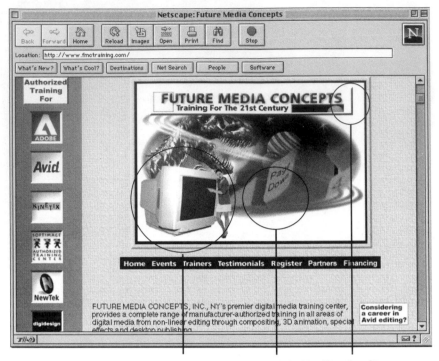

Changing logos   Moving light hit Shooting Star

Figure 9–1: The home page for Future Media Concepts' Web site at **www.fmctraining.com**

◆ Logic and ease of layout

◆ Advanced graphic design elements

The logic and ease of the site came painlessly, as navigation is always given top priority, especially for large sites. The graphic portion was a bit tougher, however, as I had to walk the fence between graphics that were dull and lifeless, leaving the user believing they would learn nothing at the school, and graphics that were so outrageous they alienated beginning students who may believe they could never achieve a certain level.

The solution I came up with was a combination of color and activity for the home page splash graphic that you see in Figure 9–1 and Color Figure 30. The areas of activity are pointed out, showing how a large portion of the design was animated for eye-catching effect. The remainder of the picture was a combination of various Photoshop effects including embossing, collaging, and shadowing that tells a full story of what FMC is all about.

The rest of this chapter will bring you through the creation of this picture, step by step, with some areas acting as review for other portions of this book, while other areas offer completely new information.

GETTING THE IDEA

Everybody works differently when it comes to design. Some people slave away for hours at a drawing table, crumpling millions of sheets of paper in a frustrated mess trying to get an idea. Others get a brainstorm just by waking up lucky. Me, I play Joe Montana Football on my Sega while listening to Led Zeppelin. Don't ask me why, I just do.

My point is that when you're going to use Photoshop for original graphic development to fit within the context of a Web site full of information, it is important to have some idea of what you want your graphic to look like.

So while my New York Giants were killing the Chicago Bears during a live rendition of Kashmir, I decided that I wanted to create a collage of computer metaphors and designs in a faded background, fronted by a display of logos for some of the manufacturers that FMC trains for. Because animation is one of the areas that FMC specializes in, I would need to have movement in at least one area of the graphic.

DESIGNING THE PICTURE

Coming up with the actual design required a combined knowledge of Photoshop, HTML, my client, and their audience.

THE OVAL BACKGROUND IMAGE

Because I had previously laid my background to create a border approximately 108 pixels wide (notice the background in the Web site in Figure 9–1—the sidebar is used for specialized navigation), I knew I had about 432 pixels in width to work with (I try to not let any graphics or combination of graphics wander much past 576 pixels.) Since I also try to make sure that a graphic won't get cut off in the center, forcing the user to scroll down to see it, I didn't want to go much beyond 252 pixels in depth. So to begin designing,

1. I opened a new file, 468 pixels by 252 pixels with a white background, and immediately created a new layer to work on. I saved and named the file "FMC Cover."

2. Considering the wide range of topics that FMC teaches, I gathered photos and elements that related to their course offerings. After much review, I decided on the 3D-rendered dinosaur, a computer keyboard, and for the rest I would rely on my own imagination. I scanned the necessary images into Photoshop, (Figure 9–2).

3. In "FMC Cover," I used my Elliptical Marquee tool to create a large oval in the center of my canvas. I then chose Select -> Feather with a feather radius of 6 to give my oval a soft edge.

Figure 9–2: The two pictures that I will use in my splash graphic.

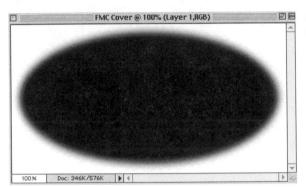

Figure 9–3: The black soft-edged oval will provide my background.

4. Because I knew that I'd be using this particular selection often, I saved it as a channel by choosing Select -> Save Selection. I named it "Oval."

5. The collage called for a spacey, ethereal background, so I started by filling my oval with black. The feathered edges made the black gradate out into the white instead of having a distinct edge, as shown in Figure 9–3.

6. Making my keyboard picture the active canvas, I selected all and copied the picture to my pasteboard. I then made "FMC Cover" active again, and chose Edit -> Paste Into to paste my keyboard picture into my selection. Figure 9–4 shows the Layers Palette indicating that a mask was created to contain my image.

7. I wanted the keyboard to be tilted and skewed a little, so I hit Command + T (Ctrl + T in Windows) to transform my image. I rotated it up to the right by dragging upward outside the grips, and made it larger proportionately by holding the Command + Option + Shift keys (Ctrl + Alt + Shift in Windows) while dragging one of the corner grips outward. The result is shown in Figure 9–4.

8. Because I didn't want the keyboard to be the focal point, I reduced the opacity of that layer to about 60%.

9. Next I did the same with the dinosaur by selecting all and copying to my clipboard, but this time when I went back to "FMC Cover," there was no selection to paste

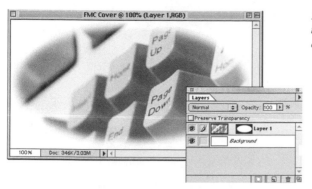

Figure 9–4: The keyboard image pasted into the oval. Pasting the image into the selection creates the mask shown in Layer 1.

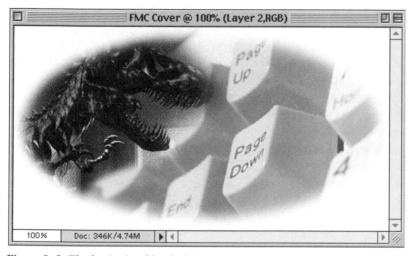

Figure 9–5: The beginning blend of the dinosaur and keyboard images.

into—it was deselected as soon as I pasted my keyboard in. I regained my selection by choosing Select -> Load Selection and choosing "Oval." (I could also have held down the Command key (Ctrl in Windows) while clicking the mask in Layer 1.)

10. I pasted the dinosaur into my selection, which appears on a new layer, directly above the keyboard layer, within it's own, identical mask.

11. I wanted the dinosaur to show off the 3D modeling that it took to create it, and also add depth and drama to the piece. I did this by enlarging him and placing him off to the left far enough that only his jaw, neck, and small, grabbing claws were visible in the picture. I erased the excess image to the right of the dinosaur.

12. Again, I didn't want the oval or its components to be the focal points of the piece, so I reduced the opacity setting for the dinosaur's layer to 60%, like the keyboard's layer. The whole picture at this point looked like Figure 9–5.

13. It looked good, but so far it was still just two pictures pasted into a feathered oval—not really a billboard for a graphics school. I continued to push for the outerspace feel by making the keyboard image the active layer and using a soft-edged eraser with a 50% opacity on the top portion of it to allow the black background to show through.

14. I loaded in some of the really cool brushes that Photoshop provides by opening the Brushes Palette and choosing "Load Brushes" from its submenu. When the navigator appeared, I found the "Brushes" folder in the Photoshop directory, and selected Assorted Brushes (this is typically named Assorted Brushes.abr in Windows). Figure 9–6 shows the brushes provided, including the star-shaped button I chose.

15. On a new layer under my keyboard layer, I used my small star-shaped brush with white foreground color to place a few stars randomly around to show through the keyboard picture.

16. I had stars, so I needed planets. On the same layer, I used my Circle Marquee tool, with the Shift key held for restraint, to make a small circle among the stars, as illustrated in Figure 9–7.

17. I filled my selection with black (even though it looks like it was already filled with black, it wasn't—the black is actually on a lower layer.)

18. With my circle still selected, I used a third-party filter, Kai Power Tools 3.0 Spheroid Designer to get a cool texture for what would become a planet. The filter, which has one of the coolest interfaces of any that I've seen is shown in Figure 9–8.

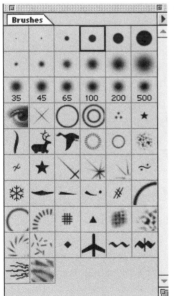

Figure 9–6: Assorted Brushes from the Brushes folder. (Located in the "Goodies" Directory).

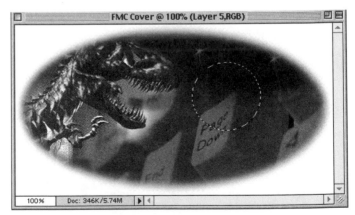

Figure 9–7: After adding the stars, I made a selection for a small planet.

*Figure 9–8: The KPT Spheroid Designer
interface*

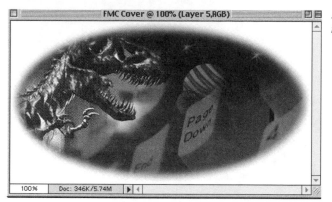

*Figure 9–9: My planets add
nice depth to the collage.*

19. I selected the design I wanted, set the desired lighting, and hit OK to put my planet in my picture. All it needed now was a moon, which I created by doing the exact same thing, this time a little smaller. The result is shown in Figure 9–9.

20. Before leaving my background oval and moving on, I wanted to do one more thing, and at that point I wasn't really sure what. I needed some other effect—something simple but eye-catching in a subtle sort of way. I made my dinosaur layer active.

21. In the Layers submenu, I chose Duplicate Layer to bring up the dialog box shown in Figure 9–10. I arranged the settings so that the dinosaur layer would duplicate within this same canvas and hit OK. The new layer is distinguished by the word "copy" in the Layers Palette.

22. Making the copy layer the active layer, I used the Move tool to position my image just below and to the right of the original dinosaur.

23. I pressed Command + I (Ctrl + I in Windows) inverting the image and giving it a ghostly, film negative quality. With the color balance dialog box, I added a bit of magenta and cyan until I was happy with the way it looked. I hit OK, getting the image that you see in Figure 9–11.

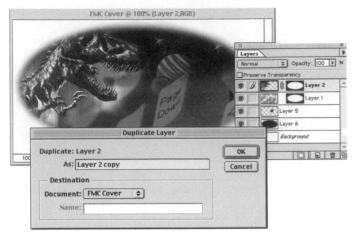

Figure 9–10: The Duplicate Layer dialog box

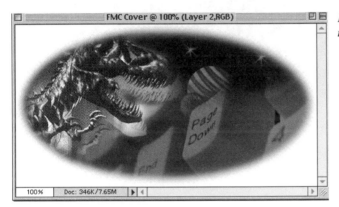

Figure 9–11: The dinosaur image moved off center and made negative.

CREATING THE TITLEBAR

My background was finished, and I was happy with it, but now I needed to put the foreground elements in. The first thing that I needed in the foreground was a titlebar so that people could see immediately who they were dealing with, as well as help to give the users' eyes a starting point to follow the graphics through the rest of the image.

1. New room was definitely in order, so I extended my canvas by choosing Image -> Canvas Size. Keeping the image in the middle, I extended the canvas 36 pixels on top and bottom.

2. I built a new layer on top of everything else, and, toward the top of my canvas, I used my Rectangular Marquee tool to draw a long rectangle from one side to the other, slightly overlapping the oval.

3. I filled the selection with white and used Layer Effects to add a bevel around the edges. I chose an inner bevel with a Depth of 14 and a Blur of only 4, with the universal 120° angle.

4. On another new layer, I used the Shift key + the Rectangular Marquee tool to make the FMC logo, and, with a vibrant purple in my foreground, I chose Edit -> Stroke to get the dialog box shown in Figure 9–12. With an Edge of only 1, I got the logo looking right and set about placing my text.

5. With the text editor, I typed the name of the company, Future Media Concepts in Frutiger Bold, 28 point and placed it at the top center of the titlebar.

6. Because Photoshop wouldn't let me apply a filter onto newly laid text, I chose Layer -> Type -> Render Layer. Now I could apply a filter, although I could no longer go back and reedit the text.

7. Flat black letters weren't doing much for me, so I chose KPT Texture Explorer (interface shown in Figure 9–13) and applied a purple and black texture to the letters. I added a bevel and shadow for depth by choosing Layer -> Effects -> Bevel and Emboss and then Drop Shadow.

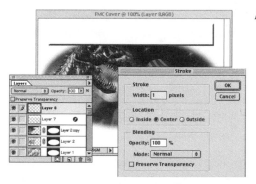

Figure 9–12: The Stroke dialog box

Figure 9–13: The KPT Texture Explorer

Figure 9–14: My splash graphic with text in the titlebar

Figure 9–15: After adding a pushed-in box on the titlebar

8. I added the tagline "Training For The 21st Century" under the company name, but this time I left the letters flat and black so that they didn't take away from the title. Figure 9–14 shows the progress at that point.

9. The white space to the right of the tagline was just enough to allow me to create one last design on the titlebar. On a new layer, I used the Rectangular Marquee tool to create a rectangular selection, then used the Layer Effects to create a bevel that goes inward this time, instead of the more traditional "pushed out" look.

10. Reducing my selection with Select -> Modify-> Contract the same amount that I had beveled inward, I filled the selection with black to give the more spacey feeling. I also added a small planet, which just peeked out from above my selection. The end result looked like Figure 9–15.

PLACING THE WOMAN AND THE MONITOR

Up to this point, I had worked to convey the general idea that FMC was a high-tech, creative, hands-on learning center. The only part that was missing from the message was the personal aspect. The instructors are as important as what they teach, and I felt it was necessary to add that to the graphic.

1. I found a photograph of a computer monitor I had taken a while back and scanned it into Photoshop. After isolating the monitor from its background, I copied it and pasted it to the topmost layer in "FMC Cover."

2. Next I found a picture of a girl I liked from the Bodyworks stock photo CD-ROM. Fortunately, the paths were already created for me by the CD-ROM manufacturer I copied her image and pasted it into "FMC Cover." A new layer was created right above my monitor. Figure 9–16 shows the image with the woman and the monitor added.

Figure 9–16: The girl and the monitor have been added to the splash graphic.

SWOOSH IT UP

I just needed one more element to give it that "ethereal" look I was after, and I thought that a simple, metallic-looking swoosh through the center would give me just what I needed.

1. On a new layer, I used the Pen tool to place points in a curve. When I finished with the outside swoosh, I opened my Paths Palette and dragged my path to the "Make Selection" icon, as shown in Figure 9–17. I did this for each individual swoosh.

2. I filled my selection with a gradient of light blue to dark blue, and did the same for the other swooshes, all of them having the same center point.

3. I selected all swooshes on the layer, and used a soft-edged airbrush to put a few light hits in various places. Figure 9–18 shows the resulting image.

CUTTING THE PICTURE

What I had so far was a very large picture that I thought would look great on the FMC Web site. My next step was to prepare the picture for the Web, including making portions of the picture animate on their own.

1. Before doing anything else, I saved my picture in layers as a Photoshop file. Even though I could not use it on the Web that way, I knew that there could be some point in the future when I might want to change it.

2. I flattened the image and then decided on which part I wanted to have animation:

   ◆ I wanted the monitor to show a series of logos for the various manufacturers that FMC teaches for.

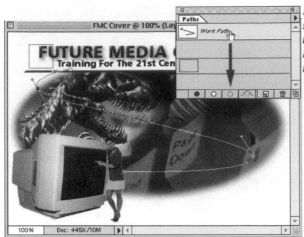

Figure 9–17: After I made a swoosh with the Pen tool, I turned the path into a selection by dragging the work path down to the stroke path icon.

Figure 9–18: The swoosh has been added.

♦ I wanted the swoosh to have a light flare running through it.

♦ I wanted the black window in the titlebar to have a shooting star go through it.

Figure 9–19 (a repeat, with variations, of Figure 9–1) shows the areas I decided to animate.

3. As I explained in Chapter 8, "Animation", when you create an animated GIF, you are basically loading in a series of pictures, or frames, that change in rapid succession. If I were to make this entire image animate, this very large picture with relatively minor changes per frame would have to load over and over again, making downloading very cumbersome. Considering that there are only a few areas that I want to animate, that would be a waste.

Instead, I carved my picture into smaller pieces and reconstructed them in HTML tables. I started doing this by designating how I wanted to break up my picture.

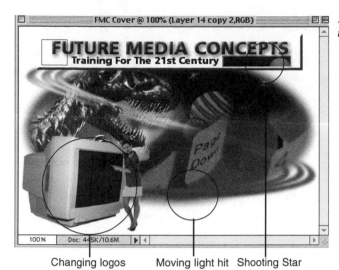

Figure 9–19: The areas of my image that I wanted to have animation.

Changing logos   Moving light hit   Shooting Star

Figure 9–20 shows the guidelines I set to determine exactly how I would disassemble my image.

4. Before I started cutting away, I set my background color to a color that was not really prevalent in my image, such as bright, neon green. When I cut, the portion that was gone would be filled with this color. When I made subsequent cuts, I'd know immediately if I had taken too much, since there would be neon green around the edges. (The crucial part was to make certain that I made my cuts as exact as possible—if I was off here, I would be off in my HTML tables.)

5. With my Rectangular Marquee tool, I started to make selections out of the area I marked off. I cut and pasted each section into its own separate file (when I cut a portion and chose File -> New, Photoshop had already set the measurements to the item on my clipboard. Figure 9–21 shows each piece as its own separate document.

6. I saved all the sections as GIFs and made the white transparent in the 3 areas that will not animate.

MAKING IT MOVE: CREATING THE ANIMATIONS

Depending on your frame of mind, this part is either the most fun, or the most tedious. I had three portions of my image left, the portions that I wanted to move or rotate in some way. I decided to start with the flashing logos in the monitor.

1. I had already collected the logos I wanted to use in a previous project, so I opened them and left them on the desktop. There were four in all, as shown in Figure 9–22.

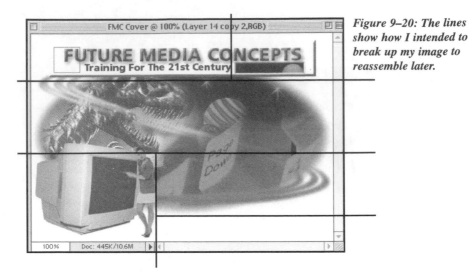

Figure 9–20: The lines show how I intended to break up my image to reassemble later.

Figure 9–21: My image broken into pieces, with each piece now its own document.

2. The monitor was going to be a slight problem because the girl I had chosen was pointing to the monitor screen—thus her hand was in the way. With the Magic Wand tool, I selected the dark monitor and then held down the Option (Alt in Windows) button and used the Lasso to subtract her hand from my selection.

3. I feathered my selection with a feather radius of 2 and saved my selection. By feathering the edges, the logos would not have stark edges, and would leave a more realistic impression of being on a computer screen.

4. I chose Image -> Duplicate, and duplicated the image four times (unfortunatley Photoshop does not allow you to specify how many duplicates you want—you just have to do this manually four times, or set up an Action for it—see Chapter 1, "Photoshop Overview" for more on establishing Actions).

5. I copied each of the logos in turn and pasted them into the feathered selection of the duplicated image. I chose Edit -> Free Transform to manipulate each logo inside of its mask. Figure 9–23 shows the finished product of what would become the frames of my animation.

6. After saving the monitors as Photoshop files, I saved each one again, this time as a GIF. I didn't bother making any portion transparent yet—I could do that in the animation program itself.

7. In GifBuilder, I started a new file, and opened my first "flashing logo" frame. I then added the remaining three frames. (See Chapter 8 for more information on animation.)

8. Selecting all of my frames with Command + A, I chose Options -> Color -> Best Palette but left the "Remove Unused Colors" active to reduce the overall number of colors as well as reduce download time.

9. I chose Options -> Loop and changed the setting to "Forever" so that the logos would not stop flashing.

10. With all of my frames still selected, I chose Options -> Interframe Delay. I changed the setting to read 250/100, which would equal 2.5 seconds between frames. Figure 9–24 illustrates Steps 8 to 10.

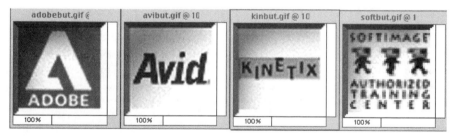

Figure 9–22: The logos that were used in my animation.

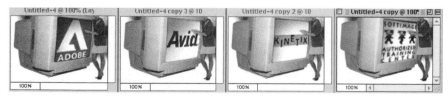

Figure 9–23: The logos in the monitor, ready to be animated.

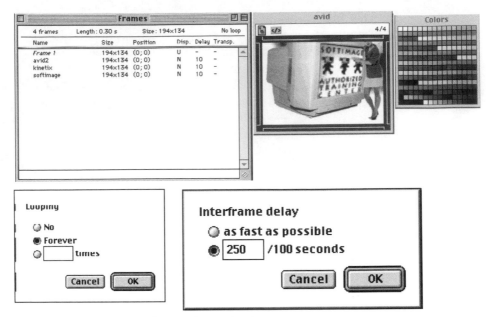

Figure 9–24: Creating my flipping logo animation.

11. I saved my animation and went through relatively the same steps for the other two areas of my splash graphic that I wanted to animate.

ASSEMBLING THE PICTURES IN HTML

Having broken up the image in Photoshop and saved the individual pieces as transparent GIFs or animated GIFs, now all I had to do was reassemble the pieces in HTML. The following is the HTML text that I wrote to put the image together. Since I haven't reviewed HTML code much throughout this book, I will provide the full HTML text and then briefly explain the coding afterward. My table starts with the following code:

```
<TABLE BORDER="3" CELLPADDING="4" CELLSPACING="4"
BGCOLOR="#000000">
<TR>
<TD>

<TABLE BORDER="0" CELLPADDING="0" CELLSPACING="0"
BGCOLOR="#FFFFFF">
<TR>
<TD width="270" height="60">
```

```
<IMG SRC="topleft.gif">
</TD>
<TD WIDTH="108" HEIGHT="60">
<IMG SRC="animation/topright.gif">
</TD>
</TR>
<TR>
<TD COLSPAN=2 WIDTH="378" HEIGHT="86">
<IMG SRC="middle.gif">
</TD>
</TR>

<TR>
<TD ROWSPAN=2 WIDTH="210" HEIGHT="116">
<IMG SRC="animation/bottomleft.gif">
</TD>
<TD WIDTH="168" HEIGHT="52">
<IMG SRC="bottomright1.gif">
</TD>
</TR>

<TR>
<TD WIDTH="168" HEIGHT="64">
<IMG SRC="animation/bottomright2.gif">
</TD>
</TR>
</TABLE>

</TD>
</TR>
</TABLE>
```

The HTML commands do not have to be in all caps. That is my personal choice, as it helps me quickly distinguish the commands from the remaider of the text.

To understand the preceding code, it is important to first understand that HTML tables are built one row at a time. In other words, the browser will put items in a row infinitely, until that particular row is ended. It will then begin to insert items and/or text into the next row until that row is filled, and so on and so on until the table is complete.

Figure 9–25 illustrates the process of building an HTML table. Each row is composed of individual data cells. These cells contain the information that will be displayed, which can be images, text, links, animations, or even other tables.

In the preceding HTML code, there are two tables—one inside of the other. If you look at the picture in the browser, repeated again in Figure 9–26, you'll see a border and black outline around the entire picture. This was done first by creating the exterior table with only one cell to contain the more complex table for my assembled image, also shown in Figure 9–26.

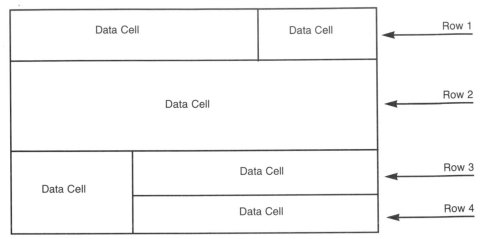

Figure 9–25: Tables in HTML are built by rows made up of cells.

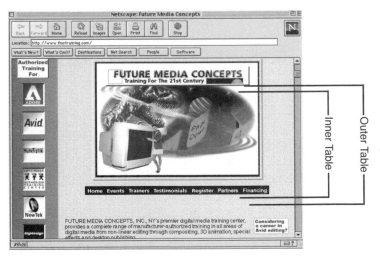

Figure 9–26: The image is actually one table within another table, the outer table creates the border and black outline all around the image.

Here is the preceding HTML code explained line by line (commands that repeat often are only listed once):

`<TABLE>`	Begins the exterior table.
`BORDER=3`	Creates a border 3 pixels thick around the table.
`CELLPADDING="4"`	Creates a space of 4 pixels between the edge of the cell and the cell content.
`CELLSPACING="4"`	Creates a space of 4 pixels between the cell borders.
`BGCOLOR="#000000"`	Sets the background of the cell to black.
`<TR>`	Starts the first table row.
`<TD>`	Starts the first table data cell.
`<TABLE>`	Begins the inner table.
`BORDER=0`	Creates a 0 pixels thick border around the table.
`CELLPADDING="0"`	Creates a space of 0 pixels between the edge of the cell and the cell content.
`CELLSPACING="0"`	Creates a space of 0 pixels between the cell borders.
`BGCOLOR="#FFFFFF"`	Sets the background of the cell to white.
`<TR>`	Starts the first table row (second table).
`<TD>`	Starts the first table data cell (second table).
`WIDTH="270" HEIGHT="60"`	Establishes the size of the cell. This helps the image load in faster.
`<IMG SRC="topleft.gif">`	Inserts the image named "topleft.gif" into the cell.
`<TR>`	Ends the data cell.
`<TD>`	Begins the second data cell.
`<IMG SRC="animation/topright.gif">`	Inserts the image named "topright.gif" into the cell. "topright.gif" is located in the "animation" folder, as indicated by the / mark.
`</TD>`	Ends the data cell.
`</TR>`	Ends the data row.
`<TD COLSPAN=2>`	Creates a cell that will span 2 columns.
`<TD ROWSPAN=2>`	Creates a cell that will span 2 rows.
`</TABLE>`	Ends the inner table.
`</TABLE>`	Ends the exterior table.

Figure 9–27 shows the inner table as an outline, and how the different HTML codes apply to the rows and cells. To see the final product in action, check out the site at www.fmctraining.com.

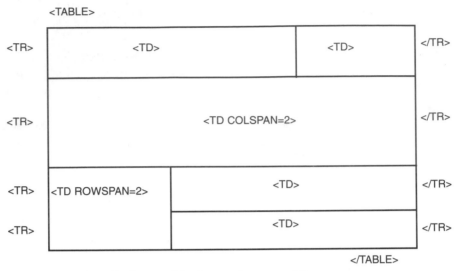

Figure 9–27: The table illustrated by the tags that created it.

 The site was completed long before I thought of writing a book, so don't be surprised if the actual graphic looks a bit different on the site than it does in this book. The HTML coding might be different as well (the coding in the book is actually a bit better than what is on the site—hey, learn as you go, right?).

To see the final product in action, check out the site at www.fmctraining.com.

SUMMARY

Of course, that's not the end of the story—after the remainder of the page was laid out, there was meticulous testing of the page, and the animation especially, on multiple browsers, monitor sizes and resolutions, and modems. However, after reading through this chapter, you should have a good idea as to how you can use some of the techniques described in other chapters to work in conjunction with one another. Collages, bevels, text, animations all work well enough on their own, but when they are used in tandem the results can be overpowering.

chapter 10

TIPS, TRICKS, AND SUGGESTIONS

The interesting part of creating Web sites is the unique combination of art and science—on the one hand, nothing but your imagination will confine you creatively, while on the other hand, current technology limits you to using certain colors, image sizes, and formats. Most of what I've tried to demonstrate in this book has fallen on the technical side—sure, I used creative examples as illustrations, but those were to demonstrate certain techniques that hopefully you will apply to your own work.

While technique, talent, and knowledge are 95% of the tools you'll need (besides equipment, of course!), sage wisdom from experienced sources never hurts. Certain pitfalls exist in creating sites that can cause frustration in those of us with little patience for problems. However in almost all cases there are work-arounds to keep problems to a minimum, and help ensure a more streamlined Web creation experience.

So let me put on my high-pointed cap, brush my beard, and take a perch at the top of a snow-capped mountain (I'm going to be the sage, wise and experienced source you just read about), while you get ready to downshift out of creative mode and learn some of the tricks of the trade. Take or leave any of the following advice in this chapter— I find them useful ideas that may or may not apply to your specific style of working. Some of these suggestions don't have anything to do with Photoshop, but may be helpful in the grand scheme of Web design (if you feel guilty accepting free advice, please feel free to send me a check directly, and consider this chapter "shareware").

THE SINGLE PIXEL TRICK

Since HTML is still somewhat archaic, you may find that as you create your Web sites you will have trouble getting everything to lay out correctly. The `<...HSPACE>` and `<...VSPACE>` commands are good in certain instances, but since they each distribute measurements equally, they are not helpful in creating one-sided space. Let's say you have two images to place on your Web page, a circle and a square, each shown in Figure 10–1. You would like the circle to be 60 pixels from the edge of the browser, and have the square kiss right up next to the circle.

The `<...HSPACE>` and `<...VSPACE>` tags are not stand-alone tags. Rather, they are attributes of other tags. In this example, they are part of the `<IMG>` tag, as shown below.

Conventional logic would say you might write your HTML code as follows:

```
<IMG SRC="circle.gif" ALIGN=LEFT HSPACE=60>
<IMG SRC="square.gif">
```

Though it may seem like the right thing to do, the `HSPACE=60` actually distributes the 60 pixels as 30 pixels before and 30 pixels after the image, so that your page looks similar to Figure 10-2. Newer programming technology such as dynamic HTML helps relieve this problem, but not all browsers can read these new codes. Most people do not use the latest browsers available, and it could be months or years before the general populace upgrades. Meanwhile, we still have a spacing problem to deal with.

One solution to this problem is known as the "single pixel trick." In Photoshop, open a new file, one pixel wide by one pixel high. Choose Image -> Mode -> Index Color and make sure that there is only one color specified. (If you're uncertain that your extremely small image is correct, compare it to Figure 10-3.) Choose File -> Export -> GIF 89a and make your one pixel transparent. (If you're not certain how to do this, check out Chapter 3, "Transparency"). Save it with a name like "pixel.gif"

Back in your HTML code, insert your pixel image with the following code:

```
<IMG SRC="pixel.gif" ALIGN=LEFT HSPACE=60>
<IMG SRC="circle.gif" ALIGN=LEFT>
<IMG SRC="square.gif">
```

Note that in the code, the `HSPACE=60` command is now being used to describe the pixel image instead of the circle. In the browser, the page now looks like Figure 10-4 Because it is transparent, the pixel remains invisible no matter what color your background is.

Figure 10–1: The circle and square graphics that will go into the Web site.

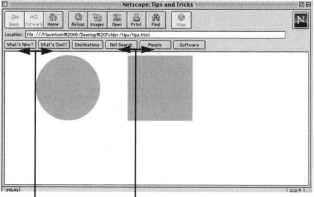

Figure 10–2: The result of using the **HSPACE** *command on one of the images.*

30 pixels   30 pixels

Figure 10–3: The single pixel

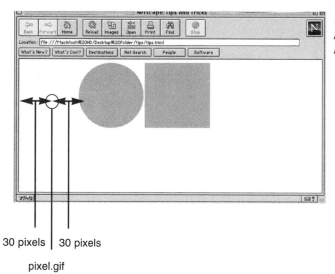

Figure 10–4: How the pixel can be used for placement.

30 pixels   30 pixels

pixel.gif

USE PHOTOSHOP FOR LAYOUT

While Photoshop is nobody's tool of choice for laying out printed pieces such as newsletters or brochures, it is gaining tremendous momentum with designers as a way to lay out entire Web pages.

Figure 10–5 and Color Figure 31 show a simple Web site that my agency created for the Metropolitan Electrical League (MEL), which can be seen at www.elec-troleague.org. The site shown in the Figure, though, is not off the Internet—it's the layout created in Photoshop. The accompanying Layers Palette shows how each element—even minor elements, all have their own layer. There are also layers that are turned off, which were eliminated as possible design elements as the site began to take shape. By using Photoshop as a layout tool rather than for creating individual elements and using HTML code to make a browser your canvas, you can quickly see how various elements will relate to each other. Beyond that, using the guides and grids, along with the rulers, the new Measurement tool and the Info Palette, you can be more precise in how each element lays out. Of course, it is difficult if not impossible to lay out a page exactly to the pixel for every platform, monitor size, resolution, and browser used, but by placing everything in Photoshop, you can be assured of coming as close as you possibly can.

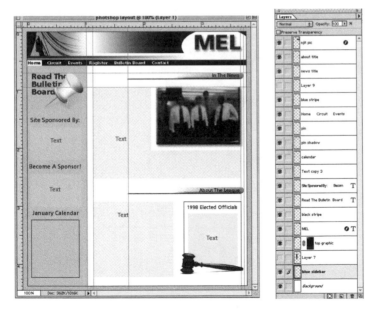

Figure 10–5: A simple Web site located at **www.electroleague.org** *was orginally laid out in Photoshop using multiple layers.*

GUIDES AND GRIDS

As you can see in Figure 10-5, the Photoshop layout uses a number of guides to align various pieces of the Web page. These guides are the same that were used when we created an image map back in Chapter 6. You can place guides by pressing Command + R (Ctrl + R in Windows) to view the rulers, and then dragging from either ruler across or down. Once the guide has been placed, you will only be able to move it again by using the Move tool (or, when using any other tool, holding the Command button [Ctrl in Windows] and dragging). You can hide the guides by pressing the Command + ; buttons (Ctrl + ; in Windows). By choosing Snap to Guides from the View menu, you ensure that elements will align correctly.

Grids are useful as well, in that they create a preset mapping of measurements. This can be particularly beneficial if you know that you will be setting up a complex table or chart on your Web site. The down side to grids, however, is that they can get in the way of seeing everything else on your page because they add lines everywhere. You can turn the grids on or off by pushing Command + " (Ctr. + " in Windows).

To change the color of the guides or the measurements of the grid, double click on a guide, or choose File -> Preferences -> Guides and Grid. You will access the dialog box shown in Figure 10-6. Both the Guides and Grid control allow you to change the color (use the pull-down menu or click on the color swatch provided), and offer a choice of line style. The Grids control also allows you to set the measurements of the grid as well as the units of measure.

USING THE MEASURE TOOL AND INFO PALETTE

Another benefit of laying out a Web site in Photoshop is the ability to control (to a certain extent) how your images will be positioned in your browser. Photoshop 5.0 is especially useful in this capacity, with the addition of the Measure tool. Used in conjunction with the Info Palette, the Measure tool will tell you the exact distance between

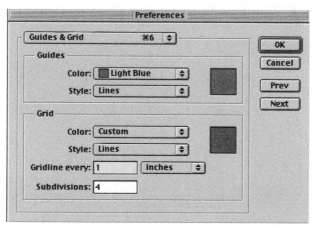

Figure 10–6: The preferences box allows you to change aspects of the guides and grids.

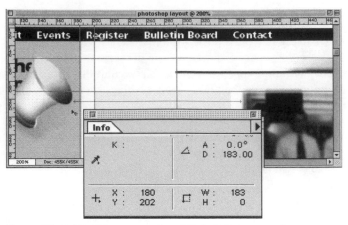

Figure 10–7: The Measure tool and Info Palette at work

two objects. As Figure 10-7 illustrates, the Measure tool was used to determine the distance between the pin on the left side of the page and the news photograph on the right. To accurately measure a distance like this:

1. Choose the Measure tool from the tool palette.

2. Place the first point at the edge of one image. Make sure that you take it from the approximate location of the actual square edge, not the end of the actual picture. For example, although the pin is the picture that users will see on the Web, it will actually be a rectangular graphic, with the area outside the pin made transparent. However I still have to measure from the rectangular edge, not just the picture.

3. Drag left or right and place the second point at the edge of another image. Hold the Shift button down for restraint.

4. If the Info Palette is not already open, it will open as soon as you set the first point. Make sure that the units of measurement are in pixels. Do this by clicking on the small arrow in the lower left quadrant of the palette and choosing Pixels.

5. The Width and/or Height of the distance between your two objects will appear in the lower right quadrant.

6. Use the measurement later to place objects in your HTML code. If you're going to be using the single pixel trick, as described earlier in this chapter, you'll want to cut the measurement number in half (see The Single Pixel Trick).

KEEP YOUR FILES ORGANIZED

As shown in Figure 10-8, I find it helpful to set up four separate folders before starting any Web job:

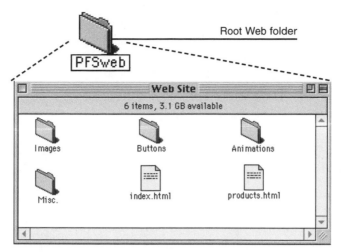

Figure 10–8: The organization of my Web folder

◆   Images   ◆   Buttons   ◆   Animations   ◆   Misc.

While my main directory houses all of my HTML files, I distribute all other media into their respective folders. This not only helps me find certain files later in life, but it is also very useful when it comes time to FTP my files to the server.

OPTIMIZING PERFORMANCE

Just because you are working with smaller file sizes for Web sites doesn't mean that you won't have just reason to heighten Photoshop's performance. The following are a few ways you can optimize Photoshop's performance both in general and for the Web.

SETTING UP SCRATCH DISKS

Even with low-res files, Photoshop can eat up RAM rather quickly. Possibly nothing is more annoying than getting really into a design, knowing in your head what you want to happen, choosing a filter, and, just as the effect is about to happen, getting that ugly message from Photoshop saying that it cannot complete the demand because of lack of RAM.

With Photoshop 5.0, you can have up to four separate scratch disk sources, combining for up to 200 GB of scratch space. You can set the sources for the extra space by choosing File -> Preferences -> Plug-Ins and Scratch Disks. Figure 10–9 shows the dialog box that appears. Since scratch space involves using empty storage memory in place of RAM when RAM runs out, you can use any source available. This includes your hard drive, any networked computers that are available, external hard drives, even

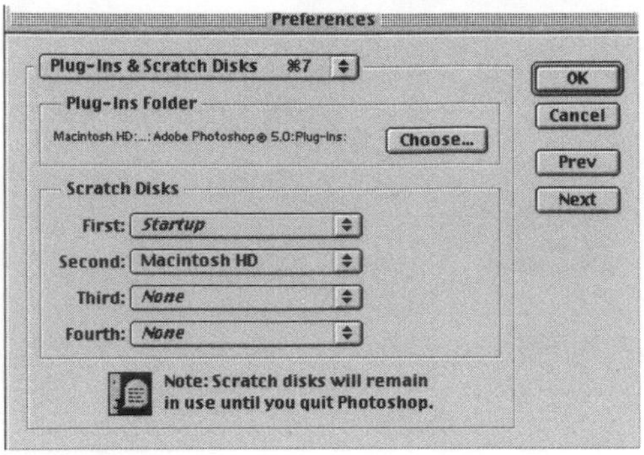

Figure 10–9: The Plug-Ins and Scratch Disks dialog box.

Jaz, Zip, SyQuest, or other storage devices (although these sources are usually frowned upon as scratch sources and will cause the program to run more slowly).

Any changes that you make to the Scratch Disk preferences will not be available until the next time that you open Photoshop, so restart Photoshop after making your choices.

OTHER SOLUTIONS TO MEMORY PROBLEMS

Because everybody's computer and hardware accessibility is different, not everyone will have access to multiple scratch sources. If you fall into this category, and do not have access to additional RAM, there are still a few things you can do:

◆ The History Palette is one of the great new features of Photoshop 5.0. But it's a veritable monster when it comes to eating RAM. In the History Palette pull-down menu, choose History Options to access the dialog box shown in Figure 10–10. Make sure that the checkbox marked Allow Non-Linear History is left unchecked. Also, make sure that Maximum History States is lowered to the lowest number of undo's you will need. The lower the number, the less memory will be used.

◆ When you do run out of RAM, choose Edit -> Purge and select either Undo, Clipboard, Pattern, Histories or All. Choosing All will free up the most amount of actual RAM, but remember—you cannot undo a purge, so make sure you really want this before you do it.

EXTENSIONS MADE EASY

Every image that you create and save for the Web has to have a file extension at the end of the name. Depending on the type of image, the extension will usually be either .jpg for JPEGs, .gif for GIFs, .or png for PNGs. Windows users will automatically have

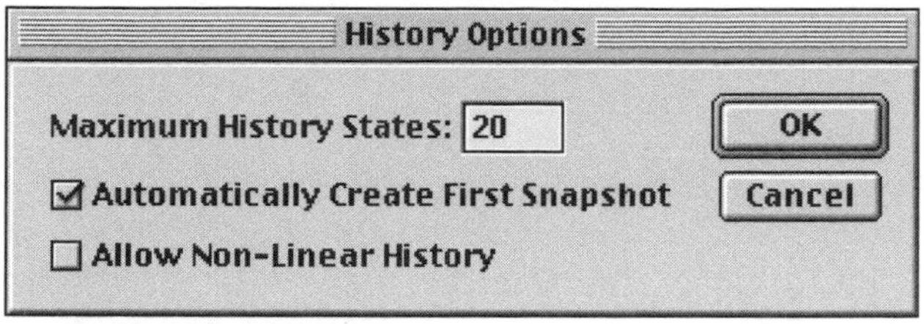

Figure 10–10: The History Options in the History Palette pull-down menu will help you optimize Photoshop's performance.

the extension put in place for them, however they will be placed with uppercase letters, which some UNIX servers will not recognize, and which would cause a headache as you referenced them in your HTML code anyway. So Windows users will have to retype the file extension no matter what.

Macintosh users, though, have an option available to them: choose File -> Preferences -> Saving Files to access the dialog box shown in Figure 10–11 (you'll be referring to this file a few times when trying to optimize Photoshop). A pull-down menu for Append File Extension gives you three choices: Never (default), Always, and Ask When Saving. Choosing Always will automatically add the extension to every file you save, in lowercase letters. If you choose Ask When Saving, you will notice an addition to the Save As dialog box, as shown in Figure 10–12. At the bottom, check the box marked Append, and then the box marked Use Lower Case.

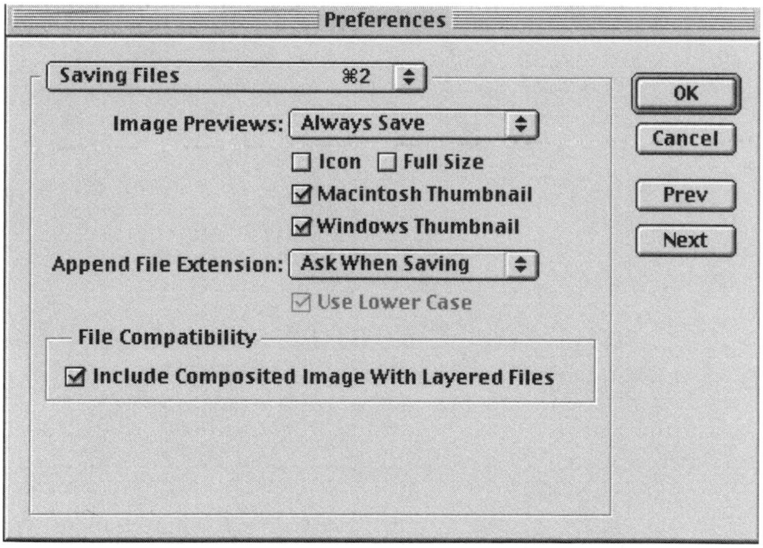

Figure 10–11: The Saving Files dialog box

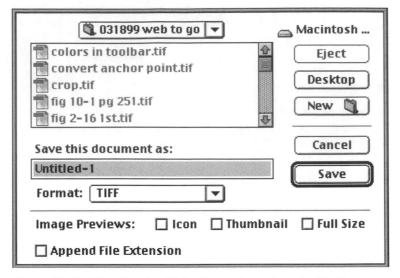

Figure 10–12: After choosing "Ask when saving... from the Preferences dialog box, a check box is added at the bottom to include the file extension.

Adding file extensions doesn't just apply to graphics. On the Web, practically everything you put on line will need a file extension, including your HTML documents. You can apply either the three-letter extension of .htm or the four-letter extension of .html. Use the shorter extension whenever possible. Macintosh users who use the .htm ending will be able to grab files from the browser when necessary, and just double click on them to open them in SimpleText. HTML documents marked .html will come off the browser as either a Netscape or IE file and you will need to first go into SimpleText and choose File -> Open and locate the file on your hard drive in order to open it.

SAVE HARD DISK SPACE. LESSON ONE: FORGET THE PAST

I've mentioned in a few areas throughout this book that you should always save multiple copies of your files, especially the original files that still have all the layers in them. Although I continue to mention it, you probably already knew to do that. What you may not know, though, is that every time you save a file with multiple layers, Photoshop is also creating a flattened version to save along with it, so that Photoshop versions that don't recognize layers (pre-version 3.0) can open up an unflattened file. This unhappy event can nearly double the file size for anything you save, and it happens by default! To keep this from happening choose File -> Preferences -> Saving Files to open the dialog box shown in Figure 10–11. Uncheck the box marked Include Composited Image With Layered Files. If you really need to open a file in Photoshop 2.5, choose File -> Save a Copy and save your file as an EPS, TIFF, JPEG, or whatever.

SAVE HARD DISK SPACE. LESSON TWO: NO PREVIEWS

Although they are convenient, image previews—those cute icons and thumbnails that let you see what an image looks like either on your desktop or in an application's Open dialog box—can add a great deal of extra bytes to any image that you save. This is especially hazardous if you are a Macintosh user uploading a JPEG file to a server: the extra bytes will be retained, and cause your Web site to load that much more slowly. Windows users and GIF images for both platforms will not have this problem. The images, on the local drive will still be larger than they need to be, though, regardless of file type or platform.

To turn off the image previews, choose File -> Preferences -> Saving Files to access the dialog box shown in Figure 10–11. In the pull-down menu for Image Previews, choose either Never Save or Ask When Saving. Don't worry about not knowing which image is which without the icons—MacOS and newer Windows versions both allow for long, descriptive file names.

Transferring files from a Mac to a PC using a Zip disk? If so, descriptive file names are out—go back to the standard 8.3 format. Zips will reduce your file names, substituting a~for anything after the seventh letter. Your HTML references could be thrown off.

SAVE MULTIPLE COPIES OF IMAGES

With hard disk space fairly easy to come by, few computers today are sold with less than 4 GB of hard disk space and for those that are, you can pick up an additional 4 gig external drive for relatively little money. Zip drives also provide an inexpensive solution for backing up and archiving files. Therefore, there is no excuse for not saving multiple copies of all images. It may seem frivolous at first, but anyone thinking ahead will realize that change is inevitable. You don't want to spend a lot of time creating a really cool graphic that needed 20 layers to perfect, just to find out six months later when you want to remove a portion that the only version you have left is a flattened GIF. Try to save the original Photoshop file, and, if you're going to be using any transparencies, save your image again as a regular GIF, and then finally as a transparent GIF. Try opening a transparent GIF in Photoshop—it's not a pretty sight.

DON'T RELY ON GRAPHICS FOR NAVIGATION

Don't worry—you didn't read the Buttons chapter in vein. Graphic buttons are an everyday part of the Web, and their creation is a primary function of any Web designer. However, if you rely solely on graphics to navigate through your site, you could be making a fatal error—a broken link or a user who has his graphics turned off will cause some people to not see your buttons, and therefore not have access to certain information.

Try putting text links at the bottom of your site as well. Even if the font size is small, it's a little extra effort that can be very helpful in the long run. (Let me stop the hoards of incoming e-mail now from protesters who actively look for sites I have created—even though the text links at the bottom of each page are a good idea, I am sometimes lazy and do not heed my own advice—believe me, I pay for it in the end.)

Add the "Alt=" command to your IMG tag to replace unviewable images with text.

IMPORTING VECTOR GRAPHICS

Many designers create graphics using other applications in conjunction with Photoshop. Illustrator, FreeHand, Painter, and CorelDRAW are among the popular applications used to do things the Photoshop cannot currently do (or do well, at least), such as certain text effects and illustrations.

Because the Web works with bitmap images (not including certain plug-in-dependent modules, such as files created with Macromedia Flash), vector images need to be *rasterized*, or converted into bitmap files. Although some of the newer versions of vector-based programs have functions that allow you to rasterize directly, this book is about using Photoshop for Web graphics, and often you'll need Photoshop to enhance a vector image in ways that Illustrator or Painter cannot. Besides, as explained earlier in this chapter, you'll want to use Photoshop to lay out all of your graphics and see how they relate to each other.

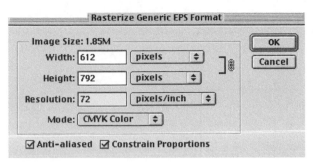

Figure 10–13: The Rasterize dialog box

There are a number of ways that you can bring a vector image into Photoshop, all of which are pretty straightforward:

◆ Choose File -> Open and select the vector file you would like to rasterize. Doing so will bring up the dialog box shown in Figure 10–13. You can choose the size and resolution you would like your image to be before you turn it into a bitmap. If you're uncertain, you're best off using a high resolution, such as 300 ppi, and resizing down later.

◆ If you are placing your vector graphic into an already-open file to become part of an existing image choose File -> Place. Your vector graphic will open on its own layer, with the Free Transform handles around it. You can manipulate the image and make it the desired size before it rasterizes.

◆ Simply cut/copy from a vector-based program and paste into Photoshop. A dialog box will give you the option of pasting as pixels or paths.

◆ Drag directly from the canvas of a vector program to an open canvas in Photoshop. You will have no choices with this method—Photoshop rasterizes and determines the size of the image by itself.

PRESENT GRAPHICS AND TEXT FROM A MARKETING STANDPOINT

The whole idea of having a Web site is to present certain information to potential viewers. Whether you are trying to sell you new invention for a better mousetrap or you simply want to meet a girl for a cyber relationship, you will want to present your information in a concise, logical order that will allow your user to gain the most from your site.

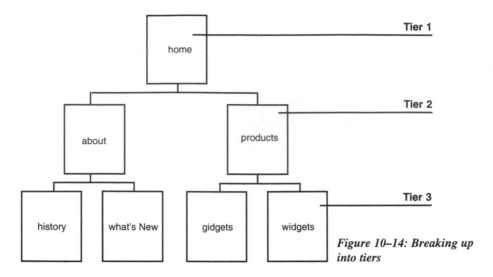

Figure 10–14: Breaking up into tiers

To do this, try to follow the basic rule of "graphics first, copy later." Let's say that you have a three-tiered Web site, as shown in Figure 10–14. Your first tier is the home page—the most crucial page on your site. Depending on how you set this page up, people will either continue to search through your site or hit the "back" button and start over again at Yahoo!. Provide just enough copy to give a general sense of what your site is all about, but concentrate on a really outstanding layout, and graphics to "grab" your audience and reel them in.

Once you've hooked your user, the second tier, which among other things could have a page for Products, for example, should try to balance the graphics with the copy. Not too much of either, but just enough to remain interesting. The third tier, which could be an explanation of one of the products, should provide significantly more copy and ease up on the graphics—by the time your user is this far into the site they are genuinely interested—you no longer need to sell them on your site. Figure 10–15 shows a site that illustrates this.

STEAL SOURCE CODE

Well, it's not really stealing, but it's a great way to learn. Spend some time just surfing around the Web. If you see something you like—an interesting layout, some unusual movement, or anything else, you can read through the HTML source code that was used to write the page. In your browser, choose View -> Document Source (Netscape) or View -> Source (Internet Explorer). The source code will appear and you can scan through it and learn what commands were used to set the page up. Save the page on your hard drive to reference later. There are a lot of brilliant Web designers out there and the best way to learn is to study their work.

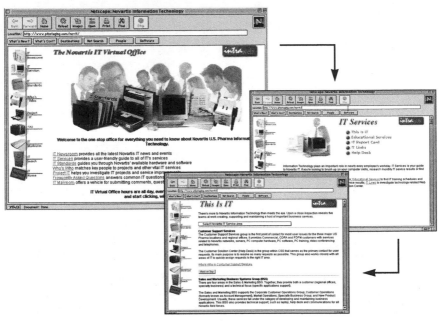

Figure 10–15: A real Web site broken into tiers

BUY A MOUSE TRAP

Mice are bad. They're great tools if you're using business applications, but will hinder your abilities in Photoshop. Buy yourself an electronic tablet. Personally, I like the WACOM Tablets, even though I sometimes find that their extension for my Mac will conflict with the extensions for other SCSI devices. The electronic tablets will give you greater design control, by allowing you to use your fingers for detailed painting and manipulating, as opposed to the mouse, which works more with your wrist.

PLAN AHEAD FOR LARGER PROJECTS

In my experience of designing Web sites for both my own agency and for corporate clients, I have learned the importance of preparing for larger projects in advance. Once a Web site is published, the customer will often want to print an accompanying brochure or catalog along with it, and advanced preparation on your part can only lead to increased payment.

Try to determine in advance the likelihood of that happening (even if a client is adamant against printing anything, oftentimes they change their minds) and prepare for it. Think about taking the following steps for future work:

◆ Scan in all photography at a high resolution and archive it someplace. Set up an Action to automate a size reduction to 72 ppi for Web graphics to save time. Your archive of hi-res files can be used for future print work.

◆ Write all text in a word processing program, such as MS Word, WordPerfect, or even layout programs such as PageMaker or QuarkXPress. It's a good thing to have on record and will help to develop other marketing material later, saving you the agony of isolating text in your HTML files and then reformatting.

◆ Design the site to be somehow interactive with a printed piece. For example, a mass mail campaign could direct users to special pages that they otherwise wouldn't have access to. Explore other unique possibilities for combining print with the Web.

Don't miss opportunities to extend contracts and earn more for yourself or your company—they're usually no more than a proposal away. Clients will appreciate the well-roundedness that you show and the ability to keep designs consistent throughout all media pieces. Keeping organized and planning ahead for these opportunities will help ensure success in these ventures.

MAKING HIGH QUALITY, SMALL FILE SIZE PDFS

PDFs are becoming all the rage on the Web, and the quicker you learn to make them, the more money you can charge when creating your Web sites. Clients will use PDFs for everything from financial records, annual reports, and catalog pages to medical forms and necessary HR paperwork.

With PDF, you can put multiple pages in one file. These pages can retain their original page layout and allow a reader to instantly jump from one page to the next and can even find a topic through a concentrated keyword search. Really advanced PDFs can imbed animations and video as well. But for most PDFs that just deal with static pages, the trick with creating PDFs is to make them as high in quality as possible, but to keep the file size down.

To do this, however, you'll need more than just Photoshop. You're also going to need another program developed by Adobe, call Acrobat, specifically Acrobat Exchange and Distiller. Once you have these, and have installed them onto your system, you'll want to complete the following steps:

1. Scan in your page at around 300 ppi (you'll need to scan in at least 200 ppi to make this process work well). Because one of the main selling points of PDFs is that you can have multiple elements and retain their particular layout, scan a page that has a good amount of text on it for this example.

While you can scan directly into Photoshop, you don't have to—you can also scan directly from Acrobat Exchange. However, you won't be able to manipulate the scan at all to any significant extent in Exchange.

Save yourself the agonizing experience of having to speak with an Acrobat tech support operator. You'll have trouble with further steps if you scan or save your PDF with more than 8-bit color.

2. Save your scan as a Photoshop PDF.

Before the next step, open a folder on the Acrobat Install CD-ROM named Drivers. Install the drivers in this folder. These will update your printer preferences. Your system printer folder now will have tons of printers in it—open the folder and delete the one you don't need, except the one named Adobe Distiller PPD. Then choose PSPrinter as your designated output source.

3. Open Acrobat Exchange.
4. Choose File -> Open and open the PDF file that you saved in Photoshop.
5. You're going to want to change the text on the page into editable text, so it doesn't eat up file size. Choose Document -> Capture from the main pull-down menu. Make the necessary choices in the ensuing dialog box, and click OK. Exchange will go through your document and pick out the portions of your image that it can recognize as text, and turn it into editable copy.
6. Choose File -> Print. The Acrobat Virtual Printer should be the printer that appears in your print dialog box. Hit OK.
7. Push the radio button for binary, and select All Fonts from the Font pull-down menu. Push OK. A PostScript file will be saved to your desired directory.

8. Open Acrobat Distiller. Choose File -> Open from the main pull-down menu and use the directory to locate the PostScript file that was saved in Step 7. Distiller will compress your file, significantly reducing the file size. When it's done, you'll have a new PDF file, ready for the Web!

 Don't take either Exchange or Distiller out of its main Acrobat folder —if you do, you may run into problems, since both programs rely on plug-ins found in a Plug-ins folder in the Acrobat directory.

USE KEYBOARD COMMANDS

You'll always need to use a mouse or an electronic tablet for drawing, painting, shading, and most other artistic functions in Photoshop. But for everything else, you're better off learning the keyboard commands as much as possible, and staying away from all the menus. There are literally hundreds of keyboard commands in Photoshop—way too many to list here.

Certain commands, like the single key shortcuts for each tool, can be found by moving your cursor over the tool and leaving it there for about two seconds (or check out Chapter 1). Many palettes can be accessed easily too by using the function keys—try each of the keys between F5–F9 to see which palette is accessed. Many other keyboard commands can be discovered by looking at the pull-down menus: each separate function that has a keyboard command will list it. But it's the many others that are not listed in Photoshop that can prove to be helpful. The following is a brief list of the keyboard commands I have found most useful when working in Photoshop (commands in parentheses indicate Windows commands):

Feather Selection:	Command (Ctrl) + Option (Alt) + D
Add to Selection:	Shift + drag/click with a selection tool
Subtract from Selection:	Option (Alt) + drag/click with a selection tool
Keep Selection Intersection:	Option (Alt) + Shift + drag/click with a selection tool
Move Marquee:	Arrows with selection tool active
Move Marquee 10 Pixels:	Shift + Arrow with selection tool active
Move Selection:	Arrows with Move tool active
Move Selection 10 Pixels:	Shift + Arrow with Move tool active
Move Up One Layer:	Option (Alt) +]
Move Down One Layer :	Option (Alt) + [
Send Layer Backward:	Command (Ctrl) + [

Send Layer Forward:	Command (Ctrl) +]
Send Layer to Back:	Command (Ctrl) + Shift + [
Send Layer to Front:	Command (Ctrl) + Shift +]
Hide All but One Layer:	Option (Alt) + click eye icon of desired layer
Create New Layer:	Command (Ctrl) + Option (Alt) + Shift + N
Preserve Layer Transparency:	/ while in active layer
Merge Linked	Command (Ctrl) + E
Change Layer Opacity	single number for increments of 10%, two number for increments of 1% while selection tool or Move tool is active
Desaturate:	Command (Ctrl) + Shift + U
Cycle through Brush Palette:	[or] while a paint tool is active
Temporarily activate Hand tool:	Spacebar
Temporarily activate Move tool:	Command (Ctrl)
Show/Hide Palettes and Toolbar:	Tab
Show/Hide just Palettes:	Shift + Tab

One of the (many) changes you may notice in version 5.0 is that you can no longer scroll through the tools in the toolbar simply by continuing to press the letter. For example, in version 4, simply hitting the m button repeatedly would scroll between the Rectangular and Elliptical Marquee tool. In version 5.0, you'll have to hold the Shift key down while hitting the letter in order to scroll.

There are plenty of other keyboard commands that can prove helpful. For a full list, please visit the Web site for this book, at `http://www.phptr.com/togo`

SUMMARY

Through the pages of this chapter, as well as all of the chapters in this book, it has become clear that there are many facets of the Internet and Photoshop that you'll need to understand to master the art of Web design. Web designing can be a uniquely creative experience that will not only challenge your imagination but could possibly prepare you for a rapidly growing segment of the job market.

I hope that you close this book with confidence that you have learned something of value and have a stronger urge to continue practicing and learning Photoshop and Web site development. Despite any negative aspects that I tried to (honestly) warn you about, there is practically nothing more rewarding than building a Web page and knowing that millions of Web surfers are viewing your work, gathering information, perhaps even marveling at your incredible Photoshop skills. If they do, make sure you let them know where you learned it....

Thanks for reading, good luck, and happy designing!

INDEX

ABOUT THE AUTHOR

Jason I, Miletsky is co–founder of PFS New Media, a full service advertising and production company, where he specializes in graphic design, web development, and print production. As an Adobe Certified Photoshop Expert, he is often called upon to conduct classes and seminars in advanced graphic design techniques, as well as teach HTML programming. He is the author of two other (yet to be released) books for the "To Go" series, *Desktop Publishing To Go* and *Illustrator 8 0 To Go*.

A graduate of Brandeis University, Jason has a B.A. in Economics and a concentration in English/Creative Writing. With no formal training in computers, graphics or de–sign, he has been self taught in a variety of media.

When he's not working or writing, Jason can be found on the rugby field, a local pool hall, or any number of NYC blues bars. But his true passion is the white beach, the glaring sun, and endless tropical drinks enjoyed on some remote island getaway. As soon as one of those islands get connected to the internet you can bet that's where he'll be, writing his next book.

FAX OR MAIL THIS ORDER FORM TO BEGIN YOUR TRAINING!

*Name or Company:*_____

*Address:*_____

*Phone:*_____ *Fax:*_____

*E-Mail:*_____ *Type of Work:*_____

QTY	Title	Price	Total
_____	*Photoshop 5.0 Level I*	*$49.95*	_____
_____	*Photoshop 5.0 Level II*	*$49.95*	_____
_____	*Photoshop 5.0 for the Web*	*$49.95*	_____
_____	*Quark XPress 4.0*	*$49.95*	_____
_____	*Digital Prepress*	*$54.95*	_____
_____	*Illustrator 8.0*	*$44.95*	_____
_____	*Director 7.0 Level I*	*$49.95*	_____
_____	*Director 7.0 Level II*	*$49.95*	_____
_____	*Video Production*	*$59.95*	_____
_____	*Video Editing*	*$59.95*	_____
_____	*Multimedia Development*	*$59.95*	_____
_____	*Authorware Attain*	*$59.95*	_____
	Sub Total:		_____
_____	*Package I: Any Two Videos*	*7% off Total*	_____
_____	*Package II: Any Three Videos*	*10% off Total*	_____
_____	*Package III: Any Five Videos*	*15% off Total*	_____
	Sales Tax (NJ Customers Only)	*Add 6%*	_____
	Shipping & Handling	*$4.95 per tape*	_____
	Total:		_____

*Payment Type:*____ *Check* ____ *Money Order* ____*Visa* ____ *MC*

*Credit Card #:*_____ *Exp. Date:*_____

*Signature:*_____

Or Order By Phone
1.800.PFS.2080
973.616.2700 • Fax 973.616.7227

Please mail check or money order for full amount to:
PFS New Media • 2422 Hamburg Tpke. • Wayne, NJ 07470
Please allow 3-5 weeks for delivery. Sorry, no COD's.